America Through the Eyes of Its People

A Collection of Primary Sources

America Through the Eyes of Its People

A Collection of Primary Sources

Carol Brown
Houston Community College

HarperCollins*CollegePublishers*

For permission to use copyrighted material, grateful acknowledgement is made to the copyright holders on pp. 227-233, which are hereby made part of this copyright page.

AMERICA THROUGH THE EYES OF ITS PEOPLE: A Collection of Primary Sources by Carol Brown

Copyright © 1993 HarperCollins College Publishers

All rights reserved. Printed in the United States of America. No part of this book may be reproduced in any manner whatsoever without written permission with the following exception: testing material may be copied for classroom testing. For information, address HarperCollins College Publishers, 10 E. 53rd St., New York, N.Y. 10022.

ISBN: 0-673-55194-6

96 97 9 8 7 6 5 4

Contents

Preface

Document Set One: Exploration and Colonization: Winners and Losers 1
- Document A: Christopher Columbus Describes the New World 3
- Document B: Alvar Nunez Cabeza de Vaca Describes the Indians of the Rio Grande Region, 1528-1536 5
- Document C: John Cabot's Voyages 7
- Document D: Thomas Mun, England's Treasure by Foreign Trade 8
- Document E: The Laws of Virginia, 1610-1611 10

Document Set Two: Life in the British Colonies: Dreams and Realties 12
- Document A: Gottlieb Mittelberger, Indentured Servants 15
- Document B: Alexander Falconbridge, The African Slave Trade 17
- Document C: William Penn: Model of Government 19
- Document D: Bacon's Rebellion: The Declaration, July 30, 1676 20
- Document E: Witchcraft in Salem 22
- Document F: Washington: Defeat in the French and Indian War 24

Document Set Three: The American Revolution: What Price Freedom? 25
- Document A: Franklin Testified Against the Stamp Act (1766) 27
- Document B: John Dickinson, Letters from a Farmer in Pennsylvania, 1768 29
- Document C: Loyalists Express Support 30
- Document D: Give Me Liberty, Give Me Death 31
- Document E: Letter from John Adams to Abigail Adams 33

Document Set Four: A New Republic: We The People 34
- Document A: George Washington: The Newburg Address, March 11, 1783 36
- Document B: Shays' Rebellion: Letters of Generals Shepherd and Lincoln 38
- Document C: Constitutional Convention of 1787: Virginia or Randoph Plan 40
- Document D: Federalist Paper #10 42

Document Set Five: The Frail New Republic 44
- Document A: Washington's Farewell Address 46
- Document B: The First Census of the United States 48
- Document C: Selections from the Journals of Lewis and Clark 49
- Document D: Madison's War Message 51

Document Set Six: An Egalitarian Society 52
- Document A: *McCulloch vs Maryland* 55
- Document B: The Monroe Doctrine 56
- Document C: Jackson Supports the Indian Removal Act 58
- Document D: David Crockett Advises Politicians 59
- Document E: Dicken's Observations of American Life 60

Document Set Seven: The Ferment of Reform 61
- Document A: A Letter from Brook Farm, 1841 63
- Document B: Horace Mann, Report of the Massachusetts Board of Education, 1848 64
- Document C: William Lloyd Garrison and The Liberator 65

Document Set Eight: Life in Antebellum America 66
    Document A: The Boston's Carpenters' Strike, 1825   69
    Document B: The Abuse of Female Workers of Lowell, 1836   71
    Document C: The Burning of a Convent School, 1834   73
    Document D: Nat Turner's Divine Mission   74
    Document E: George Fitzhugh: The Blessings of Slavery, 1856   75

Document Set Nine: Manifest Destiny and Its Consequences 77
    Document A: John L. O'Sullivan, The Great Nation of Futurity   79
    Document B: Thomas Corwin Against the Mexican War   81
    Document C: Chief Seattle's Oration   83

Document Set Ten: A Road to War 85
    Document A: Uncle Tom's Cabin   87
    Document B: The Dred Scott Decision   89
    Document C: The House Divided   90

Document Set Eleven: The World Turned Upside Down 91
    Document A: Clara Barton: Medical Life at the Battlefield   93
    Document B: The Gettysburg Address   95
    Document C: The Way We Lived, A Black Soldier Writes to Abraham Lincoln, 1863   96

Document Set Twelve: To Heal the Nation's Wounds 98
    Document A: Mississippi Black Code, 1865   100
    Document B: A Sharecrop Contract   102
    Document C: The Fourteenth Amendment, 1868   104
    Document D: The Victims of Ku Klux Klan   105

Document Set Thirteen: The Wealth of a Nation 106
    Document A: The Gilded Age   108
    Document B: The Gospel of Wealth   109
    Document C: A Century of Dishonor   111
    Document D: Account of Wounded Knee Massacre, 1890   113

Document Set Fourteen: Huddled Masses 115
    Document A: Children in the Coal Mines   117
    Document B: Letters to the *Jewish Daily Forward*, (1906-1907)   118
    Document C: Life of a Chinese Immigrant   120
    Document D: The Secret Oath of American Protective Association   122

Document Set Fifteen: City Life 123
    Document A: The Life of the Urban Poor   125
    Document B: Sanitary Conditions in New York   126
    Document C: Bathing at Coney Island   128
    Document D: The Medicine Show   129

Document Set Sixteen: The American Flag Around the Globe 131
    Document A: Our Country   133
    Document B: The March of the Flag   135
    Document C: On Empire and the Philippines   137
    Document D: McKinley Decides on Philippines   138

Document Set Seventeen: The End and the Beginning of the American Political System   139
    Document A: George Washington Plunkitt   141
    Document B: Life on the Prairie   142
    Document C: The Omaha Platform of the Populist Party   144
    Document D: *Plessy vs Ferguson*   146
    Document E: The Atlanta Compromise   147

Document Set Eighteen: Reforming American Society   148
    Document A: The Triangle Factory   150
    Document B: The New Nationalism   152
    Document C: The New Freedom (1913)   153

Document Set Nineteen: America at War   154
    Document A: Boy Scouts Support the War Effort   156
    Document B: The Treatment of German-Americans   158
    Document C: A "Doughboy" Describes the Fighting Front   159
    Document D: The Fourteen Points   161

Document Set Twenty: Hard Times   163
    Document A: The Immigration Act of 1924   165
    Document B: FDR First Inaugural Address   168
    Document C: Huey Long, "Share Our Wealth"   171
    Document D: We Want to Live, Not Merely Exist   172

Document Set Twenty-One: Peace and War   173
    Document A: The Four Freedoms   175
    Document B: A Letter to President Roosevelt   177
    Document C: A Woman Remembers the War   179
    Document D: Memories of the Internment Camp   181

Document Set Twenty-Two: The Cold War at Home and Abroad   183
    Document A: The Truman Doctrine   186
    Document B: The Marshall Plan   187
    Document C: Ronald Reagan Testifies   188
    Document D: *Brown vs Board of Education*   190

Document Set Twenty-Three: Vietnam and the Crises of Authority   192
    Document A: John Kennedy's Inaugural Address   194
    Document B: The Cuban Missile Crises   197
    Document C: The Tonkin Gulf Incident, 1964   199
    Document D: A War I Opposed and Despised   201

Document Set Twenty-Four: Liberty for All   203
    Document A: The War on Poverty   206
    Document B: Civil Rights Act of 1964, July 2, 1964   208
    Document C: Martin Luther King, Jr., "I Have a Dream"   210
    Document D: National Organization for Women   212
    Document E: Harvest of Discontent   215

Document Set Twenty-Five: The End of the U.S. Century   218
    Document A: "Malaise" Speech   220
    Document B: A Welfare Hotel   222
    Document C: Address to the Nation Announcing Allied Military Action in the Persian Gulf, January 16, 1991   224

Preface

Each semester one of the most important goals I have for my students is to have them become actively engaged with history. To me that means that the course will be a "hands-on" experience for them. As one student noted as I came into class one day, "Oh no, we are going to have to think again today." I expect them to think about history in my class; think about the process of history and form their own interpretations about the historical experiences we study in the course. In my search for teaching strategies that can help me reach this objective I took the advice of a colleague and began using primary documents. Like her, I found they were an invaluable way to have students "see history as it was." The first time student actually read the Gettysburg Address, they are often surprised at its brevity. Careful analysis of its meaning have led to fascinating discussions about Lincoln's real message in the speech.

I hope this document book will help other instructors in their quest for intellectual discourse with their students. Each set includes an introduction, three to five documents and a set of questions. In each introduction I noted ways that the document could be integrated into classroom discussion on that topic. I tried to develop "higher level" questions which asked the students to think about the document and its implication for American society in a particular time period. It was my objective in each set to highlight key events, personalities and life experiences of an age. While an instructor would probably not use all the documents in each set, I hope there will be enough variety to find some that will work within the individual classroom structure.

I want to thank several people, without whose help this project could never have been completed. Tom Hughes, a colleague and friend, spent untold hours with me searching for the right documents. Mary Davis took the manuscript and gave it form and organization. Judith Anderson had the thankless task of prodding me along. Although we have never met, I feel as if we are friends. Lastly my family, Greg, David and Lena, who supported me throughout this effort and were always there when I needed them.

America Through the Eyes of Its People

A Collection of Primary Sources

Document Set One
Exploration and Colonization: Winners and Losers

INTRODUCTION

By the end of the fifteenth century the monarchs of Western Europe were determined to find new sea routes to the East. The Portuguese paved the path with their voyages around the continent of Africa. After consolidating their power, Ferdinand and Isabella of Spain were prepared to listen to the ideas of an Italian explorer, Christopher Columbus, who believed there was a quicker and simpler way to reach the markets of the East by sailing west. The rest, of course, is history and his first historic voyages in the Caribbean opened the door to three centuries of exploration and colonization of the Western Hemisphere by Western Europe.

Before any other European nation, Spain enjoyed the political and economic power which an expansive colonial empire in the New World could provide. Under the banner of, "Glory, God and Gold," the Spanish conquistadors in the sixteenth century found riches that would make Spain the number one power in the world.

The first two selections in this set describe the reaction of two of her explorers as they experience the New World for the first time. Christopher Columbus in a letter to a leading supporter and high official in the Spanish court describes his reaction to the sights of the New World. Alvar Nunez Cabeza de Vaca was treasurer of the shipwrecked expedition of Panfilo de Narvaez in the American Southwest. His document describes the expedition's encounter with native peoples of the region. The two documents provide an interesting analysis of the first encounters the Spaniards had with native groups. It would be interesting to have students compare and contrast de Vaca and Columbus' letters and discuss how these narratives provide insight into the treatment of native groups under Spanish colonial rule.

The English were late in the game of exploration and colonization. Political and economic turmoil of the sixteenth century prevented them from focusing a national effort toward exploration and colonization. Inspired by the voyages of Columbus, a young Venetian sailed in 1497 under the flag of England and Henry VII for new western routes to the East. Like Columbus, John Cabot did not find a quicker passage to Asia, however his travels to Newfoundland provided the rationale for later colonial claims by England. In an account written by a fellow Venetian in London, Cabot is portrayed as a great hero. It is interesting to note the commitment of the monarch to future voyages by Cabot.

It would be almost a century before England would devote its energies to colonization. Unlike other Western European nations, the leadership for international greatness would come from the private sector. Successful entrepreneurs believed that the private and public sectors could jointly benefit from the wealth of the New World. Thomas Mann was a successful London merchant who served as one of the directors of the East India Company. In the late sixteenth and early seventeenth centuries most of the English ventures into the New World were capitalized by joint-stock companies. Mann's treatise, "England's Treasure by Foreign Trade," depicts how the theory of mercantilism emphasized the importance of a favorable balance of trade in order to enhance the wealth of a nation.

Virginia was one of the first colonies to be established by the English in the New World. Its early years were filled with death and disaster. It is interesting to note in the last section, "The Laws of Virginia, 1610-1611," how strictly the laws defined the actions of these first colonists.

Questions For Document Set One

1. Compare the descriptions of de Vaca and Columbus of the native Americans they encountered.

2. How did native Americans treat de Vaca and Columbus?

3. What was the reaction in England to the first voyage of John Cabot?

4. Describe Munn's vision of a merchant and decide how realistic it was for the times.

5. According to Munn, how can a nation enrich itself?

6. Would it have been difficult to live under the laws of Virginia?

Document A
Christopher Columbus Describes the New World

Sir,

As I know that you will have pleasure of the great victory which out Lord hath given me in my voyage, I write you this, by which you shall know that in [thirty-three] days I passed over the Indies with the fleet which the most illustrious King and Queen, our Lords, gave me: where I found very many islands peopled with inhabitants beyond number. And, of them all, I have taken possession for their Highnesses, with proclamation and the royal standard displayed; and I was not gainsaid. On the first which I found, I put the name Sant Salvador, in commemoration of His High Majesty, who marvelously hath given all this: the Indians call it [Guanhani]. The second I named the Island of Santa Maria de Concepcion, the third Ferrandina, the fourth Fair Island, the fifth La Isla Juana; and so for each one a new name. When I reached Juana, I followed its coast westwardly, and found it so large that I thought it might be the mainland province of Cathay. And as I did not thus find any towns and villages on the sea-coast, save small hamlets with the people whereof I could not get speech, because they all fled away forthwith, I went on further in the same direction, thinking I should not miss of great cities or towns. And at the end of many leagues, seeing that there was no change, ...and turned back as far as a port agreed upon; from which I sent two men into the country to learn if there were a king, or any great cities. They traveled for three days, and found interminable small villages and a numberless population, but nought of ruling authority; wherefore they returned. I understood sufficiently from other Indians...that this land, ...was an island; and so I followed its coast eastwardly for a hundred and seven leagues as far as where it terminated; from which headland I saw another island to the east [eighteen] leagues distant from this, to which I at once gave the name La Spanola. And I proceeded thither, and followed the northern coast, as with La Juana, eastwardly for a hundred and [eighty-eight] great leagues in a direct easterly course, as with La Juana. The which, and all the others, are more [fertile] to an excessive degree, and this extremely so. In it, there are many havens on the sea-coast, incomparable with any others that I know in Christendom, and plenty of rivers so good and great that it is a marvel. The lands thereof are high, and in it are very many ranges of hills, and most lofty mountains incomparably beyond the Island of [Tenerife]; all most beautiful in a thousand shapes, and all accessible, and full of trees of a thousand kinds, so lofty that they seem to reach the sky. And I am assured that they never lose their foliage; as may be imagined, since I saw them as green and as beautiful as they are in Spain during May...And the nightingale was singing, and other birds of a thousand sorts, in the month of November, round about the way I was going. There are palm-trees of six or eight species, wondrous to see for their beautiful variety; but so are the other trees, and fruits, and plants therein. There are wonderful pine-groves, and very large plains of verdure, and there is honey, and many kinds of birds, and many various fruits. In the earth there are many mines of metals; and there is a population of incalculable number. Spanola is a marvel; the mountains and hills, and plains, and fields, and land, so beautiful and rich for planting and sowing, for breeding cattle of all sorts, for building of towns and villages. There could be no believing, without seeing, such harbours as are here, as well as the many and great rivers, and excellent waters, most of which contain gold. In the trees and fruits and plants, there are great differences from those of Juana. In [La Spanola], there are many spiceries, and great mines of gold and other metals. The people of this island, and of all the others that I have found and seen, or not seen, all go naked, men and women, just as their mothers bring them forth; although some women cover a single place with the leaf of a plant, or a cotton something which they make for that purpose. They have no iron or steel, nor any weapons; nor are they fit thereunto; not be because they be not a well-formed people and of fair stature, but that they are most wondrously timorous. They have no other weapons than the stems of reeds in their seeding state, on the end of which they fix little sharpened stakes. Even these, they dare not use; for many times has it happened that I sent two or three men ashore to some village to parley, and countless numbers of them sallied forth, but as soon as they saw those approach, they fled away in such wise that even a father would not wait for this son. And this was not because any hurt had ever done to any of them:—but such they are, incurably timid. It is true that since they have become more assured, and are losing that terror, they are artless and generous with what they have, to such a degree as no one would believe but him who had seen it. Of anything they have, if it be asked for, they never say no, but do rather invite the person to accept it, and show as much lovingness as though they would give their hearts. And whether it be a thing of value, or one of little worth, they are straightways content with whatsoever trifle of whatsoever kind may be given them in return for it. I forbade that anything so worthless as fragments of broken platters, and pieces of broken glass, and strapbuckles, should be given them; although when they were able to get such things, they seemed to think they had the best jewel in the world...And they knew no sect, nor idolatry; save that they all believe that power and goodness are in the sky, and they believed very firmly that I, with these ships and crew, came from the sky; and in such opinion, they received me at every place were I landed, after they had lost their terror. And this comes not because they are ignorant; on the contrary, they are men of very subtle wit, who navigate all those seas, and who give a marvellously good account of everything—but because they never saw men wearing clothes nor the like of our ships. And as soon as I arrived in the Indies, in the first island that I found, I took some of them by force to the intent that they should learn [our speech] and give me information of what there was in those parts. And so it was, that very soon they understood [us] and we them, what by speech or what by signs; and those [Indians] have been of much service...with loud cries of "Come! come to see the people from heaven!" Then, as soon as their minds were reassured about us, every one came, men as well as women, so that there remained none behind, big or little; and they all brought something to eat and drink, which they gave with wondrous lovingness...It seems to me that in all those islands, the men are all content with a single wife; and to their chief or king they give as many as twenty. The women, it appears to me, do more work than the men. Nor have I been able to learn whether they held personal property, for it seemed to me that whatever one had, they all took share of, especially of eatable things. Down to the present, I have not found in those islands any monstrous men, as many expected, but on the contrary all the people are very comely; nor are they black like those in Guinea, but have flowing hair; and they are not begotten where there is an excessive violence of the rays of the sun...In those islands, where there are lofty mountains, the cold was very keen there, this winter; but they endured it by being accustomed thereto, and by the help of the meats which they eat with many and inordinately hot spices...Since thus our Redeemer has given to our most illustrious King and Queen, and to their famous kingdoms, this victory in so high a matter, Christendom should take gladness therein and make great festivals, and give solemn thanks to the Holy Trinity for the great exaltation they shall have by the conversion of so many peoples to our holy faith; and next for the temporal benefit which will bring hither refreshment and profit, not only to Spain, to all Christians. This briefly, in accordance with the facts. Dated, on the caravel, off the Canary Islands, the 15 February of the year 1493.

Document B
Alvar Nunez Cabeza de Vaca Describe the
Indians of the Rio Grande Region, 1528-1536

...They are so accustomed to running that, without resting or getting tired, they run from morning till night in pursuit of a deer, and kill a great many, because they follow until the game is worn out, sometimes catching it alive. Their huts are of matting placed over four arches. They carry them on their back and move every two or three days in quest of food; they plant nothing that would be of any use.

They are very merry people, and even when famished do not cease to dance and celebrate their feasts and ceremonials. Their best times are when "tunas" (prickly pears) are ripe, because then they have plenty to eat and spend the time in dancing and eating day and night. As long as these tunas last they squeeze and open them and set them to dry. When dried they are put in baskets like figs and kept to be eaten on the way. The peelings they grind and pulverize.

All over this country there are a great many deer, fowl and other animals which I have before enumerated. Here also they come up with cows; I have seen them thrice and have eaten their meat. They appear to me of the size of those in Spain. Their horns are small, like those of the Moorish cattle; the hair is very long, like fine wool and like a peajacket; some are brownish and others black, and to my taste they have better and more meat than those from here. Of the small hides the Indians make blankets to cover themselves with, and of the taller ones they make shoes and targets. These cows come from the north, across the country further on, to the coast of Florida, and are found all over the land for over four hundred leagues. On this whole stretch, through the valleys by which they come, people who live there descend to subsist upon their flesh. And a great quantity of hides are met with inland.

We remained with the Avavares Indians for eight months, according to our reckoning of the moons. During that time they came for us from many places and said that verily we were children of the sun. Until then Donates and the negro had not made any cures, but we found ourselves so pressed by the Indians coming from all sides, that all of us had to become medicine men. I was the most daring and reckless of all in undertaking cures. We never treated anyone that did not afterwards say he was well, and they had such confidence in our skill as to believe that none of them would die as long as we were among them....

The women brought many mats, with which they built us houses, one for each of us and those attached to him. After this we would order them to boil all the game, and they did it quickly in ovens built by them for the purpose. We partook of everything a little, giving the rest to the principal man among those who had come with us for distribution among all. Every one then came with the share he had received for us to breathe on it and bless it, without which they left it untouched. Often we had with us three to four thousand persons. And it was very tiresome to have to breathe on and make the sign of the cross over every morsel they ate or drank. For many other things which they wanted to do they would come to ask our permission, so that it is easy to realize how greatly we were bothered. The women brought us tunas, spiders, worms, and whatever else they could find, for they would rather starve than partake of anything that had not first passed through our hands.

While travelling with those, we crossed a big river coming from the north and, traversing about thirty leagues of plains, met a number of people that came from afar to meet us on the trail, who treated us like the foregoing ones.

Thence on there was a change in the manner of reception, insofar as those who would meet us on the trail with gifts were no longer robbed by the Indians of our company, but after we had entered their homes they tendered us all they possessed, and the dwellings also. We turned over everything to the principals for distribution. Invariably those who had been deprived of their belongings would follow us, in order to repair their losses, so that our retinue became very large. They would tell them to be careful and not conceal anything of what they owned, as it could not be done without our knowledge, and then we would cause their death. So much did they frighten them that on the first few days after joining us they would be trembling all the time, and would not dare to speak or lift their eyes to Heaven.

Those guided us for more than fifty leagues through a desert of very rugged mountains, and so arid that there was no game. Consequently we suffered much from lack of food, and finally forded a very big river, with its water reaching to our chest. Thence on many of our people began to show the effects of the hunger and hardships they had undergone in those mountains, which were extremely barren and tiresome to travel.

The next morning all those who were strong enough came along, and at the end of three journeys we halted. Alonso del Castillo and Estevanico, the negro, left with the women as guides, and the woman who was a captive took them to a river that flows between mountains where there was a village in which her father lived, and these were the first adobes we saw that were like unto real houses. Castillo and Estevanico went to these and, after holding parley with the Indians, at the end of three days Castillo returned to where he had left us, bringing with him five or six of the Indians. He told how he had found permanent houses, inhabited, the people of which ate beans and squashes, and that he had also seen maize.

Of all things upon earth that caused us the greatest pleasure, and we gave endless thanks to our Lord for this news. Castillo also said that the negro was coming to meet us on the way, near by, with all the people of the houses. For that reason we started, and after going a league and a half met the negro and the people that came to receive us, who gave us beans and many squashes to eat, gourds to carry water in, robes of cowhide, and other things. As those people and the Indians of our company were enemies, and did not understand each other, we took leave of the latter, leaving them all that had been given to us, while we went on with the former and, six leagues beyond, when night was already approaching, reached their houses, where they received us with great ceremonies. Here we remained one day, and left on the next, taking them with us to other permanent houses, where they subsisted on the same food also, and thence on we found a new custom....

Having seen positive traces of Christians and become satisfied they were very near, we gave many thanks to our Lord for redeeming us from our sad and gloomy condition. any one can imagine our delight when he reflects how long we had been in that land, and how many dangers and hardships we had suffered. That nigh I entreated one of my companions to go after the Christians, who were moving through the part of the country pacified and quieted by us, and who were three days ahead of where we were. They did not like my suggestion, and excused themselves from going, on the ground of being tired and worn out, although any of them might have done it far better than I, being younger and stronger.

Seeing their reluctance, in the morning I took with me the negro and eleven Indians and, following the trail, went in search of the Christians. On that day we made ten leagues, passing three places where they slept. The next morning I came upon four Christians on horseback, who, seeing me in such a strange attire, and in company with Indians, were greatly startled. They stared at me for quite awhile, speechless; so great was their surprise that they could not find words to ask me anything. I spoke first, and told them to lead me to their captain, and we went together to Diego de Alcaraz, their commander.

Document C
John Cabot's Voyages

The Venetian, our countryman, who went with a ship from Bristol in quest of new islands, is returned, and says that 700 leagues hence he discovered land, the territory of the Grand Cham [Khan]. He coasted for 300 leagues and landed; saw no human beings, but he has brought hither to the King certain snares which had been set to catch game, and a needle for making nets. He also found some felled trees, wherefore he supposed there were inhabitants, and returned to his ship in alarm.

He was three months on the voyage, and on his return he saw two islands to starboard, but would not land, time being precious, as he was short of provisions. He says that the tides are slack and do not flow as they do here. The King of England is much pleased with this intelligence.

The King has promised that in the spring our countryman shall have then ships, armed to his order, and at his request has conceded him all the prisoners, except such as are confined for high treason, to man his fleet. The King has given him money wherewith to amuse himself till then, and he is now at Bristol with his wife, who is also Venetian, and with his sons. His name is Zuan Cabot, and he is styled the Great Admiral. Vast honor is paid him; he dresses in silk. And these English run after him like mad people, so that he can enlist as many of them as he pleases, and a number of our own rogues besides.

Document D
Thomas Mun
England's Treasure
by Foreign Trade

The Qualities which are required in a perfect Merchant of Forraign Trade

The Love and service of our Country consisteth not so much in the knowledge of those duties which are to be performed by others, as in the skilful practice of that which is done by our selves; and therefore it is now fit that I say something of the Merchant...for the Merchant is worthily called the Steward of the Kingdoms Stock, by way of Commerce with other Nations; a work of no less Reputation than Trust, which ought to be performed with great skill and conscience, that so the private gain may ever accompany the publique good....I will briefly set down the excellent qualities which are required of a perfect Merchant.

1. He ought to be a good Penman, a good Arithmetician, and a good Accomptant, by that noble order of Debtor and Creditor, which is used onely amongst Merchants; also to be expert in the order and form of Charter-parties, Bills of Lading, Invoyces, Contracts, Bills of Exchange, and Policies of Ensurance.
2. He ought to know the Measures, Weights, and Monies of all forraign Countries, especially where we have Trade, & the Monies not onely by their several denominations, but also by their intrinsique values in weight & fineness, compared with the Standard of this Kingdom, without which he cannot well direct his affaires.
3. He ought to know the Customs, Tools, Taxes, Impositions, Conducts and other charges upon all manner of Merchandize exported or imported to and from the said Forraign Countries.
4. He ought to know in what several commodities each Country abounds, and what be the wares which they want, and how and from whence they are furnished with the same.
5. He ought to understand, and to be a diligent observer of the rates of Exchanges by Bills, from one State to another, whereby he may the better direct his affairs, and remit over and receive home his Monies to the most advantage possible.
6. He ought to know what goods are prohibited to be exported or imported in the said forraign Countreys, lest otherwise he should incur great danger and loss in the ordering of his affairs.
7. He ought to know upon what rates and conditions to fraight his Ships, and ensure his adventures from one Countrey to another, and to be well acquainted with the laws, orders and customes of the Ensurance office both here and beyond the Seas, in the many accidents which may happen upon the damage or loss of Ships and goods, or both these.
8. He ought to have knowledge in the goodness and in the prices of all the several materials which are required for the building and repairing of Ships, and the divers workmanships of the same, as also for the Masts, Tackling, Cordage, Ordnance, Victuals, Munition, and Provisions of many kinds; together with the ordinary wages of Commanders, Officers, and Mariners, all which concern the Merchant as he is an Owner of Ships.
9. He ought (by the divers occasions which happen sometimes in the buying and selling of one commodity and sometimes in another) to have indifferent if not perfect knowledge in all manner of Merchandize or wares, which is to be as it were a man of all occupations and trades.
10. He ought by his voyaging on the Seas to become skilful in the Art of Navigation.
11. He ought, as he is a Traveller, and sometimes abiding in forraign Countreys, to attain to the speaking of divers Languages, and to be a diligent observer of the ordinary Revenues and expences of forraign Princes, together with their strength both by Sea and Land, their laws, customes, policies, manners, religions, arts, and the like; to be able to give account thereof in all occasions for the good of his Countrey.
12. Lastly, although there be no necessity that such a Merchant should be a great Scholar; yet it is (at least) required, that in his youth he learn the Latine tongue, which will the better enable him in all the rest of his endeavours.

The Means to Enrich this Kingdom, and to Encrease Our Treasure

The ordinary means therefore to increase our wealth and treasure is by Forraign Trade, wherein wee must ever observe this rule; to sell more to strangers yearly than wee consume of theirs in value. For suppose that when this Kingdom is plentifully served with the Cloth, Lead, Tinn, Iron, Fish and other native commodities, we doe yearly export the overplus to forraign Countreys to the value of twenty two hundred thousand pounds; by which means we are enable beyond the Seas to buy and bring in forraign wares for our use and Consumptions, to the value of twenty hundred thousand pounds.

The Exportation of our Moneys in Trade of Merchandize in a Means to Encrease our Treasure.

If we have such a quantity of wares as doth fully provide us of all things needful from beyond the seas: why should we then doubt that our monys sent out in trade, must not necessarily come back again in treasure; together with the great gains which it may procure in such manner as is before set down? And on the other side, if those Nations which send out their monies do it because they have but few wares of their own, how come they then to have so much Treasure as we ever see in those places which suffer it freely to be exported at all times and by whomsoever? I answer, Even by trading with their Moneys; for by what other means can they get it, having no Mines of Gold or Silver?

Document E
The Laws of Virginia, 1610-1611

...Whereas his Majesty, like himself a most zealous prince, has in his own realms a principal care of true religion and reverence to God and has always strictly commanded his generals and governors, with all his forces wheresoever, to let their ways be, like his ends, for the glory of God.

And forasmuch as no good service can be performed, or were well managed, where military discipline is not observed, and military discipline cannot be kept where the rules or chief parts thereof be not certainly set down and generally know, I have, with the advice and counsel of Sir Thomas Gates, Knight, Lieutenant-General, adhered unto the laws divine and orders politic and martial of his lordship, the same exemplified, as addition of such others as I found either the necessity of the present state of the colony to require or the infancy and weakness of the body thereof as yet able to digest, and do now publish them to all persons in the colony, that they may as well take knowledge of the laws themselves as of the penalty and punishment, which, without partiality, shall be inflicted upon the breakers of the same.

1. First, Since we owe our highest and supreme duty, our greatest, and all our allegiance to him from whom all power and authority is derived and flows as from the first and only fountain, and being especial soldiers impressed in this sacred cause, we must alone expect our success from him, who is only the blesser of all good attempts, the king of kings, the commander of commanders, and lord of hosts, I do strictly command and charge all captains and officers, of what quality or nature soever, whether commanders in the field or in town or towns, forts or fortresses, to have a care that the Almighty God be duly and daily served and that they call upon their people to hear sermons, as that also they diligently frequent morning and evening prayer themselves by their own exemplar and daily life and duty herein, encouraging others thereunto, and that such who shall often and willfully absent themselves be duly punished according to the martial law in that case provided.

2. That no man speak impiously or maliciously against the holy and blessed Trinity or any of the three persons, that is to say, against God the Father, God the Son, and God the Holy Ghost, or against the known articles of the Christian faith, upon pain of death.

3. That no man blaspheme God's holy name upon pain of death, or use unlawful oaths, taking the name of God in vain, curse, or bane upon pain of severe punishment for the first offense so committed and for the second to have a bodkin thrust through his tongue; and if he continue the blaspheming of God's holy name, for the third time so offending, he shall be brought to a martial court and there receive censure of death of his offense.

4. No man shall use any traitorous words against his Majesty's person or royal authority, upon pain of death.

5. No man shall speak any word or do any act which may tend to the derision or despite of God's holy word, upon pain of death; nor shall any man unworthily demean himself unto any preacher or minister of the same, but generally hold them in all reverent regard and dutiful entreaty; otherwise he the offender shall openly be whipped three times and ask public forgiveness in the assembly of the congregation three several Sabbath days.

6. Every man and woman duly, twice a day upon the first tolling of the bell, shall upon the working days repair unto the church to hear divine service upon pain of losing his or her day's allowance for the first omission, for the second to be whipped, and for the third to be condemned to the galleys for six months. Likewise, no man or woman shall dare to violate or break the Sabbath by any gaming, public or private abroad or at home, but duly sanctify and observe the same, both himself and his family, by preparing themselves at home with private prayer that they may be the better fitted for the public, according to the commandments of God and the orders of our church. As also every man and woman shall repair in the morning to the divine service and sermons preached upon the Sabbath day in the afternoon to divine service and catechising, upon pain for the first fault to lose their provision and allowance for the whole week following, for the second to lose the said allowance and also to be whipped, and for the third to suffer death.

7. All preachers and ministers within this our colony or colonies shall, in the forts where they are resident, after divine service, duly preach every Sabbath day in the forenoon and catechise in the afternoon and weekly say the divine service twice every day and preach every Wednesday. Likewise, every minister where he is resident, within the same fort or fortress, towns or town, shall choose unto him four of the most religious and better disposed as well to inform of the abuses and neglects of the people in their duties and service of God, as also to the due reparation and keeping of the church handsome and fitted with all reverent observances thereunto

belonging. Likewise, every minister shall keep a faithful and true record of church book of all christenings, marriages, and deaths of such our people as shall happen within their fort or fortress, towns or town, at any time, upon the burden of a neglectful conscience and upon pain of losing their entertainment.

8. He that, upon pretended malice, shall murder or take away the life of any man, shall be punished with death.

9. No man shall commit the horrible and detestable sins of sodomy, upon pain of death; and he or she that can be lawfully convict of adultery shall be punished with death. No man shall ravish or force any woman, maid or Indian, or other, upon pain of death; and know that he or she that shall commit fornication, and evident proof made thereof, for their first fault shall be whipped, for their second they shall be whipped, and for their third they shall be whipped three times a week for one month and ask public forgiveness in the assembly of the congregation.

10. No man shall be found guilty of sacrilege, which is a trespass as well committed in violating and abusing any sacred ministry, duty, or office of the church irreverently or prophanely, as by being a church robber to filch, steal, or carry away anything out of the church appertaining thereunto or unto any holy and consecrated place to the divine service of God, which no man shall do upon pain of death. Likewise, he that shall rob the store of any commodities therein of what quality soever, whether provisions of victuals, or of arms, trucking stuff, apparel, linen, or woolen, hose or shoes, hats or caps, instruments or tools of steel, iron, etc., or shall rob from his fellow soldier or neighbor anything that is his, victuals, apparel, household stuff, tool, or what necessary else soever, by water or land, out of boat, house, or knapsack, shall be punished with death....

...Every minister or preacher shall, every Sabbath day before catechising, read all these laws and ordinances publicly in the assembly of the congregation upon pain of his entertainment checked for that week....

Document Set Two
Life in the British Colonies: Dreams and Realities

Within a hundred years of the first settlement in Virginia, England established thirteen colonies along the North American coastline. These settlements fostered the transplantation of immigrants whose colonial societies were shaped by their traditions and the environment of the New World. Many came voluntarily, motivated by hopes and dreams of political, social and economic opportunities.

Enslaved Africans, however, had no choice and were brought over by involuntary means to fill the need for permanent enslaved labor in the southern colonies.

This set of documents depicts the development of colonial life during this period. They highlight important events and characteristics which helped to shape an American identity. What should be noted is the contrast between the hopes and dreams of these colonists and the reality of their environment.

The first two documents contrast voluntary and involuntary servitude in the colonies. Indentured servants during the eighteenth century were an important source of labor. In exchange for their labor, they were given transportation to the New World. Gottlieb Mittelberger in, "Journey to the New World," narrates the horror of the trans-Atlantic trip. He describes how the end of the journey brought further terror as these servants were auctioned off for their labor. Of particular interest is his description of what happened to families at these auctions.

As difficult as life was for indentured servants, they had the hope that their bondage was not permanent and, eventually, freedom could be achieved. This was not the situation for African slaves. In the second piece, "The African Salve Trade," by Alexander Falconbridge, the reader is given a precise description of the inhumanity of the middle passage to the New World. Falconbridge served as a surgeon on slave ships during the 1770s and 1780s. After reading this piece it is easy to understand why the mortality rate was so high on slave ships.

For William Penn the founding of a colony meant an opportunity to implement his dream for a perfect society in which people lived in perfect harmony. The third document is a discourse by him on the relationship between government and the citizenry. The piece was written prior to the settlement in Pennsylvania was established and therefore it would be interesting to contrast his dream with the reality of how the colony actually functioned.

In the next set of documents on Virginia and Massachusetts, the reader is given the opportunity to see what happens when dreams clash with reality. By 1676, Virginia had developed a distinct lifestyle which included the best land being held by a small group of planters. Under the leadership of Governor Berkeley, they dominated the political and economic life of the colony. Later arrivals to the colony were forced to settle further inland in an environment which was hostile and not as fertile. Realizing the inequity of their situation and, believing that they had little support from the colonial government, their frustrations manifested in an attempt to take over control of the colony. "Bacon's Rebellion: The Declaration" details their specific grievances and challenged the authority of colonial rule. It is an important example of the tensions which developed throughout the colonies between the frontier and coastal regions.

Massachusetts was intended to be "The City Upon The Hill." It was to have been a perfect Christian community that could serve as a model society for the rest of the world. Founded by the Puritans, there was never any doubt for them that they would succeed in achieving their objective. However, the economic success of the colony doomed its religious mission. As the colony grew and prospered it was difficult to focus on maintaining a closed Christian community. The influx of non-Puritans diverted the attention from the covenant to dollar signs. The hysteria of the Salem Witchtrials channeled the frustrations of many Puritans as they lost control of their colony. In the document, "Witchcraft in Salem," note the speculations of Cotton Mather about witches. It would be interesting to compare his thoughts to Ann Foster's confession concerning how pervasive this evil was throughout Salem.

By the mid 1750s it was clear that the colonies were not insulated from world events. Territorial expansion brought them into the world conflict occurring between Great Britain and France. In the last piece, George Washington narrates to his mother the military difficulties which were encountered during the French and Indian war. The letter was written just after the disastrous defeat by General Braddock. Note his comparison between the actions of the British and colonial troops.

Questions for Document Set Two

1. Compare the treatment of indentured servants and slaves on the passage to the New World.

2. Describe Penn's vision for a perfect society. Could any society have achieved this goal?

3. What specific grievances did the participants in Bacon's Rebellion have against the governor?

4. What examples did Ann Foster cite to show the devil had appeared?

5. According to Washington's description, compare the actions of the British and colonial troops under fire?

6. How difficult was life in colonial America? Given the problems which were described why would an individual be motivated to settle in the New World?

Document A
Gottlieb Mittelberger
Indentured Servants

Both in Rotterdam and in Amsterdam the people are packed densely, like herrings so to say, in the large sea-vessels. One person receives a place of scarcely 2 feet width and 6 feet length in the bedstead, while many a ship carries four to six hundred souls; not to mention the innumerable implements, tools, provisions, water-barrels and other things which likewise occupy such space.

On account of contrary winds it takes the ships sometimes 2, 3, and 4 weeks to make the trip from Holland to...England. But when the wind is good, they get there in 8 days or even sooner. Everything is examined there and the custom-duties paid, whence it comes that the ships ride there 8, 10 or 14 days and even longer at anchor, till they have taken in their full cargoes. During that time every one is compelled to spend his last remaining money and to consume his little stock of provisions which had been reserved for the sea; so that most passengers, finding themselves on the ocean where they would be in greater need of them, must greatly suffer from hunger and want. Many suffer want already on the water between Holland and Old England.

When the ships have for the last time weighed their anchors near the city of Kaupp [Cowes] in Old England, the real misery begins with the long voyage. For from there the ships, unless they have good wind, must often sail 8, 9, 10 to 12 weeks before they reach Philadelphia. But even with the best wind the voyage lasts 7 weeks.

But during the voyage there is on board these ships terrible misery, stench, fumes, horror, vomiting, many kinds of sea-sickness, fever, dysentery, headache, heat, constipation, boils, scurvy, cancer, mouth rot, and the like, all of which come from old and sharply salted food and meat, also from very bad and foul water, so that many die miserably.

Add to this want of provisions, hunger, thirst, frost, heat, dampness, anxiety, want, afflictions and lamentations, together with other trouble, as...the lice abound so frightfully, especially on sick people, that they can be scraped off the body. The misery reaches the climax when a gale rages for 2 or 3 nights and days, so that every one believes that the ship will go to the bottom with all human beings on board. In such a visitation the people cry and pray most piteously.

Children from 1 to 7 years rarely survive the voyage. I witnessed...misery in no less than 32 children in our ship, all of whom were thrown into the sea. The parents grieve all the more since their children find no resting-place in the earth, but are devoured by the monsters of the sea.

That most of the people get sick is not surprising, because, in addition to all other trials and hardships, warm food is served only three times a week, the rations being very poor and very little. Such meals can hardly be eaten, on account of being so unclean. The water which is served out of the ships is often very black, thick and full of worms, so that one cannot drink it without loathing, even with the greatest thirst. Toward the end we were compelled to eat the ship's biscuit which had been spoiled long ago; though in a whole biscuit there was scarcely a piece the size of a dollar that had not been full of red worms and spiders' nests....

At length, when, after a long and tedious voyage, the ships come in sight of land, so that the promontories can be seen, which the people were so eager and anxious to see, all creep from below on deck to see the land from afar, and they weep for joy, and pray and sing, thanking and praising God. The sight of the land makes the people on board the ship, especially the sick and the half dead, alive again, so that their hearts leap within them; they shout and rejoice, and are content to bear their misery in patience, in the hope that they may soon reach the land in safety. But alas!

When the ships have landed at Philadelphia after their long voyage, no one is permitted to leave them except those who pay for their passage or can give good security; the others, who cannot pay, must remain on board the ships till they are purchased, and are released from the ships by their purchasers. The sick always fare the worst, for the healthy are naturally preferred and purchased first; and so the sick and wretched must often remain on board in front of the city for 2 or 3 weeks, and frequently die, whereas many a one, if he could pay his debt and were permitted to leave the ship immediately, might recover and remain alive.

The sale of human beings in the market on board the ship is carried out thus: Every day Englishmen, Dutchmen and High-German people come from the city of Philadelphia and other places, in part from a great distance, say 20, 30, or 40 hours away, and go on board the newly arrived ship that has brought and offers for sale passengers from Europe, and select among the healthy persons such as they deem suitable for their business, and bargain with them how long they will serve for their passage money, which most of them are still in debt for. When they have come to an agreement, it happens that adult persons bind themselves in writing to serve 3, 4, 5 or 6 years for the amount due by them, according to their age and strength. But very young people, from 10 to 15 years, must serve till they are 21 years old.

Many parents must sell and trade away their children like so many head of cattle; for if their children take the debt upon themselves, the parents can leave the ship free and unrestrained; but as the parents often do not know where and to what people their children are going, it often happens that such parents and children, after leaving the ship, do not see each other again for many years, perhaps no more in all their lives.

Document B
Alexander Falconbridge
The African Slave Trade

Treatment of the Slaves

As soon as the wretched Africans, purchased at the fairs, fall into the hands of the black traders, they experience an earnest of those dreadful sufferings which they are doomed in future to undergo. And there is not the least room to doubt, but that even before they can reach the fairs, great numbers perish from cruel usage, want of food, travelling through inhospitable deserts, etc. They are brought from the places where they are purchased to Bonny, etc. in canoes; at the bottom of which they lie, having their hands tied with a kind of willow twigs, and a strict watch is kept over them. Their usage in other respects, during the time of passage, which generally lasts several days, is equally cruel. Their allowance of food is so scanty, that it is barely sufficient to support nature. They are, besides, much exposed to the violent rains which frequently fall here, being covered only with mats that afford but a slight defense; and as there is usually water at the bottom of the canoes, from their leaking, they are scarcely every dry.

Nor do these unhappying beings, after they become the property of the Europeans (from whom as a more civilized people, more humanity might naturally be expected), find their situation in the least amended. Their treatment is no less rigorous. The men Negroes, on being brought aboard the ship, are immediately fastened together, two and two, by handcuffs on their wrists, and irons riveted on their legs. They are then sent down between the decks, and placed in an apartment partitioned off for that purpose. The women likewise are placed in a separate room, on the same deck, but without being ironed. And an adjoining room, on the same deck is besides appointed for the boys. Thus are they placed in different apartments.

But at the same time, they are frequently stowed so close, as to admit of no other posture than lying on their sides. Neither will the height between decks, unless directly under the grating, permit them the indulgence of an erect posture; especially where there are platforms, which is generally the case. These platforms are a kind of shelf, about eight or nine feet in breadth, extending from the side of the ship towards the centre. They are placed nearly midway between the decks, at the distance of two or three feet from each deck. Upon these the Negroes are stowed in the same manner as they are on the deck underneath.

...About eight o'clock in the morning the Negroes are generally brought upon deck. Their irons being examined, a long chain, which is locked to a ring-bolt, fixed in the deck, is run through the rings of the shackles of the men, and then locked to another ring-bolt, fixed also in the deck. By this means fifty or sixty, and sometimes more, are fastened to one chain, in order to prevent them from rising, or endeavoring to escape. If the weather proves favorable, they are permitted to remain in that situation till four or five in the afternoon, when they are disengaged from the chain, and sent down.

...Upon the Negroes refusing to take sustenance, I have seen coals of fire, glowing hot, put a shovel, and placed so near their lips, as to scorch and burn them. And this has been accompanied with threats, of forcing them to swallow the coals, if they any longer persisted in refusing to eat. These means have generally had the desired effect. I have also been credibly informed that a certain captain in the slave trade poured melted lead on such of the Negroes as obstinately refused their food.

Exercise being deemed necessary for the preservation of their health, they are sometimes obligated to dance, when the weather will permit their coming on deck. If they go about it reluctantly, or do not move with agility, they are flogged; a person standing by them all the time with at cat-o'-nine-tails in his hand for that purpose. Their music, upon these occasions, consists of a drum, sometimes with only one head; and when that is worn out, they do not scruple to make use of the bottom of one of the tubs before described. The poor wretches are frequently compelled to sing also; but when they do so, their songs are generally, as may naturally be expected, melancholy lamentations of their exile from their native country.

...On board some ships, the common sailors are allowed to have intercourse with such of the black women whose consent they can procure. And some of them have been known to take the inconstancy of their paramours so much to heart, as to leap overboard and drown themselves. The officers are permitted to indulge their passions among them at pleasure, and sometimes are guilty of such brutal excesses as disgrace human nature.

The hardships and inconveniences suffered by the Negroes during the passage are scarcely to be enumerated or conceived. They are far more violently affected by the seasickness than the Europeans. It frequently terminates in death, especially among the women. But the exclusion of the fresh air is among the most intolerable. For the purpose of admitting this needful refreshment, most of the ships in the slave trade are provided, between the decks, with five or six air-ports on each side of the ship, of about six inches in length, and four in breadth; in addition to which, some few ships, but not one in twenty, have what they denominate wind-sails. But whenever the sea is rough and the rain heavy, it becomes necessary to shut these, and every other conveyance by which the air is admitted. The fresh air being thus excluded, the Negroes' rooms very soon grow intolerably hot. The confined air, rendered noxious by the effluvia exhaled from their bodies, and by being repeatedly breathed, soon produces fevers and fluxes, which generally carries off great numbers of them.

...One morning, upon examining the place allotted for the sick Negroes, I perceived that one of them, who was so emaciated as scarcely to be able to walk, was missing, and was convinced that he must have gone overboard in the night, probably to put a more expeditious period to his sufferings. And, to conclude on this subject, I could not help being sensibly affected, on a former voyage, at observing with what apparent eagerness a black woman seized some dirt from off an African yam, and put it into her mouth, seeming to rejoice at the opportunity of possessing some of her native earth.

From these instances I think it may have been clearly deduced that the unhappy Africans are not bereft of the finer feelings, but have a strong attachment to their native country, together with a just sense of the value of liberty. And the situation of the miserable beings above described, more forcibly urges the necessity of abolishing a trade which is the source of such evils, than the most eloquent harangue, or persuasive arguments could do.

Document C
William Penn: Model of Government

For particular frames and models [of government] it will become me to say little....My reasons are: First, that the age is too nice and difficult for it, there being nothing the wits of men are more busy and divided upon.... Secondly, I do not find a model in the world that time, place, and some singular emergencies have not necessarily altered; nor is it easy to frame a civil government that shall serve all places alike.

Thirdly, I know what is said by the several admirers of monarchy, aristocracy, and democracy, which are the rule of one, a few, and many, and are the three common ideas of government when men discourse on that subject. But I choose to solve the controversy with this small distinction, and it belongs to all three: any government is free to the people under it (whatever to be the frame) where the laws rule, and the people are a party to those laws; and more than this is tyranny, oligarchy, and confusion.

Document D
Bacon's Rebellion: The Declaration, July 30, 1676

1. For having, upon specious pretences of public works, raised great unjust taxes upon the commonalty for the advancement of private favorites and other sinister ends, but no visible effects in any measure adequate; for not having, during this long time of his government, in any measure advanced this hopeful colony either by fortifications, towns, or trade.
2. For having abused and rendered contemptible the magistrates of justice by advancing to places of judicature scandalous and ignorant favorites.
3. For having wronged his Majesty's prerogative and interest by assuming monopoly of the beaver trade and for having in it unjust gain betrayed and sold his Majesty's country and the lives of his loyal subjects to the barbarous heathen.
4. For having protected, favored, and emboldened the Indians against his Majesty's loyal subjects, never contriving, requiring, or appointing any due or proper means of satisfaction for their many invasions, robberies, and murders committed upon us.
5. For having, when the army of English was just upon the track of those Indians, who now in all places burn, spoil, murder and when we might with ease have destroyed them who then were in open hostility, for then having expressly countermanded and sent back our army by passing his word for the peaceable demeanor of the said Indians, who immediately prosecuted their evil intentions, committing horrid murders and robberies in all places, being protected by the said engagement and word past of him the said Sir William Berkeley, having ruined and laid desolate a great part of his majesty's country, and have now drawn themselves into such obscure and remote places and are by their success so emboldened and confirmed by their confederacy so strengthened that the cries of blood are in all places, and the terror and consternation of the people so great, are now become not only difficult but a very formidable enemy who might at first with ease have been destroyed.
6. And lately, when, upon the loud outcries of blood, the assembly had, with all care, raised and framed an army for the preventing of further mischief and safeguard of this his Majesty's colony.
7. For having, with only the privacy of some few favorites without acquainting the people, only by the alteration of a figure, forged a commission, by we know not what hand, not only without but even against the consent of the people, for the raising and effecting civil war and destruction, which being happily and without bloodshed prevented; for having the second time attempted the same, thereby calling down our forces from the defense of the frontiers and most weakly exposed places.
8. For the prevention of civil mischief and ruin amongst ourselves while the barbarous enemy in all places did invade, murder, and spoil us, his Majesty's most faithful subjects.

Of this and the aforesaid articles we accuse Sir William Berkeley as guilty of each and every one of the same, and as one who has traitorously attempted, violated, and injured his Majesty's interest here by a loss of a great part of this his colony and many of his faithful loyal subjects by him betrayed and in a barbarous and shameful manner exposed to the incursions and murder of the heathen. And we do further declare these the ensuing persons in this list to have been his wicked and pernicious councillors, confederates, aiders, and assisters against the commonalty in these our civil commotions.

Sir Henry Chichley
Lt. Col. Christopher Wormeley
Phillip Ludwell
Robt. Beverley
Ri. Lee
Thomas Ballard
William Cole

Richard Whitacre
Nicholas Spencer
Joseph Bridger
William Claiburne, Jr.
Thomas Hawkins
William Sherwood
John Page Clerke
John Clauffe Clerk

John West, Hubert Farrell, Thomas Reade, Math. Kempe

And we do further demand that the said Sir William Berkeley with all the persons in this list be forthwith delivered up or surrender themselves within four days after the notice hereof, or otherwise we declare as follows. That in whatsoever place, house, or ship, any of the said persons shall reside, be hid, or protected, we declare the owners, masters, or inhabitants of the said places to be confederates and traitors to the people and the estates of them is also of all the aforesaid persons to be confiscated. And this we, the commons of Virginia, do declare, desiring a firm union amongst ourselves that we may jointly and with one accord defend ourselves against the common enemy. And let not the faults of the guilty be the reproach of the innocent, or the faults or crimes of the oppressors divide and separate us who have suffered by their oppressions.

These are, therefore, in his Majesty's name, to command you forthwith to seize the persons abovementioned as traitors to the King and country and them to bring to Middle Plantation and there to secure them until further order, and, in case of opposition, if you want any further assistance you are forthwith to demand it in the name of the people in all the counties of Virginia.

Nathaniel Bacon
General by Consent of the people.

William Sherwood

Document E
Witchcraft in Salem

1. Cotton Mather on Witchcraft

In all the Witchcraft which now Grievously Vexes us, I know not whether anything be more unaccountable, than the Trick which the Witches have to render themselves, and their Tools Invisible. Witchcraft seems to be the Skill of Applying the Plastic Spirit of the World, unto some unlawful purposes, by means of a Confederacy with Evil Spirits.

2. The Examination and Confession of Ann Foster at Salem Village, 15 July, 1692

After a while Ann ffoster conffesed that the devil apered to her in the shape of a bird at several Times, such a bird as she neuer saw the like before; & that she had had this gift (viz. of striking ye afflicted downe with her eye euer since) & being askt why she thought yt bird was the diuill she answered because he came white & vanished away black & yt the diuill told her yt she should haue this gift & yt she must beliue him & told her she should haue prosperity & she said yt he had apeared to her three times & was always as a bird, and the last time was about half a year since, & sat upon a table had two legs & great eyes & yt it was the second time of his apearance that he promised her prosperity & yt it was Carriers wife about three weeks agoe yt came & perswaded her to hurt these people.

16 July 1692. Ann ffoster Examined confessed yt it was Goody Carrier yt made her a witch yt she came to her in person about Six yeares agoe & told her it she would not be a witch ye diuill should tare her in peices & carry her away at which time she promised to Serve the diuill yt she had bewitched a hog of John Loujoys to death & that she had hurt some persons in Salem Villige, yt goody Carier came to her & would have her bewitch two children of Andrew Allins & that she had then two popets made & stuck pins in them to bewitch ye said children by which one of them dyed ye other very sick, that she was at the meeting of the witches at Salem Vilige, yt Goody Carier came & told her of the meeting and wonld haue her goe, so they got upon Sticks & went said Jorny & being there did see Mr. Buroughs ye minister who spake to them all, & this was about two months agoe that there was then twenty five persons meet together, that she tyed a knot in a Rage & threw it into the fire to hurt Tim. Swan & that she did hurt the rest yt complayned of her by Squesing popets like them & so almost choked them.

18 July 1692. Ann ffoster Examined confessed yt ye deuil in shape of a man apeared to her wth Goody carier about six yeare since when they made her a witch & that she promised to serve the diuill two years, upon which the diuill promised her prosperity and many things but neuer performed it, that she & martha Carier did both ride on a stick or pole when they went to the witch meeting at Salem Village & that the stick broak: as they were caried in the aire aboue the tops of the trees, & they fell but she did hang fast about the neck of Goody Carier & ware presently at the vilage, that she was then much hurt of her Leg, she further saith that she heard some of the witches say there was three hundred & fiue in the whole Country & that they would ruin that place ye Vilige, also said there was present at that meetting two men besides Mr. Burroughs ye minister & one of them had gray haire, she saith yt she formerly frequented the publique metting to worship god. but the diuill had such power ouer her yt she could not profit there & yt was her undoeing: she saith yt about three or foure yeares agoe Martha Carier told her she would bewitch James Hobbs child to death & the child dyed in twenty four hours.

21. July 92. Ann ffoster Examined Owned her former conffesion being read to her and further conffesed that the discourse amongst ye witches at ye meeting at Salem village was that they would afflict there to set up the Diuills Kingdome. This confesion is true as witness my hand.

Ann ffoster Signed & Owned the aboue Examination & Conffesion before me
Salem 10th September 1692.   John Higginson, Just Peace.

3. The Examination of George Jacobs, Sr., and Margaret Jacobs

Warrant V. Geo. Jacobs Sr.

To the Constables in Salem.

You are in theire Majests names hereby required to apprehend and forthwith bring before vs George Jacobs Senr of Salem And Margaret Jacobs, the daughter of George Jacobs Junr of Salem, Singlewoman, Who stand accused of high suspition of sundry acts of witchcraft by them both Committed on sundry persons in Salem to theire great wrong and Injury and hereof faile not. (Dated Salem, May 10th, 1692)

John Hathorne,
Jonathan Corwin, Assists.

Indictment V. Geo. Jacobs Sr.

On the 12th of May, 1692, George Jacobs, sen., of Salem Village, was committed to Boston jail for witchcraft, and remained there six weeks and a few days. On the fifth day of August, the same year at a Court of Oyer and Terminer held at Salem, he was tried with five other–the Rev. Geo. Burroughs, a former minister of Salem Village, John Proctor and his wife Elizabeth, John Willard and Martha Carryer of Andover, who were all brought in by the jury guilty of the crime of Witchcraft.

They were all executed on the nineteenth of August, with the exception of Elizabeth Proctor, on Gallows Hill in Salem.

The witnesses in these trials were Margaret Jacobs, grand-daughter of George Jacobs, Mary Wolcott, Elizabeth Hubbard, Ann Putnam, Mercy Lewis and Mary Warren.

It is probable that Margaret Jacobs testified against her grandfather and Mr. Burroughs to save her own life, for she acknowledged to Mr. B., the day before the execution, that she had belied him and begged his forgiveness, who not only forgave her, but also prayed with and for her.

Document F
Washington: Defeat in the French and Indian War

Honored Madam: As I doubt not but you have heard of our defeat, and perhaps have it represented in a worse light (if possible) than it deserves, I have taken this earliest opportunity to give you some account of the engagement, as it happened within seven miles of the French fort, on Wednesday the 9th instant.

We marched on to that place without any considerable loss, having only now and then a straggler picked up by the French scouting Indians. When we came here, we were attacked by a body of French and Indians whose number (I am certain) did not exceed 300 men; ours consisted of about 1300 well-armed troops, chiefly of the English soldiers, who were stuck with such a panic that they behaved with more cowardice than it is possible to conceive. The officers behaved gallantly in order to encourage their men, for which they suffered greatly; there being near 60 killed and wounded; a large proportion out of the number we had!

The Virginia troops showed a good deal of bravery, and were near all killed; for I believe out of three companies that were there, there is scarce 30 men left alive. Capt. Peyrouny and all his officers down to a corporal was killed. Capt. Polson shared near as hard a fate; for only one of his was left. In short, the dastardly behavior of those they call regulars exposed all others that were inclined to do their duty to almost certain death. And at last, in despite of all the efforts of the officers to the contrary, they broke and run as sheep pursued by dogs; and it was impossible to rally them.

The General was wounded, of which he died three days after. Sir Peter Halkett was killed in the field, where died many other brave officers. I luckily escaped without a wound, though I had four bullets through my coat, and two horses shot under me. Captains Orme and Morris, two of the General's aides-de-camp, were wounded early in the engagement, which rendered the duty hard upon me, as I was the only person then left to distribute the General's orders, which I was scarcely able to do, as I was not half recovered from a violent illness that confined me to my bed and a wagon for above ten days. I am still in a weak and feeble condition, which induces me to halt here [Fort Cumberland] two or three days in hopes of recovering a little strength, to enable me to proceed homewards; from whence I fear I shall not be able to stir till towards September....

Document Set Three
The American Revolution: What Price Freedom?

It is difficult to discern the exact moment that the path of the American colonies and the British government diverged. Perhaps it was inevitable given the changes within the colonies as they developed an American identity. Prior to 1756, the British imperial government made a number of attempts at controlling the economic and political arrangement it had with the colonies. However, turmoil within its own political system made it almost difficult to achieve these objectives. It was only after the French and Indian War that a new imperial policy developed that called for tighter restrictions over them. Within a ten year period their differences would develop into an ideological and political dispute that would drive them apart. This set of documents centers on the major political debates of the period. It follows the path of the American colonists as they formulate their view and prepare for independence.

In 1765 Parliament passed the first internal tax on the colonists, the Stamp Act. Benjamin Franklin was a colonial agent at the time and, as colonial opposition to the act grew, found himself representing these views to the British government. In Franklin's Testimony to The Parliament he describes the role of taxes in the Pennsylvania colony. Students could be asked to analyze his arguments concerning internal and external taxes and why the colonists objected to the imposition of the former by Parliament. They could discuss what actions Franklin suggests the colonists would take if the tax was not rescinded.

John Dickinson's, "Letters From a Pennsylvania Farmer," were written in protest to the passage of the Townshend Duties in 1767. It was widely read throughout the colonies to help Americans justify their refusal to be taxed by Parliament. As in Franklin's testimony, Dickinson defines the political and economic relationship of Britain and the American colonies. An interesting discussion for students could focus on his arguments and what Dickinson feared would happen if the taxes were collected.

Not all colonists believed that the British government should not have the right to impose taxes on them. The third document is a letter sent by colonial Loyalists to the North Carolina governor. Students could discuss the perception these colonists had of their relationship with the British government. They might surmise which type of colonists might have written this type of letter.

There are few Americans who are not familiar with Patrick Henry's cry, "Give me liberty or give me death." In the fourth document students have an opportunity to read the speech which included this statement. He argues that the colonists have no other choice after exhausting all the avenues for reconciliation with Britain. An interesting comparison could be made between his speech and the letter of the Loyalists. Why would they have entirely different perceptions of the relationship between Britain and the colonies? Why would Henry's speech have been so popular throughout the colonies?

The document set ends with a letter from John Adams to his wife Abigail on July 3, 1776. He carefully explains to her why it was important to wait to declare independence. Would the course of the revolution have changed if independence had come earlier? As most of the other authors in this set of documents, Adams believes that Americans had no other choice but to declare independence.

Questions for Document Set Three

1. Compare the similarities and differences in the arguments of Franklin and Dickinson concerning the passage of internal colonial taxes by Parliament.

2. According to Franklin, what actions were the colonists willing to take to show their disapproval of the passage of the Stamp Act.

3. What did Dickinson fear would happen if the Townshend duties were collected?

4. Why did the Loyalists feel it was necessary to express their feelings about colonial-British relations?

5. What fundamental political principles were expressed in Patrick Henry's speech?

6. Which of the authors was most convincing in their arguments?

Document A
Franklin Testifies Against the Stamp Act (1766)

Q. What is your name, and place of abode?
A. Franklin, of Philadelphia.
Q. Do the Americans pay any considerable taxes among themselves?
A. Certainly many, and very heavy taxes.
Q. What are the present taxes in Pennsylvania, laid by the laws of the colony?
A. There are taxes on all estates, real and personal; a poll tax; a tax on all offices, professions, trades, and businesses, according to their profits; an excise on all wine, rum, and other spirit; and a duty of ten pounds per head on all Negroes imported, with some other duties.
Q. For what purposes are those taxes laid?
A. For the support of the civil and military establishments of the country, and to discharge the heavy debt contracted in the last [Seven Years'] war....
Q. Are not all the people very able to pay those taxes?
A. No. The frontier counties, all along the continent, have been frequently ravaged by the enemy and greatly impoverished, are able to pay very little tax....
Q. Are not the colonies, from their circumstances, very able to pay the stamp duty?
A. In my opinion there is not gold and silver enough in the colonies to pay the stamp duty for one year.
Q. Don't you know that the money arising from the stamps was all to be laid out in America?
A. I know it is appropriated by the act to the American service; but it will be spent in the conquered colonies, where the soldiers are, not in the colonies that pay it....
Q. Do you think it right that America should be protected by this country and pay no part of the expense?
A. That is not the case. The colonies raised, clothed, and paid, during the last war, near 25,000 men, and spent many millions.
Q. Where you not reimbursed by Parliament?
A. We were only reimbursed what, in your opinion, we had advanced beyond our proportion, or beyond what might reasonably be expected from us; and it was a very small part of what we spent. Pennsylvania, in particular, disbursed about 500,000 pounds, and the reimbursements, in the whole, did not exceed 60,000 pounds....
Q. Do you think the people of America would submit to pay the stamp duty, if it was moderated?
A. No, never, unless compelled by force of arms....
Q. What was the temper of America towards Great Britain before the year 1763?
A. The best in the world. They submitted willingly to the government of the Crown, and paid, in all their courts, obedience to acts of Parliament....
Q. What is your opinion of a future tax, imposed on the same principle with that of the Stamp Act? How would the Americans receive it?
A. Just as they do this. They would not pay it.
Q. Have not you heard of the resolutions of this House, and of the House of Lords, asserting the right of Parliament relating to America, including a power to tax the people there?
A. Yes, I have heard of such resolutions.
Q. What will be the opinion of the Americans on those resolutions?
A. They will think them unconstitutional and unjust.
Q. Was it an opinion in America before 1763 that the Parliament had no right to lay taxes and duties there?
A. I never heard any objection to the right of laying duties to regulate commerce; but a right to lay internal taxes was never supposed to be in Parliament, as we are not represented there....
Q. Did the Americans ever dispute the controlling power of Parliament to regulate the commerce?
A. No.
Q. Can anything less than a military force carry the Stamp Act into execution?
A. I do not see how a military force can be applied to that purpose.

Q. Why may it not?
A. Suppose a military force sent into America; they will find nobody in arms; what are they then to do? They cannot force a man to take stamps who chooses to do without them. They will not find a rebellion; they may indeed make one.
Q. If the act is not repealed, what do you think will be the consequences?
A. A total loss of the respect and affection the people of America bear to this country, and of all the commerce that depends on that respect and affection.
Q. How can the commerce be affected?
A. You will find that, if the act is not repealed, they will take very little of your manufactures in a short time.
Q. Is it in their power to do without them?
A. I think they may very well do without them.
Q. Is it their interest not to take them?
A. The goods they take from Britain are either necessaries, mere conveniences, or superfluities. The first, as cloth, etc., with a little industry they can make at home; the second they can do without till they are able to provide them among themselves; and the last, which are mere articles of fashion, purchased and consumed because the fashion in a respected country; but will now be detested and rejected. The people have already struck off, by general agreement, the use of all goods fashionable in mourning....
Q. If the Stamp Act should be repealed, would it induce the assemblies of America to acknowledge the right of Parliament to tax them, and would they erase their resolutions [against the Stamp Act]?
A. No, never.
Q. Is there no means of obliging them to erase those resolutions?
A. None that I know of; they will never do it, unless compelled by force of arms.
Q. Is there a power on earth that can force them to erase them?
A. No power, how great soever, can force men to change their opinions....
Q. What used to be the pride of the Americans?
A. To indulge in the fashions and manufactures of Great Britain.
Q. What is now their pride?
A. To wear their old clothes over again, till they can make new ones.

Document B
John Dickinson
Letters From a Farmer in Pennsylvania
1768

Letter II

There is [a] late act of Parliament, which seems to me to be...destructive to the liberty of these colonies, ...that is the act for granting duties on paper, glass, etc. It appears to me to be unconstitutional.

The Parliament unquestionable possesses a legal authority to regulate the trade of Great Britain and all its colonies. Such an authority is essential to the relation between a mother country and its colonies and necessary for the common good of all. He who considers these provinces as states distinct from the British Empire has very slender notions of justice or of their interests. We are but parts of a whole; and therefore there must exist a power somewhere to preside, and preserve the connection in due order. This power is lodged in the Parliament, and we are as much dependent on Great Britain as a perfectly free people can be on another.

I have looked over every statute relating to these colonies, from their first settlement to this time; and I find every one of them founded on this principle till the Stamp-Act administration. All before are calculated to preserve or promote a mutually beneficial intercourse between the several constituent parts of the Empire. And though many of them imposed duties on trade, yet those duties were always imposed with design to restrain the commerce of one part that was injurious to another, and thus to promote the general welfare....Never did the British Parliament, till the period abovementioned, think of imposing duties in American for the purpose of raising a revenue....This I call an innovation, and a most dangerous innovation.

That we may be legally bound to pay any general duties on these commodities, relative to the regulation of trade, is granted. But we being obliged by her laws to take them from Great Britain, any special duties imposed on their exportation to us only, with intention to raise a revenue from us only, are as much taxes upon us as those imposed by the Stamp Act....It is nothing but the edition of a former book with a new title page,....and will be attended with the very same consequences to American liberty.

Sorry I am to learn that there are some few persons, [who] shake their heads with solemn motion, and pretend to wonder what can be the meaning of these letters....I will now tell the gentlemen....The meaning of them is to convince the people of these colonies that they are at this moment exposed to the most imminent dangers, and persuade them immediately, vigorously, and unanimously to exert themselves, in the most firm, but most peaceable manner for obtaining relief. The cause of liberty is a cause of too much dignity to be sullied by turbulence and tumult. It ought to be maintained in a manner suitable to her nature....I hope, my dear countrymen, that you will in every colony be upon your guard against those who may at any time endeavour to stir you up, under pretences of patriotism, to any measures disrespectful to our sovereign and our mother country. Hot, rash, disorderly proceedings injure the reputation of a people as to wisdom, valour and virtue, without procuring them the least benefit....

Every government, at some time or other, falls into wrong measures. They may proceed from mistake or passion. But every such measure does not dissolve the obligation between the governors and the governed. The mistake may be corrected, the passion may pass over. It is the duty of the governed to endeavour to rectify the mistake and appease the passion. They have not at first any other right than to represent their grievances and to pray for redress....

Document C
Loyalists Express Support

Address of the Inhabitants of Anson County to Governor Martin

To His Excellency, Josiah Martin Esquire, Captain General, Governor, &c,

Most Excellent Governor:

Permit us, in behalf of ourselves, and many others of His Majesty's most dutiful and loyal subjects within the County of Anson, to take the earliest opportunity of addressing your Excellency, and expressing our abomination of the many outrageous attempts now forming on this side of the Atlantick, against the peace and tranquillity His Majesty's Dominions in North America, and to witness to your Excellency, by this our Protest, a disapprobation and abhorence of the many lawless combinations and unwarrantable practices actually carrying on by a gross tribe of infatuated anti-Monarchists in the several Colonies in these Dominions; the baneful consequence of whose audacious contrivance can, in fine, only tend to extirpate the fundamental principles of all Government, and illegally to shake off their obedience to, and dependence upon, the imperial Crown and Parliament of Great Britain; the infection of whose pernicious example being already extended to this particular County, of which we now bear the fullest testimony.

It is with the deepest concern (though with infinite indignation) that we see in all public places and papers disagreeable votes, speeches and resolutions, said to be entered into by our sister Colonies, in the highest contempt and derogation of the superintending power of the legislative authority of Great Britain. And we further, with sorrow, behold their wanton endeavors to vilify and arraign the honour and integrity of His Majesty's most honourable Ministry and Council, tending to sow the seed of discord and sedition, in open violation of their duty and allegiance....

...We are truly invigorated with the warmest zeal and attachment in favour of the British Parliament, Constitution and Laws, which our forefathers gloriously struggled to establish, and which are now become the noblest birthright and inheritance of all Britannia's Sons....

We are truly sensible that those invaluable blessings which we have hitherto enjoyed under His Majesty's auspicious Government, can only be secured to us by the stability of his Throne, supported and defended by the British Parliament, the only grand bulwark and guardian of our civil and religious liberties.

Duty and affection oblige us further to express our grateful acknowledgements for the inestimate blessings flowing from such a Constitution. And we do assure your Excellency that we are determined, by the assistance of Almighty God, in our respective stations, steadfastly to continue His Majesty's loyal Subjects, and to contribute all in our power for the preservation of the publick peace; so, that, by our unanimous example, we hope to discourage the desperate endeavours of a deluded multitude, and to see a misled people turn again from their atrocious offences to a proper exercise of their obedience and duty.

And we do furthermore assure your Excellency, that we shall endeavor to cultivate such sentiments in all those under our care, and to warm their breasts with a true zeal for His Majesty, and affection for his illustrious family. And may the Almighty God be pleased to direct his Councils, his Parliament, and all those in authority under him, that their endeavors may be for the advancement of piety, and the safety, honour and welfare of our Sovereign and his Kingdoms, that the malice of his enemies may be assuaged, and their evil designs confounded and defeated; so that all the world may be convinced that his sacred person, his Royal family, his Parliament, and our Country, are the special objects of Divine dispensation and Providence.

[Signed by two hundred and twenty-seven of the Inhabitants of the county of Anson.]

Document D
Give Me Liberty, Give Me Death

Mr. President:

It is natural to man to indulge in the illusions of hope. We are apt to shut our eyes against a painful truth, and listen to the song of the siren till she transforms us into beasts. Is this the part of wise men, engaged in a great and arduous struggle for liberty? Are we disposed to be of the number of those who having eyes see not, and having ears hear not, the things which so nearly concern their temporal salvation? For my part, whatever anguish of spirit it may cost, I am willing to know the whole truth; to know the worst and to provide for it.

I have but one lamp by which my feet are guided; and that is the lamp of experience. I know of no way of judging of the future but by the past. And judging by the past, I wish to know what there has been in the conduct of the British ministry for the last ten years, to justify those hopes with which gentlemen have been pleased to solace themselves and the house? Is it that insidious smile with which our petition has been lately received? Trust it not, sir: It will prove a snare to your feet. Suffer not yourselves to be betrayed with a kiss. Ask yourselves how this gracious reception of our petition comports with those warlike preparations which cover our waters and darken our land. Are fleets and armies necessary to a work of love and reconciliation? Have we shown ourselves so unwilling to be reconciled that force must be called in to win back our love? Let us not deceive ourselves, sir. These are the implements of war and subjugation—the last arguments to which kings resort. I ask gentlemen, sir, what means this martial array, if its purpose be not to force us to submission? Can gentlemen assign any other possible motive for it? Has Britain any enemy in this quarter of the world, to call for all this accumulation of navies and armies? No, sir, she has none. They are meant for us; they can be meant for no other. They are sent over to bind and rivet upon us those chains which the British ministry have been so long forging. And what have we to oppose them? Shall we try argument? Sir, we have been trying that for the last ten years. Have we anything new to offer upon the subject? Nothing. We have held the subject up in every light of which it is capable; but it has been all in vain. Shall we resort to entreaty and humble supplication? What terms shall we find which have not been already exhausted? Let us not, I beseech you, sir, deceive ourselves longer.

Sir, we have done everything that could be done to avert the storm which is now coming on. We have petitioned, we have remonstrated, we have supplicated, we have prostrated ourselves before the throne, and have implored its interposition to arrest the tyrannical hands of the ministry and Parliament. Our petitions have been slighted; our remonstrances have produced additional violence and insult; our supplications have been disregarded; and we have been spurned with contempt from the foot of the throne. In vain, after these things, may we indulge the fond hope of peace and reconciliation. There is no longer any room for hope. If we wish to be free, if we mean to preserve inviolate those inestimable privileges for which we have been so long contending, if we mean not basely to abandon the noble struggle in which we have been so long engaged, and which we have pledged ourselves never to abandon until the glorious object of our contest shall be obtained—we must fight! I repeat, sir, we must fight! An appeal to arms and to the God of Hosts is all that is left us!

They tell us, sir, that we are weak—unable to cope with so formidable an adversary. But when shall we be stronger? Will it be the next week, or the next year? Will it be when we are totally disarmed, and when a British guard shall be stationed in every house? Shall we gather strength by irresolution and inaction? Shall we acquire the means of effectual resistance by lying supinely on our backs, and hugging the delusive phantom of hope until our enemies shall have bound us hand and foot? Sir, we are not weak, if we make a proper use of those means which the God of nature hath placed in our power. Three millions of people, armed in the holy cause of liberty, and in such a country as that which we possess, are invincible by any force which our enemy can send against us. Besides, sir, we shall not fight our battles alone. There is a just God who presides over the destinies of nations; and who will raise up friends to fight our battles for us. The battle, sir, is not to the strong alone; it is to the vigilant, the active, the brave. Besides, sir, we have no election. If we were base enough to desire it, it is not too late to retire from the contest. There is no retreat but in submission and slavery! Our chains are forged; their clanking may be heard on the plains of Boston! The war is inevitable—and let it come! I repeat it, sir, let it come!

It is in vain, sir, to extenuate the matter. Gentlemen may cry, Peace, peace; but there is no peace. The war is actually begun. The next gale that sweeps from the north will bring to our ears the clash of resounding arms. Our brethren are already in the field. Why stand we here idle? What is it that gentlemen wish? What would they have? If life so dear, or peace sweet, as to be purchased at the price of chains and slavery? Forbid it Almighty God—I know not what course others may take; but as for me, give me liberty or give me death!

Document E
Letter from John Adams to Abigail Adams

Philadelphia July 3d. 1776

Had a Declaration of Independency been made seven Months ago, it would have been attended with many great and glorious Effects....We might before this Hour, have formed Alliances with foreign States.—We should have mastered Quebec and been in Possession of Canada....You will perhaps wonder, how such a Declaration would have influenced our Affairs, in Canada, but if I could write with Freedom I could easily convince you, that it would, and explain to you the manner how.—Many Gentlemen in high Stations and of great Influence have been duped, by the ministerial Bubble of Commissioners to treat....And in real, sincere Expectation of this Event, which they so fondly wished, they have been slow and languid, in promoting Measures for the Reduction of that Province. Others there are in the Colonies who really wished that our Enterprise in Canada would be defeated, that the Colonies might be brought into Danger and Distress between two Fires, and be thus induced to submit. Others really wished to defeat the Expedition to Canada, lest the Conquest of it, should elevate the Minds of the People too much to hearken to those Terms of Reconciliation which they believed would be offered Us. These jarring Views, Wishes and Designs, occasioned an opposition to many salutary Measures, which were proposed for the support of that Expedition, and caused Obstructions, Embarrassments and studied Delays, which have finally, lost Us the Province.

All these Causes however in Conjunction would not have disappointed Us, if it had not been for a Misfortune, which could not be foreseen, and perhaps could not have been prevented, I mean the Prevalence of the small Pox among our Troops...This fatal Pestilence compleated our Destruction.—It is a Frown of Providence upon Us, which We ought to lay to heart.

But on the other Hand, the Delay of this Declaration to this Time, has many great Advantages attending it.—The Hopes of Reconciliation, which we fondly entertained by Multitudes of honest and well meaning tho weak and mistaken People, have been gradually and at least totally extinguished.—Time has been given for the whole People, maturely to consider the great Question of Independence and to ripen their Judgments, dissipate their Fears, and allure their Hopes, by discussing it in News Papers and Pamphletts, by debating it, in Assemblies, Conventions, Committees of Safety and Inspection, in Town and County Meetings, as well as in private Conversations, so that the whole People in every Colony of the 13, have now adopted it, as their own Act.—This will cement the Union, and avoid those Heats and perhaps Convulsions which might have been occasioned, by such a Declaration Six Months ago.

But the Day is past. The Second Day of July 1776, will be the most memorable Epocha, in the History of America. —I am apt to believe that it will be celebrated, by succeeding Generations, as the great anniversary Festival. It ought to be commemorated, as the Day of Deliverance by solemn Acts of Devotion to God Almighty. It ought to be solemnized with Pomp and Parade, with Shews, Games, Sports, Guns, Bells, Bonfires and Illuminations from one End of this Continent to the other from this Time forward forever more.

You will think me transported with Enthusiasm but I am not.—I am well aware of the Toil and Blood and Treasure, that it will cost Us to maintain this Declaration, and support and defend these States.—Yet through all the Gloom I can see the Rays of ravishing Light and Glory. I can see that the End is more than worth all the Means. And that Posterity will tryumph in that Days Transaction, even although We should rue it, which I trust in God We shall not.

Document Set Four
A New Republic: We the People

As the American Revolution drew to a close in the early 1780s, the new nation took its first shaky steps toward unity. Many Americans hoped that the sacrifices of war meant a better future for them and the nation. Unfortunately, they met frustration and disappointment as the country learned the difficulties of self government. They would spend the decade searching to create national and local governments which could provide stability, unity and protect their liberties. This set of documents provides an overview of this "Critical Period" in American history. It highlights the major events of the period and how the nation dealt with this difficult time.

It became evident during the American Revolution that the central government was in a financial dilemma. Determined to maintain a level of solvency, it had withheld the pay of the soldiers and officers in the early 1780s. After offering a compromise, which was rejected by the national government, a number of officers met in Newburgh, New York in 1783 to discuss alternate ways to address their grievances. As the officers debated over a course of action, Washington appeared and addressed them. In Document A, "The Newburgh Address," he acknowledges the hardships under which they won the war. Washington appeals to them to find, "greater strength not to succumb" to their anger. Students reading this document may find a different side of Washington. They might consider the reasons why he chose to appear before the officers. Why was Washington worried about a "tyranny of a different sort?" After careful analysis, what conclusions would they reach as to why the speech did prevent further actions by the officers?

The first national government, The Articles of Confederation, was unable to deal with the economic problems of the postwar period. A lack of a national currency, runaway inflation, interstate tariffs and little foreign trade combined to drive the nation into a depression by the mid 1780s. With a restricted market place and mounting debts many American farmers were driven to economic disaster. In western Massachusetts, believing they had no other alternative, a group of farmers led by Daniel Shay marched to the state government to force it to address their problems. The second document is a set of letters written to the governor by two state militia generals, Shepherd and Lincoln. While students may be familiar with Shays Rebellion, these letters give them an opportunity to read first hand accounts of the incident. While neither general wanted bloodshed, students could discuss why Shepherd and Lincoln found it necessary to take action against the farmers. Were other alternatives available to the state government?

In 1787 there was little doubt that the national government was no longer able to govern in its present form. Delegates from 12 states met in Philadelphia in May to revise the Articles. Document C is the plan presented by Virginia to re-structure the national government. Students will quickly realize that the Virginia Plan became the basis for the new national government created in the constitution. Class discussion could center on the plan's concept for representation, how the executive was to be chosen, the role of the judiciary and the Council of Revision. Was republican government guaranteed under this model? Why would Virginia have taken the leadership in presenting a new structure of government?

The newly written Constitution made a powerful argument for a republican form of government that created a strong central government. Ratification was not easy given the memories of living under the rule of the British government. In 85 articles, Hamilton, Jay and Madison argued the strengths of this new government. Today, the Federalist Papers still provide the clearest analysis of American Federalism. The most well known of these documents is "Federalist Paper #10," written by James Madison. In Document D Madison outlines how a republican government should balance the needs of the minority and majority. Students could identify the factions which were present in American society in 1787. They could also discuss whether or not his argument is still valid today. Is the Constitution still able to maintain "equilibrium"" between the factions of modern society?

Questions for Document Set Four

1. What did Washington mean when he told the officers, "give the world another subject of wonder...an army victorious over its enemies-victorious over itself."

2. What fears did Washington express regarding the threatened actions of the army?

3. Can a comparison be made between the actions of the officers at Newburgh and the group led by Daniel Shay?

4. Given the tone of the letters by Shepherd and Lincoln, what were their feelings concerning the rebellion?

5. What are the similarities and differences between the Virginia Plan of government and the present federal government?

6. According to James Madison how would the new constitution balance the "cabals of a few" with the "confusion of the multitude."

7. Define the differences between pure democracy and a republic.

Document A
George Washington: The Newburgh Address,
March 11, 1783

To the Officers of the Army

Gentlemen-A fellow soldier, whose interest and affections bind him strongly to you, whose past sufferings have been as great, and whose future fortune may be as desperate as yours—would beg leave to address you.

Age has its claims, and rank is not without its pretensions to advise: but, though unsupported by both, he flatters himself, that the plain language of sincerity and experience will neither be unheard nor unregarded.

Like many of you, he loved private life, and left it with regret. He left it, determined to retire from the field, with the necessity that called him to it, and not till then—not till the enemies of his country, the slaves of power, and the hirelings of injustice, were compelled to abandon their schemes, and acknowledge America as terrible in arms as she had been humble in remonstrance. With this object in view, he has long shared in your toils and mingled in your dangers. He has felt the cold hand of poverty without a murmur, and has seen the insolence of wealth without a sigh. But, too much under the direction of his wishes, and sometimes weak enough to mistake desire for opinion, he has till lately—very lately—believed in the justice of his country. He hoped that, as the clouds of adversity scattered, and as the sunshine of peace and better fortune broke in upon us, the coldness and severity of government would relax, and that, more than justice, that gratitude would blaze forth upon those hands, which had upheld her, in the darkest stages of her passage, from impending servitude to acknowledged independence. But faith has its limits as well as temper, and there are points beyond which neither can be stretched, without sinking into cowardice or plunging into credulity.—This, my friends, I conceive to be your situation.—Hurried to the very verge of both, another step would ruin you forever.—To be tame and unprovoked when injuries press hard upon you, is more than weakness; but to look up for kinder usage, without one manly effort of your own, would fix your character, and shew the world how richly you deserve those chains you broke. To guard against this evil, let us take a review of the ground upon which we now stand, and from thence carry our thoughts forward for a moment, into the unexplored field of expedient.

After a pursuit of seven long years, the object for which we set out is at length brought within our reach. Yes, my friends, that suffering courage of yours was active once—it has conducted the United States of America through a doubtful and a bloody war. It has placed her in the chair of independency, and peace returns again to bless—whom? A country willing to redress your wrongs, cherish your worth and reward your services, a country courting your return to private life, with tears of gratitude and smiles of admiration, longing to divide with you that independency which your gallantry has given, and those riches which your wounds have preserved? Is this the case? Or is it rather a country that tramples upon your rights, disdains your cries and insults your distresses? Have you not, more than once, suggested your wishes, and made known your wants to Congress? Wants and wishes which gratitude and policy should have anticipated, rather than evaded. And have you not lately, in the meek language of entreating memorials, begged from their justice, what you would no longer expect from their favour? How have you been answered? Let the letter which you are called to consider to-morrow make reply.

If this, then, be your treatment, while the swords you wear are necessary for the defence of America, what have you to expect from peace, when your voice shall sink, and your strength dissipate by division? When those very swords, the instruments and companions of your glory, shall be taken from your sides, and no remaining mark of military distinction left but your wants, infirmities and scars? Can you then consent to be the only sufferers by this revolution, and retiring from he field, grow old in poverty, wretchedness and contempt? Can you consent to wade through the vile mire of dependency, and owe the miserable remnant of that life to charity, which has hitherto been spent in honor? If you can—GO—and carry with you the jest of tories and scorn of whigs—the ridicule, and what is worse, the pity of the world. Go, starve, and be forgotten! But, if your spirit should revolt at this; if you have sense enough to discover, and spirit enough to oppose tyranny under whatever garb it may assume; whether it be the plain coat of republicanism, or the splendid robe of royalty; if you have yet learned to discriminate between a people and a cause, between men and principles—awake; attend to your situation and redress yourselves. If the present moment be lost, every future effort is in vain; and your threats then, will be as empty as your entreaties now.

I would advise you, therefore, to come to some final opinion upon what you can bear, and what you will suffer. If your determination be in any proportion to your wrongs, carry your appeal from the justice to the fears of government. Change the milk-and-water style of your last memorial; assume a bolder tone—decent, but lively, spirited and determined, and suspect the man who would advise to more moderation and longer forbearance. Let two or three men, who can feel as well as write, be appointed to draw up your last remonstrance; for, I would no longer give it the sueing, soft, unsuccessful epithet of memorial. Let it be represented in language that will neither dishonor you by its rudeness, nor betray you by its fears, what has been promised by Congress, and what has been performed, how long and how patiently you have suffered, how little you have asked, and how much of that little has been denied. Tell them that, though you were the first, and would wish to be the last to encounter danger: though despair itself can never drive you into dishonor, it may drive you from the field: that the wound often irritated, and never healed, may at length become incurable; and that the slightest mark of indignity from Congress now, must operate like the grave, and part you forever: that in any political event, the army has its alternative. If peace, that nothing shall separate them from your arms but death: if war, that courting the auspices, and inviting the direction of your illustrious leader, you will retire to some unsettled country, smile in your turn, and "mock when their fear cometh on." But let it represent also, that should they comply with the request of your late memorial, it would make you more happy and them more respectable. That while war should continue, you would follow their standard into the field, and when it came to an end, you would withdraw into the shade of private life, and give the world another subject of wonder and applause; and army victorious over its enemies—victorious over itself.

Document B
Shays' Rebellion: Letters of Generals William Shepard and Benjamin Lincoln
To Governor James Bowdoin of Massachusetts, January 1787

General Shepard to Governor Bowdoin
Springfield
January 26, 1787

The unhappy time is come in which we have been obliged to shed blood. Shays, who was at the head of about twelve hundred men, marched yesterday afternoon about four o'clock, towards the public buildings in battle array. He marched his men in an open column by platoons. I sent several times by one of my aides, and two other gentlemen, Captains Buffington and Woodbridge, to him to know what he was after, or what he wanted. His reply was, he wanted barracks, and barracks he would have and stores. The answer returned was he must purchase them dear, if he had them.

He still proceeded on his march until he approached within two hundred and fifty yards of the arsenal. He then make a halt. I immediately sent Major Lyman, one of my aides, and Capt. Buffington to inform him not to march his troops any nearer the arsenal on his peril, as I was stationed here by order of your Excellency and the Secretary at War, for the defence of the public property; in case he did I should surely fire on him and his men. A Mr. Wheeler, who appeared to be one of Shays' aides, met Mr. Lyman, after he had delivered my orders in the most peremptory manner, and made answer, that was all he wanted. Mr. Lyman returned with his answer.

Shays immediately put his troops in motion, and marched on rapidly near one hundred yards. I then ordered Major Stephens, who commanded the artillery, to fire upon them. He accordingly did. The two first shots he endeavored to overshoot them, in hopes they would have taken warning without firing among them, but it had no effect on them. Major Stephens then directed his shot through the center of his column. The fourth or fifth shot put their whole column into the utmost confusion. Shays made an attempt to display the column, but in vain. We had one howitz which was loaded with grapeshot, which when fired, gave them great uneasiness.

Had I been disposed to destroy them, I might have charged upon their rear and flanks with my infantry and the two field pieces, and could have killed the greater part of his whole army within twenty-five minutes. There was not a single musket fired on either side. I found three men dead on the spot, and one wounded, who is since dead. One of our artillery men by inattention was badly wounded. Three muskets were taken up with the dead, which were all deeply loaded.

I have received no reinforcement yet, and expect to be attacked this day by their whole force combined.

General Lincoln to Governor Bowdoin
Head Quarters, Springfield
January 28th, 1787

We arrived here yesterday about noon with one regiment from Suffolk, one from Essex, one from Middlesex, and one from Worcester, with three companies of artillery, a corps of horse, and a volunteer corps under the command of Colonel Baldwin; the other company of artillery with the other regiment from Middlesex and another from Worcester which were as a cover to our stores arrived about eight o'clock in the evening. On my arrival, I found that Shays had taken a post at a little village six miles north of this, with the whole force under his immediate command, and that Day had taken post in West Springfield, and that he had fixed a guard at the ferry house on the west side of the river, and that he had a guard at the bridge over Agawam river. By this disposition all communication from the north and west in the usual paths was cut off.

From a consideration of this insult on Government, that by an early move we should instantly convince the insurgents of its ability and determination speedily to disperse them; that we wanted the houses occupied by these men to cover our own troops; that General Patterson was on his march to join us, which to obstruct was an object with them; that a successful movement would give spirits to the troops; that it would be so was reduced to as great a certainty, as can be had in operations of this kind; from these considerations, Sir, with many others, I was induced to order the troops under arms at three o'clock in the afternoon, although the most of them had been so from one in the morning.

We moved about half after three, and crossed the river upon the ice, with the four regiments; four pieces of artillery; the light horse, and the troops of this division, under General Shepard moved up the river on the ice, with an intention to fall in between Shays who was on the east side of the river, and Day on the west, and to prevent a junction as well as to cut off Day's retreat. We supposed that we should hereby encircle him with a force so superior that he would not dare to fire upon us which would effectually prevent bloodshed, as our troops were enjoined in the most positive manner not to fire without orders. The moment we showed ourselves upon the river the guard at the ferry house turned out and left the pass open to us. They made a little show of force for a minute or two near the meeting house, and then retired in the utmost confusion and disorder. Our horse met them at the west end of the village, but the insurgents found means by crossing the fields and taking to the woods to escape them; some were taken who are aggravatedly guilty, but not the most so.

The next news we had of them, was by an express form Northampton, that part of them arrived in the south end of their town about eleven o'clock. Shays also in a very precipitate manner left his post a[t] Chickabee, and some time in the night passed through South Hadley, on his way to Amherst.

As soon as our men are refreshed this morning, we shall move northward, leaving General Shepard here as a cover to the magazines; perhaps we may overtake Shays and his party, we shall do it, unless they disperse. If they disperse, I shall cover the troops in some convenient place, and carry on our operations in a very different way.

Document C
Constitutional Convention of 1787:
Virginia or Randolph Plan,
May 29, 1787

1. Resolved that the Articles of Confederation ought to be so corrected and enlarged as to accomplish the objects proposed by their institution; namely "common defence, security of liberty and general welfare."
2. Resolved therefore that the rights of suffrage in the National Legislature ought to be proportioned to the Quotas of contribution, or to the number of free inhabitants, as the one or the other rule may seem best in different cases.
3. Resolved that the National Legislature ought to consist of two branches.
4. Resolved that the members of the first branch of the National Legislature ought to be elected by the people of the several States every for the terms of: to be of the age of years at least, to receive liberal stipends by which they may be compensated for the devotion of their time to public service, to be ineligible to any office established by a particular State, or under the authority of the United States, except those peculiarly belonging to the functions of the first branch, during the term of service, and for the space of after its expiration; to be incapable of reelection for the space of after the expiration of their term of service, and to be subject to recall.
5. Resolved that the members of the second branch of the National Legislature ought to be elected by those of the first, out of a proper number of persons nominated by the individual Legislatures, to be of the age of years at least; to hold their offices for a term sufficient to ensure their independency; to receive liberal stipends, by which they may be compensated for the devotion of their time to public service; and to be ineligible to any office established by a particular State, or under the authority of the United States, except those peculiarly belonging to the functions of the second branch, during the term of service, and for the space of after the expiration thereof.
6. Resolved that each branch ought to possess the right of originating Acts; that the National Legislature ought to be impowered to enjoy the Legislative Rights vested in Congress by the Confederation and moreover to legislate in all cases to which the separate States are incompetent, or in which the harmony of the United States may be interrupted by the exercise of individual Legislation; to negative all laws passed by the several States, contravening in the opinion of the national Legislature the articles of Union; and to call forth the force of the Union against any member of the Union failing in its duty under the articles thereof.
7. Resolved that a National Executive be instituted; to be chosen by the National Legislature for the terms of years; to be chosen by the National Legislature for the terms of years; to receive punctually, at stated times, a fixed compensation for the services rendered, in which no increase or diminution shall be made so as to affect the Magistracy, existing at the time of the increase of diminution, and to be ineligible a second time; and that besides a general authority to execute the National laws, it ought to enjoy the Executive rights vested in Congress by the Confederation.
8. Resolved that the Executive and a convenient number of the national Judiciary, ought to compose a Council of revision with authority to examine every act of the National Legislature before it shall operate, and every act of a particular Legislature before a Negative thereon shall be final; and that the dissent of the said Council shall amount to a rejection, unless the Act of the National Legislature be passed again, or what of a particular Legislature be again negatived by the members of each branch.
9. Resolved that National Judiciary be established to consist of one or more supreme tribunals, and of inferior tribunals to be chosen by the National Legislature, to hold their offices during good behaviour; and to receive punctually at stated times fixed compensation for their services, in which no increase or diminution shall be made so as to affect the persons actually in office at the time of such increase or diminution. That the jurisdiction of the inferior tribunals shall be to hear and determine in the dernier resort, all piracies and felonies on the high seas, captures from an enemy; cases in which foreigners or citizens of other States applying to such jurisdictions may be interested, or which respect the collection of the National revenue; impeachments of any National officers, and questions which may involve the national peace and harmony.

10. Resolved that provision ought to be made for the admission of States Lawfully arising within the limits of the United States, whether from a voluntary junction of Government and Territory or otherwise, with the consent of a number of voices in the National legislature less than the whole.

11. Resolved that a Republican Government and the territory of each State, except in the instance of a voluntary junction of Government and territory, ought to be guaranteed by the United States to each State.

12. Resolved that provision ought to be made for the continuance of Congress and their authorities and privileges, until a given day after the reform of the articles of Union shall be adopted, and for the completion of all their engagements.

13. Resolved that provision ought to be made for the amendment of the Articles of Union whensoever it shall seem necessary, and that the assent of the National Legislature ought not to be required thereto.

14. Resolved that the Legislative Executive and Judiciary powers within the several States ought to be bound by oath to support the articles of Union.

15. Resolved that the amendments which shall be offered to the Confederation, by the Convention ought at a proper time, or times, after the approbation of Congress to be submitted to an assembly or assemblies of Representatives, recommended by the several Legislatures to be expressly chosen by the people, to consider and decide thereon.

Document D
Federalist Paper #10

...[I]t may be concluded that a pure democracy, by which I mean a society, consisting of a small number of citizens, who assemble an administer the government in person, can admit of no cure for the mischiefs of faction. A common passion or interest will, in almost every case, be felt by a majority of the whole; a communication and concert results from the form of government itself; and there is nothing to check the inducements to sacrifice the weaker party, or an obnoxious individual. Hence it is, that such democracies have ever been spectacles of turbulence and contention; have ever been found incompatible with personal security, or the rights of property; and have in general been a short in their lives, as they have been violent in their deaths. Theoretic politicians, who have patronized this species of government, have erroneously supposed, that by reducing mankind to a perfect equality in their political rights, they would, at the same time, be perfectly equalized, and assimilated in their possessions, their opinions, and their passions.

A republic, by which I mean a government in which the scheme of representation takes place, opens a different prospect, and promises the cure for which we are seeking. Let us examine the points in which it varies from pure democracy, and we shall comprehend both the nature of the cure, and the efficacy which it must derive from the union.

The two great points of difference between a democracy and a republic, are first, the delegation of the government, in the latter, to a small number of citizens elected by the rest; secondly, the greater number of citizens, and greater sphere of country, over which the latter may be extended.

The effect of the first difference is, on the one hand, to refine and enlarge the public views, by passing them through the medium of a chosen body of citizens, whose wisdom may best discern the true interest of their country, and whose patriotism and love of justice, will be least likely to sacrifice it to temporary or partial considerations. Under such a regulation, it may well happen that the public voice pronounced by the representatives of the people, will be more consonant to the public good, than if pronounced by the people themselves convened for the purpose. On the other hand, the effect may be inverted. Men of factious tempers, of local prejudices, or of sinister designs, may by intrigue, by corruption, or by other means, first obtain the suffrages, and then betray the interests of the people. The question resulting is, whether small or extensive republics are most favourable to the election of proper guardians of the public wealth; and it is clearly decided in favour of the latter by two obvious considerations.

In the first place it is to be remarked, that however small the republic may be, the representatives must be raised to a certain number, in order to guard against the cabals of a few; and that however large it may be, they must be limited to a certain number, in order to guard against the confusion of a multitude. Hence the number of representatives in the two cases not being in proportion to that of the constituents, and being proportionally greatest in the small republic, it follows, that if the proportion of fit characters be not less in the large than in the small republic, the former will present a greater opinion, and consequently a greater probability of a fit choice.

In the next place, as each representative will be chosen by a greater number of citizens in the large than in the small republic, it will be more difficult for unworthy candidates to practise with success the vicious arts, by which elections are too often carried; and the suffrages of the people being more free, will be more likely to centre on men who possess the most attractive merit, and the most diffusive and established characters.

It must be confessed, that in this, as in most other cases, there is a mean, on both sides of which inconveniences will be found to lie. By enlarging too much the number of electors, you render the representative too little acquainted with all their local circumstances and lesser interests; as by reducing it too much, you render him unduly attached to these, and too little fit to comprehend and pursue great and national objects. The federal constitution forms a happy combination in this respect; the great and aggregate interests being referred to the national, the local and particular to the state legislatures.

The other point of difference is, the greater number of citizens and extent of territory which may be brought within the compass of republican, than of democratic government; and it is this circumstance principally which renders factious combinations less to be dreaded in the former, than in the latter. The smaller the society the fewer probably will be the distinct parties and interests composing it; the fewer the distinct parties and interests, the more frequently will a majority be found of the same party; and the smaller the number of individuals composing a majority, and the smaller the compass within which they are placed, the more easily will they concert and execute their plans of oppression. Extend the sphere, and you take in a greater variety of parties and interests; you make it less probable that a majority of the whole will have a common motive to invade the rights of other citizens; or if such a common motive exists, it will be more difficult for all who feel it to discover their own strength, and to act in unison with each other. Besides other impediments, it may be remarked, that where there is a consciousness of unjust dishonourable purposes, communication is always checked by distrust, in proportion to the number whose concurrence is necessary.

Hence it clearly appears, that the same advantage, which a republic has over a democracy, in controlling the effects of faction, is enjoyed by a large over a small republic—is enjoyed by the union over the states composing it. Does this advantage consist in the substitution of representatives, whose enlightened views and virtuous sentiments render them superior t local prejudices and to schemes of injustice? It will not be denied, that the representation of the union will be most likely to possess these requisite endowments. Does it consist in the greater security afforded by a greater variety of parties, against the event of any one party being able to outnumber or oppress the rest? In an equal degree does the encreased variety of parties, comprised within the union, encrease this security. Does it, in fine, consist in the greater obstacles opposed to the concert and accomplishment of the secret wishes of an unjust and interested majority? Here, again, the extent of the union gives it the most palpable advantage.

The influence of factious leaders may kindle a flame within their particular states, but will be unable to spread a general conflagration through the other states: A religious sect, may degenerate into a political faction in a part of the confederacy; but the variety of sects dispersed over the entire face of it, must secure the national councils against any danger from that source: A range of paper money, for an abolition of debts, for an equal division of property, or for any other improper or wicked project, will be less apt to pervade the whole body of the union, than a particular member of it; in the sample proportion as such a malady is more likely to taint a particular county or district, than an entire sate.

In the extent an proper structure of the union, therefore, we behold a republican remedy for the diseases most incident to republican government. And according to the degree of pleasure and pride, we feel in being republicans, ought to be our zeal in cherishing the spirit, and supporting the character of federalists.

Publius.

Document Set Five
The Frail New Republic

The writers of the Constitution provided a framework for a government for the new nation. It would be left to the first four administrations of Washington, Adams, Jefferson and Madison to prove it was a workable form of government. Their path would be a difficult one as policies, programs and procedures had to be developed for the nation. Divisions quickly appeared within the leadership over what path should be followed and which policies and programs would be the most effective for the nation. These differences led to the rise of political parties, an institution that the framers of the Constitution had hoped to avoid. By the end of the War of 1812, The country had almost doubled in size, withstood a war with a major European power and had learned to integrate politics became a natural part of the political process.

By the time George Washington left office he was very disheartened by the state of the nation. He had watched the country divide over economic policies and foreign affairs. Unable to stay above the dispute, many believed that Washington was guided by his own political loyalties to the Federalist Party. Students will find Document A, "Washington's Farewell Address," an interesting speech. They could discuss why Washington chose to focus on foreign affairs and did not discuss the other major issues of the period? How much did the difficulty of the passage of the Jay Treaty effect his speech? They could be asked to analyze whether or not the speech supports Federalist ideology or if it was driven by his genuine concern for the American people. Was it realistic to expect the nation to ,"...steer clear of permanent alliances?"

In 1790 the United States Congress authorized the first national census. Students should find the information in Document B very interesting. Several different class exercises could be used to have them analyze the data. They should note the types of categories used. Why were free, white males divided into two categories but not free white females? What conclusions could be drawn about the institution of slavery during this period? If the only information the students had was this census what conclusion would they make about American society?

In 1801 Thomas Jefferson became the third president of the United States. Given Jefferson's political stance, he proved to be much more moderate in office and followed a path which was dictated by his inaugural theme, "We Are All Republicans, We Are All Democrats." The Louisiana Purchase is considered one of the greatest accomplishments of his administration. Casting aside his own ideology, Jefferson doubled the size of the nation and laid the foundation for one of the largest territorial expansions in history.

Jefferson asked his private secretary, Meriwether Lewis, to lead an expedition across the newly purchased land. With his partner, William Clark, the party took almost two years to trek to the Pacific. Document C is a series of selections from the journals they kept during their journey. Students should pay attention to the important role of native Americans throughout the trip. Was Lewis reflecting popular sentiment in his statement, "...sensible...their dependance on the will of the government." What specific evidence was found in the journal entries of the importance of native Americans to the success of the trip. Why were the Indians interested in trading for guns?

In 1803 the respite the United States enjoyed from the war in Europe ended. With the ascension of Napoleon to power in France, war quickly broke out again. Unlike Washington and Adams, Jefferson and Madison believed the United States could use economics as a diplomatic weapon. Unfortunately their politics proved to be failures and by 1812 the nation was drawn into a war with Great Britain. Madison's War Message to Congress in Document D expresses the prevailing belief that Britain was, "violating the American flag on the great highway of nations." Ironically, while the message focuses on trade and commerce, support for the war came primarily from the western states. Students could be asked to evaluate why little mention was made of territorial grievances against Britain. Why didn't the trading states of the North support his actions? Had Washington's prophetic warning come true about foreign alliances?

Questions for Document Set Five

1. What did Washington mean in his statement, "...the jealousy of a free people ought to be constantly awake."

2. When Washington wrote, "...foreign influences is one of the most baneful foes of republican government..." was he concerned about a particular country?

3. Was it realistic in 1796 to expect the nation to "...steer clear of permanent alliances."

4. After careful analysis of the 1790 census what picture can be drawn of the nation from the data?

5. Why did the census use these categories?

6. How would the Louisiana Purchase affect native Americans living within its territory?

7. Why were native Americans receptive to the Lewis and Clark expedition?

8. Were Madison's reasons for war realistic or could war have been avoided?

Document A
Washington's Farewell Address

Observe good faith and justice toward all nations. Cultivate peace and harmony with all. Religion and morality enjoin this conduct. And can it be that good policy does not equally enjoin it? It will be worthy of a free enlightened, and, at no distant period, a great nation to give to mankind the magnanimous and too novel example of a people always guided by an exalted justice and benevolence....

In the execution of such a plan nothing is more essential than that permanent, inveterate antipathies against particular nations and passionate attachments for others should be excluded, and that, in place of them just and amicable feelings toward all should be cultivated. The nation which indulges toward another an habitual hatred or an habitual fondness is in some degree a slave. It is a slave to its animosity or to its affection either of which is sufficient to lead it astray from its duty and its interest....

The nation prompted by ill will and resentment sometimes impels to war the government, contrary to the best calculations of policy. The government sometimes participates in the national propensity, and adopts through passion what reason would reject....

So, likewise, a passionate attachment of one nation for another produces a variety of evils. Sympathy for the favorite nation, facilitating the illusion of an imaginary common interest in cases where no real common interest exists, and infusing into one the enmities of the other, betrays the former into a participation in the quarrels and wars of the latter without adequate inducement or justification....

As avenues to foreign influence in innumerable ways, such attachments are particularly alarming to the truly enlightened and independent patriot. How many opportunities do they afford to tamper with domestic factions to practice the arts of seduction, to mislead public opinion, to influence or awe the public councils! Such an attachment of a small or weak toward a great and powerful nation dooms the former to be the satellite of the latter.

Against the insidious wiles of foreign influence (I conjure you to believe me, fellow citizens) the jealousy of a free people ought to be constantly awake, since history and experience prove that foreign influence is one of the most baneful foes of republican government....

The great rule of conduct for us in regard to foreign nations is, in extending our commercial relation, to have with then as little political connection as possible. So far as we have already formed engagements [French treaty], let them be fulfilled with perfect good faith. Here let us stop.

Europe has a set of primary interests which to us have none, or a very remote, relation. Hence she must be engaged in frequent controversies, the causes of which are essentially foreign to our concerns. Hence, therefore, it must be unwise in us to implicate ourselves by artificial ties in the ordinary vicissitudes of her politics, or the ordinary combinations and collisions of her friendships or enmities.

Our detached and distant situation invites and enables us to pursue a different course. If we remain one people, under an efficient government, the period is not far off when we may defy material injury from external annoyance; when we may take such an attitude as will cause the neutrality we may at any time resolve upon to be scrupulously respected; when belligerent nations, under the impossibility of making acquisitions upon us, will not lightly hazard the giving us provocation; when we may choose peace or war, as our interest, guided by justice, shall counsel.

Why forego the advantages of so peculiar a situation? Why quit our own to stand upon foreign ground? Why, by interweaving our destiny with that of any part of Europe, entangle our peace and prosperity in the toils of European ambition, rivalship, interest, humor, or caprice?

It is our true policy to steer clear of permanent alliances with any portion of the foreign world, so far, I mean, as we are now at liberty to do it. For let me not be understood as capable of patronizing infidelity to existing engagements. I hold the maxim of less applicable to public than to private affairs that honesty is always the best policy. I repeat, therefore, let those engagements be observed in their genuine sense. But in my opinion it is unnecessary and would be unwise to extend them.

Taking care always to keep ourselves by suitable establishments on a respectable defensive posture, we may safely trust to temporary alliances for extraordinary emergencies.

Harmony, liberal intercourse with all nations, are recommended by policy, humanity, and interest. But even our commercial policy should hold an equal an impartial hand, neither seeking nor granting exclusive favors or preference;...constantly keeping in view that it is folly in one nation to look for disinterested favors from another; that it must pay with a portion of its independence for whatever it may accept under that character; that by such acceptance it may place itself in the condition of having given equivalents for nominal favors, and yet of being reproached with ingratitude for not giving more. There can be no greater error than to expect or calculate upon real favors from nation to nation. It is an illusion which experience must cure, which a just pride ought to discard.

Summary of the First Census of the United States
Document B

Population of the United States as Returned at the First Census, by States: 1790

District.	Free White Males of 16 Years and Upward, Including Heads of Families.	Free White Males Under 16 Years.	Free White Females, Including Heads of Families.	All Other Free Persons.	Slaves.	Total.
Vermont	22,435	22,328	40,505	255	16	85,539
New Hampshire	36,086	34,851	70,160	630	158	141,885
Maine	24,384	24,748	46,870	538	None.	96,540
Massachusetts	95,453	87,289	190,582	5,463	None.	378,787
Rhode Island	16,019	15,799	32,652	3,407	948	68,825
Connecticut	60,523	54,403	117,448	2,808	2,764	237,946
New York	83,700	78,122	152,320	4,654	21,324	340,120
New Jersey	45,251	41,416	83,287	2,762	11,423	184,139
Pennsylvania	110,788	106,948	206,363	6,537	3,737	434,373
Delaware	11,783	12,143	22,384	3,899	8,887	59,094
Maryland	55,915	51,339	101,395	8,043	103,036	319,728
Virginia	110,936	116,135	215,046	12,866	292,627	747,610
Kentucky	15,154	17,057	28,922	114	12,430	73,677
North Carolina	69,988	77,506	140,710	4,975	100,572	393,751
South Carolina	35,576	37,722	66,880	1,801	107,094	249,073
Georgia	13,103	14,044	25,739	398	29,264	82,548
Total number of inhabitants of the United States exclusive of S. Western and N. territory	807,094	791,850	1,541,263	59,150	694,280	3,893,635
	Free White Males of 21 Years and Upward.	Free Males Under 21 Years of Age.	Free White Females.	All Other Persons.	Slaves.	Total.
S. W. territory	6,271	10,277	15,365	361	3,417	35,691
N. "						

Data excerpted from U.S. Bureau of the Census, *Heads of Families at the First Census* (Baltimore: Genealogical Publishing Company): *South Carolina* (1978), p. 8 and *Pennsylvania* (1966), pp. 6–8, 218–229.

Document C
Selection From the Journals of Lewis and Clark

[Lewis] Saturday August 17th 1805

we made them [the Indians] sensible of their dependance on the will of our government for every species of merchandize as well for their defence & comfort; and apprized them of the strength of our government and its friendly dispositions toward them. we also gave them as a reason why we wished to pe[ne]trate the country as far as the ocean to the west of them was to examine and find out a more direct way to bring merchandize to them. that as no trade could by carryed on with them before our return to our homes that it was mutually advantageous to them as well as to ourselves that they should render us such aids as they had in their power to furnish in order to haisten our voyage and of course our return home. that such were their horses to transport our baggage without which we could not subsist, and that a pilot to conduct us through the mountains was also necessary if we could not decend the river by water. but that we did not ask either their horses or their services without giving a satisfactory compensation in return. that at present we wished them to collect as many horses as were necessary to transport our baggage to their village on the Columbia where we would then trade with them at our leasure for such horses as they could spare us.

the chief thanked us for friendship towards himself and nation & declared his wish to serve us in every rispect. that he was sorry to find that it must yet be some time before they could be furnished with firearms but said they could live as they had done heretofore until we brought them as we had promised. he said they had not horses enough with them at present to remove our baggage to their village over the mountain, but that he would return tomorrow and encourage his people to come over with their horses and that he would bring his own and assist us. this was complying with all we wished at present.

Sunday August 18th 1805

this morning while Capt. Clark was busily engaged in preparing for his rout, I exposed some articles to barter with the Indians for horses as I wished a few at this moment to releive the men who were going with Capt Clark from the labour of carrying their baggage, and also one to keep here in order to pack the meat to camp which the hunters might kill. i soon obtained three very good horses for which I gave an uniform coat, a pair of legings, a few handkerchiefs, three knives and some other small article the whole of which did not cost more than about 20$ in the U'States. the Indians seemed quite as well pleased with their bargin as I was. the men also purchased one for an old checked shirt a pair of old legings and a knife. two of those I purchased Capt. C. took on him. At 10 a.m. Capt. Clark departed with his detachment and all the Indians except 2 men and 2 women who remained with us.

Lewis Tuesday August 20, 1805

i now prevailed on the Chief to instruct me with rispect to the geography of his country. his he undertook very cheerfully, by delineating the rivers on the ground. but I soon found that his information fell far short of my expectation or wishes. e drew the river on which we now are [the Lemhi] to which he placed two branches just above us, which he shewed me from the openings on the mountains were in view; he next made it discharge itself into a large river which flowed from the S.W. about ten miles below us {the Salmon], then continued this joint stream in the same direction of this valley or N.W. for one days march and then enclined to the West for 2 more days march. here we placed a number of heaps of sand on each side which he informed me represented the vast mountains of rock eternally covered with snow through which the river passed. that the perpendicular and even juting rocks so closely hemned in the river that there was no possibil[it]y of passing along the shore; that the bed of the river was obstructed by sharp pointed rocks and the rapidity of the stream such that the whole surface of the river was beat into perfect foam as far as the eye could reach. that the mountains were also inaccessible to man or horse. he said that this being the state of the country in that direction that himself nor none of his nation had ever been further down the river than these mountains.

in this manner I spend the day smoking with them and acquiring what information I could with respect to their country. they informed me that they could pass the Spaniards by the way of the yellowstone river in 10 days. I can discover that these people are by no means friendly to the Spaniards. their complaint is, that the Spaniards will not let them have fire arms and ammunition, that they put them off by telling them that if they suffer them to have guns they will kill each other, thus leaving them defenceless and an easy prey to their bloodthirsty neighbours to the East of them who being in possession of fire arms hunt them up and murder them without rispect to sex or age an plunder them of their horses on all occasions. they told me that to avoid their enemies who were eternally harrassing them that they were obliged to remain in the interior of these mountains at least two thirds of the year where the[y] suffered as we then saw great hardships for the want of food sometimes living for weeks without meat and only a little fish roots and berries. but this added Cameahwait, with his ferce eyes and lank jaws grown meager for the want of food, would not be the case if we had guns, we could then live in the country of buffaloe and eat as our enimies do an not be compelled to hide ourselves in these mountains and live on roots and berries as the bear do. whitemen would come to them with an abundance of guns and every other article necessary to their defence and comfort, and that they would be enabled to supply themselves with these articles on reasonable terms in exchange for the skins of the beaver Otter and Ermin so abundant in their country. they expressed great pleasure at this information and said they had been long anxious to see the whitemen that traded guns; and that we might rest assured of their friendship and that they would do whatever we wished them.

Document D
Madison's War Message

Scholars once believed that Madison—mild-mannered and highly intellectual—was prodded into war by the purposeful War Hawks from the West. The truth is that the President, unable to wring concessions from the British, worked hand in glove with the War Hawks. In reading his following War Message, ascertain whether he seems more concerned with purely Western grievances than with national grievances. Decide which of his numerous charges against England carries the least conviction, and note the additional evidence that the West had an economic stake in a free sea.

British cruisers had been in the continued practice of violating the American flag on the great highway of nations, and seizing and carrying off persons sailing under it, not in the exercise of a belligerent right founded on the law of nations against an enemy, but of a municipal [internal] prerogative over British subject. British jurisdiction is thus extended to neutral vessels....

The practice...is so far from affecting British subjects alone that, under the pretext of searching for these, thousands of American citizens, under the safeguard of public law and of their national flag, have been torn from there country and from everything dear to them; have been dragged on board ships of war of a foreign nation and exposed, under the severities of their discipline, to be exiled to the most distant and deadly climes, to risk their lives in the battles of their oppressors, and to be the melancholy instrument of taking away those of their own brethren.

Against this crying enormity, which Great Britain would be so prompt to avenge if committed against herself, the United States have in vain exhausted remonstrances and expostulations. And that no proof might be wanting of their conciliatory dispositions, and no pretext left for a continuance of the practice, the British government was formally assured of the readiness of the United States to enter into arrangements such as could not be rejected if the recovery of British subjects were the real and the sole object. The communication passed without effect.

British cruisers have been in the practice also of violating the rights and the peace of our coasts. They hover over and harass our entering and departing commerce. To the most insulting pretensions they have added the most lawless proceedings in our very harbours, and have wantonly split American blood within the sanctuary of our territorial jurisdiction....

Under pretended blockades, our commerce has been plundered in every sea...the great staples of our country have been cut off from their legitimate markets, and a destructive blow aimed at our agricultural and maritime interests....Not content with these occasional expedients for laying waste our neutral trade, the Cabinet of Britain resorted at length to the sweeping system of trade, the Cabinet of Britain resorted at length to the sweeping system of blockades, under the name of Orders in Council....

It has become, indeed, sufficiently certain that the commerce of the United States is to be sacrificed, not as interfering with the belligerent rights of Great Britain; not as supplying the wants of her enemies, which she herself supplies; but as interfering with the monopoly which she covets for her own commerce and navigation....
In reviewing the conduct of Great Britain toward the United States, our attention is necessarily drawn to the warfare just renewed by the savages on one of our extensive frontiers—a warfare which is known to spare neither age nor sex and to be distinguished by features peculiarly shocking to humanity. It is difficult to account for the activity and combinations which have for some time been developing themselves among tribes in constant intercourse with British traders and garrisons, without connecting their hostility with that influence, and without recollecting the authenticated examples of such interpositions heretofore furnished by the officers and agents of that government.

Document Set Six
An Egalitarian Society

With the end of the War of 1812, the American nation turned its energy inward to begin drawing upon its own internal resources. Ironically, while there were few victories from the experience, the war fostered a new spirit of nationalism. It laid the foundation for a period of enormous political, economic and territorial activity. This set of documents highlights some of the changes which occurred at this time. It begins with the second administration of James Monroe and ends as Andrew Jackson leave office.

The period between 1816-1824 has been characterized as the Era of Good Feeling. It was a time of political harmony in which the national government provided leadership in promoting a national market economy. Under the leadership of John Marshall, an activist Supreme Court encouraged this economic growth and supported the concept of a strong national government. In Document A, *McCulloch v Maryland*, students have an opportunity to read one of the most influential court decisions of this period. They should note how Marshall's own Federalist beliefs are prevalent throughout the document. Class discussion might focus on the impact of the statement, "The Power to tax is the Power to Destroy." What long term impact did this belief have shall invoke the necessary and proper clause in his decision?

For many Americans the War of 1812 finally convinced them that it was important to heed Washington's warnings and avoid foreign alliances. However, that would not be an easy path to follow. By the early 1820s the Spanish colonies of Latin America had declared their independence at a time in which the major powers of Europe had formed new alliances. The United States was particularly concerned about the activities of Russia on the Pacific coast. James Madison and his Secretary of State, John Adams concluded that it was important for the United States to state its policies concerning European activities in the Western Hemisphere. "The Monroe Doctrine," Document B, became the basis for American foreign policy in this region. Students might speculate how far the United States would be willing to go to keep "European influences" out of the region. Why did the United States turn down the British offer to issue a joint declaration? Can the Monroe Doctrine be seen as another extension of American nationalism during the period? Students might draw parallels between American foreign policy in Latin America during this period their own.

The election of Andrew Jackson in 1828 symbolized a revolution in American politics. After a short period of one party rule, it ushered in a return to the two party system but with marked changes from the era of the Federalists and Republicans. This period has been characterized as the Age of Political Democratization as major changes occurred within the party system as a result of the enfranchisement of lower class white voters and the rise of political power in the new West. The last three documents present different perspectives on these changes. Document C centers on Andrew Jackson's Administration. Much has been written about Jackson's actions as President and the consequences of them for the nation. He utilized the powers of his office to enact policies and programs that Jackson believed represented his constituents.

By 1829 it had become clear that Western expansion would require a national policy for Native Americans. Since most of the expansion was confined to east of the Mississippi, Americans believed transplanting them west of the river could resolve the problem. In an annual address to Congress, Jackson acknowledges the importance of passage of the Indian Removal Act. As a former frontiersman, students could speculate about his concern for Native Americans. Did he really believe that Native Americans were "...surrounded by the whites...(who)...destroying the resources of the savages." Did "humanity and national honor" really demand the removal of these tribes? The document could be tied to the larger issue of territorial expansion and its effect on American society. What choices was the nation willing to make in order to march westward to the Pacific.

One of the most well-known figures from this time period is Davey Crockett. A frontiersman from Tennessee, Crockett symbolized the New America. He served three terms in the House of Representatives. Document D provides Crockett's advise to eager young politicians. Interesting parallels can be drawn between 1836 and the present. Should the same advice be given to politicians running for office today? Do Crockett's suggestions reflect the political changes which occurred at that time? What picture can be drawn from the speech about politics in the 1830s?

Charles Dickens visited the United States in 1842 and his observations were compiled in his *American Notes*. As a foreign observer Dickens was very critical of most Americans and characterized them as greedy, brash, immoral and concerned with the "smart deal." Dickens' portrayal was colored by his financial losses in an American business venture. Students could compare the Dickens and Crockett articles. How similar are their characterizations of American life? Was Dickens being unduly harsh on American morals and values? Were Americans willing to risk everything for the "Smart Deal?"

Questions for Document Set Six

1. Would McCulloch v Maryland be considered a "Federalist" document?

2. Why is Marshall so concerned with the, "consequence of allowing states to tax one instrument of the Federal government?"

3. Compare the Monroe Doctrine to the Untied States' pre-war foreign policy.

4. Was it realistic to assume that the United States could enforce the Monroe Doctrine in 1824?

5. What were Jackson's motives in supporting the Indian Removal Bill?

6. According to Jackson, what were the benefits for Native Americans in removing them to lands west of the Mississippi?

7. As a new politician, how would you utilize Davey Crockett's advice about getting elected?

8. Has politics changed since 1836?

9. How correct was Charles Dickens in his analysis of the characteristics of Americans in 1842?

Document A
McCulloch vs Maryland

That the power of taxation is one of vital importance; that it is retained by the states; that it is not abridged by the grant of a similar power to the government of the Union; that it is to be concurrently exercised by the two governments—are truths which have never been denied. But such is the paramount character of the Constitution that its capacity to withdraw any subject from the action of even this power is admitted. The states are expressly forbidden to lay any duties on imports or exports, except what may be absolutely necessary for executing their inspection laws....The same paramount character would seem to restrain...a state from such other exercise of this power as is in its nature incompatible with, and repugnant to, the constitutional laws of the Union. A law absolutely repugnant to another, as entirely repeals that other as if express terms of repeal were used.

On this ground the counsel for the Bank place its claim to be exempted from the power of a state to tax its operations. There is no express provision for the case, but the claim has been sustained on a principle which so entirely pervades the Constitution, is so intermixed with the materials which compose it, so interwoven with its web, so blended with its texture, as to be incapable of being separated from it without rending it into shreds.

This great principle is that the Constitution, and laws made in pursuance thereof, are supreme; that they control the constitutions and laws of the respective states, and cannot be controlled by them. From this, which may be almost termed an axiom, other propositions are deduced as corollaries....These are: 1. That a power to create implies a power to preserve. 2. That a power to destroy, if wielded by a different hand, is hostile to, and incompatible with, these powers to create an preserve. 3. That where this repugnancy exists, that authority which is supreme must control, not yield to that over which it is supreme....

That the power to tax involves the power to destroy; that the power to destroy may defeat and render useless the power to create; that there is a plain repugnance in conferring on one government a power to control the constitutional measures of another...are propositions not to be denied....

If we apply the principle for which the state of Maryland contends, to the Constitution generally, we shall find it capable of changing totally the character of that instrument. We shall find it capable of arresting all the measures of the government, and of prostrating it at the foot of the states. The American people have declared their Constitution, and the laws made in pursuance thereof, to be supreme; and this principle would transfer the supremacy, in fact, to the states.

If the states may tax one instrument employed by the government in the execution of its powers, they may tax any and every other instrument. They may tax the mail; they may tax the mint; they may tax patent rights; they may tax the papers of the custom-house; they may tax judicial process; they may tax all the means employed by the government, to an excess which would defeat all the ends of government. This was not intended by the American people. They did not design to make their government dependent on the states....

The question is, in truth, a question of supremacy. And if the right of the states to tax the means employed by the general government be conceded, the declaration that the Constitution, and the laws made in pursuance thereof, shall be the supreme law of the land, is empty and unmeaning declamation.

Document B
The Monroe Doctrine

In the discussion to which this interest [Russia's on the northwest coast] has given rise, the occasion has been judged proper for asserting, as a principle in which the rights and interests of the United States are involved, that the American continents, by the free and independent condition which they have assumed and maintain, are henceforth not to be considered as subjects for the future colonization by any European powers....

The political system of the Allied Powers [Holy Alliance] is essentially different...from that of America. This difference proceeds from that which exists in their perspective [monarchical] governments; and to the defense of our own...this whole nation is devoted. We owe it, therefore, to candor and to the amicable relations existing between the United States and those powers to declare that we should consider any attempt on their part to extend their system to any portion of this hemisphere as dangerous to our peace and safety.

With the existing colonies or dependencies of any European power, we have not interfered and shall not interfere. But with the governments [of Spanish America] who have declared their independence and maintained it, and whose independence we have, on great consideration and on just principles, acknowledged, we could not view any interposition for the purpose of oppressing them, or controlling in any other light than as the manifestation of an unfriendly disposition toward the United States....

Our policy in regard to Europe, which was adopted at an early stage of the wars which have so long agitated that quarter of the globe, nevertheless remains the same, which is, not to interfere in the internal concerns of any of its powers; to consider the government de facto as the legitimate government for us; to cultivate friendly relations with it, and to preserve those relations by a frank, firm, and manly policy, meeting in all instances the just claims of every power, submitting to injuries from none.

But in regard to those [American] continents, circumstances are eminently and conspicuously different. It is impossible that the Allied Powers should extend their political system to an portion of either continent without endangering our peace and happiness. Nor can anyone believe that our southern brethren, if left to themselves, would adopt it of their own accord. It is equally impossible, therefore, that we should behold such interposition in any form with indifference.

Reactions to the Monroe Doctrine
A Baltimore Editor Exults (1823)

Monroe's defiant pronouncement touched a patriotic chord and evoked near-unanimous acclaim. The Vermont Gazette, with remarkable foresight, predicted that the message would "go down in our annals along with Washington's Farewell Address." Other journals guessed that the President must have had some secret information as to a possible hostile move by the "crowned conspirators' of Europe. The Baltimore Morning Chronicle gave vent to the following editorial bombast. Observe the evidences of blatant nationalism and particularly the world-dominating role envisaged for the United States.

We can tell...further that this high-toned, independent, and dignified message will not be read by the crowned heads of Europe without a revolting stare of astonishment. The conquerors of Bonaparte, with their laurels still green and blooming on their brows, and their disciplined animal machines, called armies, at their backs, could not have anticipated that their united force would so soon be defied by a young republic, whose existence, as yet, cannot be measured with the ordinary life of man.

This message itself constitutes an era in American history, worthy of commemoration....We are confident that, on this occasion, we speak the great body of American sentiment, such as exulting millions are ready to re-echo....We are very far from being confident that, if Congress occupy the high and elevated ground taken in the Message, it may not, under the smiles of Divine Providence, be the means of breaking up the Holy Alliance.

Of this we are positively sure: that all timidity, wavering , imbecility, an backwardness on our part will confirm these detested tyrants in their confederacy; paralyze the exertions of freedom in every country; accelerate the fall of those young sister republics whom we have recently recognized; and, perhaps, eventually destroy our own at the feet of absolute monarchy.

Document C
Jackson Supports the Indian Removal Act

The Condition and ulterior destiny of the Indian tribes within the limits of some of our states have become objects of much interest and importance. It has long been the policy of government to introduce among them the arts of civilization, in the hope of gradually reclaiming them from a wandering life. This policy has, however, been coupled with another wholly incompatible with its success. Professing a desire to civilize and settle them, we have at the same time lost no opportunity to purchase their lands and thrust them farther into the wilderness. By this means they have not only been kept in a wandering state, but been led to look upon us as unjust and indifferent to their fate....

Our conduct toward these people is deeply interesting to our national character. Their present condition, contrasted with what they once were, makes a most powerful appeal to our sympathies. Our ancestors found them the uncontrolled possessors of these vast regions. By persuasion and force they have been made to retire from river to river and from mountain to mountain, until some of the tribes have become extinct and others have left but remnants to preserve for awhile their once terrible names. Surrounded by the whites with their arts of civilization, which, by destroying the resources of the savage, doom him to weakness and decay, the fate of the Mohegan, the Narragansett, and the Delaware is fast overtaking the Choctaw, the Cherokee, and the Creek. That this fate surely awaits them if they remain within the limits of the states does not admit of a doubt. humanity and national honor demand that every effort should be made to avert so great a calamity....

As a means of effecting this end, I suggest for our consideration the propriety of setting apart an ample district west of the Mississippi, and without [outside] the limits of any state or territory now formed, to be guaranteed to the Indian tribes as long as they shall occupy it, each tribe having a distinct control over the portion designated for its use. There they may be secured in the enjoyment of governments of their own choice, subject to no other control from the United States than such as may be necessary to preserve peace on the frontier and between the several tribes. There the benevolent may endeavor to teach them the arts of civilization, and, by promoting union and harmony among them, to raise up an interesting commonwealth, destined to perpetuate the race and to attest the humanity and justice of this government.

This emigration should be voluntary, for it would be as cruel as unjust to compel the aborigines to abandon the graves of their fathers and seek a home in a distant land. But they should be distinctly informed that if they remain within the limits of the states they must be subject to their laws.

Document D
David Crockett Advises Politicians

"Attend all public meetings," says I, "and get some friend to move that you take the chair. If you fail in this attempt, make a push to be appointed secretary. The proceeding of course will be published, and your name is introduced to the public. But should you fail in both undertakings, get two or three acquaintances, over a bottle of whisky, t pass some resolutions, no matter on what subject. publish them, even if you pay the printer. It will answer the purpose of breaking the ice, which is the main point in these matters.

"Intrigue until you are elected an officer of the militia. This is the second step toward promotion, and can be accomplished with ease, as I know an instance of an election being advertised, and no one attending, the innkeeper at whose house it was to be held, having a military turn, elected himself colonel of his regiment." Says I, "You may not accomplish your ends with as little difficulty, but do not be discouraged—Rome wasn't built in a day."

"If your ambition or circumstances compel you to serve your country and earn three dollars a day, by becoming a member of the legislature, you must first publicly avow that the constitution of the state is a shackle upon free and liberal legislation, and is, therefore, of as little use in the present enlightened age as an old almanac of the year in which the instrument was framed. There is policy in this measure, for by making the constitution a mere dead letter, your headlong proceedings will be attributed to a bold and unshackled mind; whereas, it might otherwise be thought they arose from sheer mulish ignorance. "The Government' has set the example in his [Jackson's] attack upon the Constitution of the United States, and who should fear to follow where 'the Government' leads?

"When the day of election approaches, visit your constituents far and wide. Treat liberally, and drink freely, in order to rise in their estimation, though you fall in your own. True, you may be called a drunken dog by some of the clean-shirt and silk-stocking gentry, but the real roughnecks will style you a jovial fellow. Their votes are certain, and frequently count double."

"Do all you can to appear to advantage in the eyes of the women. That's easily done. You have but to kiss and slabber [slobber over] their children, wipe their noses, and pat them on the head. This cannot fail to please their mothers, and you may rely on your business being done in that quarter."

"Promise all that is asked," said I, "and more if you can think of anything. Offer to build a bridge or a church, to divide a county, create a batch of new offices, make a turnpike, or anything they like. Promises cost nothing; therefore, deny nobody who has a vote or sufficient influence to obtain one."

"Get up on all occasions, and sometimes on no occasion at all, and make long-winded speeches, though composed of nothing else than wind. Talk of your devotion to your country, your modesty and disinterestedness, or on any such fanciful subject. Rail against taxes of all kinds, officeholders, and bad harvest weather; and wind up with a flourish abut the heroes who fought and bled for our liberties in the times that tried men's souls. To be sure, you run the risk of being considered a bladder of wind, or an empty barrel. But never mind that; you will find enough of the same fraternity to keep you in countenance."

"If any charity be going forward, be at the top of it, provided it is to be advertised publicly. If not, it isn't worth your while. None but a fool would place his candle under a bushel on such an occasion."

These few directions." said I, "if properly attended to, will do your business. And when once elected—why, a fig for the dirty children, the promises, the bridges, the churches, the taxes, the offices, and the subscriptions. For it is absolutely necessary to forget all these before you can become a thoroughgoing politician, and a patriot of the first water."

Document E
Dicken's Observations of American Life

Another prominent feature [of America] is the love of "smart" dealing, which gilds over many a swindle and gross breach of trust, many a defalcation, public and private; and enables many a knave to hold his head up with the best, who well deserves a halter; though it has not been without its retributive operation, for this smartness has done more in a few years to impair the public credit, and to cripple the public resources, than dull honesty, however rash, could have effected in a century. The merits of a broken speculation, or a bankruptcy, or of a successful scoundrel, are not gauged by its or his observance of the golden rule, "Do as you would be done by," but are considered with reference to their smartness.

I recollect, on both occasions of our passing that ill-fated Cairo on the Mississippi, remarking on the bad effects such gross deceits must have when they exploded, in generating a want of confidence abroad, and discouraging foreign investment. But I was given to understand that this was a very smart scheme by which a deal of money had been made; and that its smartest feature was that they forgot these things abroad in a very short time, and speculated again, as freely as ever.

The following dialogue I have held a hundred times:
"Is it not a very disgraceful circumstance that such a man as So-and-so should be acquiring a large property by the most infamous and odious means, and, notwithstanding all the crimes of which he has been guilty, should be tolerated an abetted by your citizens? He is a public nuisance, is he not?"
"Yes, sir."
"A convicted liar?"
"Yes, sir."
"He has been kicked, and cuffed, and caned?"
"Yes, sir."
"And he is utterly dishonorable, debased, and profligate?"
"Yes, sir."
"In the name of wonder, then, what is his merit?"
"Well, sir, he is a smart man."

Document Set Seven
The Ferment of Reform

American society in the antebellum period experienced many rapid cultural, economic and social changes. One of the responses to these changes was a reform movement which permeated all parts of society. Rooted in the ideals of the Second Great Awakening, many American reformers believed in the perfectibility of man. While some groups focused on individual reform, others looked toward reforming specific American institutions. Most of the reform groups were located in the North where the Industrial Revolution had begun to affect all aspects of its society.

Ironically, while many of these groups wanted to perfect life in America, they would end up accelerating the growing tensions and strains between the North and the South.

As the Northern economy underwent industrialization, there were many who questioned its effect on the people of the region. Some withdrew and created their own 'utopian' communities. George Ripley, a Boston Unitarian minister organized Brook Farm in Massachusetts in 1841. He believed that self realization could be found through communal sharing. Among the literary figures who came to the farm was Nathaniel Hawthorne. In the first document Hawthorne writes to his wife about his experiences on the farm. Students should note his description of the type of labor he was expected to do on the farm. Hawthorn states that "...the worker and the thinker...are the same individual and that he has"..."gained strength wonderfully..." from his farming experience. Do utopian communities have a function in society? Could they make contributions to society or were they attempting to isolate themselves from reality?

One of the most effective reforms of this period concerned the changes within Northern schools. As industrialization took hold, it became painfully clear that the educational system was inadequate. Classical education had no relevance in preparing a workforce necessary for an industrial economic system. Massachusetts, under the leadership of Horace Mann, created the blueprint for the modern American school system. Appointed the first state superintendent of schools in 1837, Mann's programs led to universal public education in American society.

In the second document, Report of the Massachusetts Board of Education, Mann explains why public education is integral to the success of the united States. Students should analyze how the "common school" would support the basic ideals of the Republic. How does Mann differentiate between American and European societies? Students should note what Mann claims will happen if universal education is not adopted throughout the nation. Is this concept of public education outdated today?

No reform movement had a more dramatic effect on antebellum America than the Abolitionist movement. The movement had a long history that began with the Quakers during the colonial period. However, after 1830, its activity would be centered in the North. Earlier groups, like the American Colonization Society, had sought amicable solutions for planters and slaves. The new reformers sought immediate abolition of an institution they defined as immoral and a blight on mankind.

The catalyst for this change in ideology was William Lloyd Garrison. Beginning with the first articles published in the Liberator, Garrison's extreme views challenged Northern society to consider its relationship to the institution of slavery. The last document is a short article from the Liberator. Students can assess Garrison's depiction of Northern society. Was there a need for a great revolution in public sentiment concerning slavery? Were his words harsh and uncompromising? What might have been the reaction of many Northerners to this article? Discussion could concentrate on why Northerners did not hold the same beliefs as Garrison.

Questions For Document Set Seven

1. Describe Nathaniel Hawthorne's description of life on Brook Farm.

2. Did Brook Farm reflect the philosophy of Transcendentalism?

3. According to Horace Mann, what role should the common school play in American society?

4. How can education be "the great equalizer?"

5. How correct was Garrison's depiction of Northern slavery?

Document A
A Letter from Brook Farm, 1841

As the weather precludes all possibility of ploughing, hoeing, sowing and other such operations, I bethink me that you may have no objection to hear something of my whereabout and whatabout. You are to know then, that I took up my abode here on the 12th ultimo, in the midst of a snowstorm, which kept us all idle for a day or two. At the first glimpse of fair weather, Mr. Ripley summoned us into the cowyard and introduced me to an instrument with four prongs, commonly called a dung-fork. With this tool, I have already assisted to load twenty or thirty carts of manure, and shall take part in loading nearly three hundred more. Besides, I have planted potatoes and peas, cut straw and hay for the cattle, and done various other mighty works. This very morning, I milked three cows; and I milk two or three every night and morning. The weather has been so unfavorable, that we have worked comparatively little in the fields; but, nevertheless, I have gained strength wonderfully—grown quite a giant, in fact—and can do a day's work without the slightest inconvenience. In short, I am transformed into a complete farmer.

This is one of the most beautiful places I ever say in my life, and as secluded as if it were a hundred miles from any city or village. There are woods, in which we can ramble all day, without meeting anybody, or scarcely seeing a house. Our house stands apart from the main road; so that we are not troubled even with passengers looking at us. Once in a while, we have a transcendental visitor, such as Mr. [Bronson] Alcott; but, generally, we pass whole days without seeing a single face, save those of the brethren. At this present time, our effective force consists of Mr. Ripley, Mr. Farley (a farmer from the far west) Rev. Warren Burton (author of various celebrated works), three young men and boys, who are under Mr. Ripley's care, and William Allen, his hired man, who has the chief direction of our agricultural labors. In the female part of the establishment there is Mrs. Ripley and two women folks. The whole fraternity eat together; and such a delectable way of life has never been seen on earth, since the days of the early Christians. We get up at half-past four, breakfast at half-past six, dine at half-past twelve, and go to bed at nine.

The thin frock, which you made for me, is considered a most splendid article; and I should not wonder if it were to become the summer uniform of the community. I have a thick frock, likewise; but it is rather deficient in grace, though extremely warm and comfortable. I wear a tremendous pair of cow-hide boots, with soles two inch thick. Of course, when I come to see you, I shall wear my farmer's dress.

We shall be very much occupied during most of this month, ploughing and planting; so that I doubt whether you will see me for two or three weeks. you have the portrait by this time, I suppose; so you can very well dispense with the original. When you write to me (which I beg you will do soon) direct your letter to West Roxbury, as there are two post offices in the town. I would write more; but William Allen is going to the village, and must have this letter; so good-bye.

Nath Hawthorne
Ploughman

Document B
Horace Mann
Report of the Massachusetts Board of Education
1848

Without undervaluing any other human agency, it may be safely affirmed that the common school, improved and energized as it can easily be, may become the most effective and benignant of all the forces of civilization. Two reasons sustain this position. In the first place, there is an universality in its operation, which can be affirmed of no other institution whatever. If administered in the spirit of justice and conciliation, all the rising generation may be brought within the circle of its reformatory and elevating influences. And, in the second place, the materials upon which it operates are so pliant and ductile as to be susceptible of assuming a greater variety of forms than any other earthly work of the Creator....

According to the European theory, men are divided into classes—some to toil and earn, others to seize and enjoy. According to the Massachusetts theory, all are to have an equal chance for earning, and equal security in the enjoyment of what they earn. A republican form of government, without intelligence in the people, must be, on a vast scale, what a mad-house without superintendent or keepers would be on a small one....However elevated the moral character of a constituency may be, however, well informed in maters of general science or history, yet they must, if citizens of a republic, understand something of the true nature and functions of the government under which they live....

The establishment of a republican government, without well-appointed and efficient means for the universal education of the people, is the most rash and foolhardy experiment ever tried by man....It may be an easy thing to make a republic, but it a very laborious thing to make republicans; and woe to the republic that rests upon no better foundations than ignorance, selfishness, and passion!...

Such, then,...is the Massachusetts system of common schools. reverently it recognizes and affirms the sovereign rights of the Creator, sedulously and sacredly it guards the religious rights of the creature....In a social and political sense, it is a free school system. It knows no distinction of rich and poor, of bond and free, or between those, who, in the imperfect light of this world, are seeking, through different avenues, to reach the gate of heaven. Without money and without price, it throws open its doors, and spreads the table of its bounty, for all the children of the State. Like the sun, it shines not only upon the good, but upon the evil, that they may become good; and, like the rain, its blessings descend not only upon the just, but upon the unjust, that their injustice may depart from them, and be know no more.

Document C
William Lloyd Garrison and The Liberator

During my recent tour for the purpose of exciting the minds of the people by a series of discourses on the subject of slavery, every place that I visited gave fresh evidence of the fact that a great revolution in public sentiment was to be effected in the free states--and particularly in New England—than at the South. I fund contempt more bitter, opposition more active, detraction more relentless, prejudice more stubborn, and apathy more frozen, than among slaveowners themselves. Of course, there were individual exceptions to the contrary.

This state of things afflicted but did not dishearten me. I determined, at every hazard, to lift up the standard of emancipation in the eyes of the nation, within sight of Bunker Hill and in the birthplace of liberty. That standard is now unfurled; and long may it float, unhurt by the spoliations of time or the missiles of a desperate foe—yea, till every chain be broken, and every bondman set free! Let Southern oppressors tremble—let all the enemies of the persecuted blacks tremble....

Assenting to the "self-evident truth" maintained in the American Declaration of Independence "that all men are created equal, and endowed by their Creator with certain inalienable rights—among which are life, liberty, and the pursuit of happiness," I shall strenuously contend for the immediate enfranchisement of our slave population....In Park Street Church, on the Fourth of July, 1829, in an address on slavery, I unreflectingly assented to the popular but pernicious doctrine of gradual abolition. I seize this opportunity to make a full and unequivocal recantation, and thus publicly to ask pardon of my God, of my country, and of my brethren the poor slaves, for having uttered a sentiment so full of timidity, injustice, and absurdity....

I am aware that many object to the severity of my language; but is there not cause for severity? I will be as harsh as truth, and as uncompromising as justice. On this subject I do not wish to think, or speak, or write, with moderation. No! No! Tell a man whose house is on fire to give a moderate alarm; tell him to moderately rescue his wife from the hands of the ravisher; tell the mother to gradually extricate her babe from the fire into which it has fallen—but urge me not to use moderation in a cause like the present. I am in earnest- will not equivocate--I will not excuse—I will not retreat in a single inch—and I will be heard. The apathy of the people is enough to make every statue leap from its pedestal, and to hasten the resurrection of the dead.

It is pretended that I am retarding the cause of emancipation by the coarseness of my invective and the precipitancy of my measures. The charge is not true. On this question my influence—humble as it is—is felt at this moment to a considerable extent, and shall be felt in coming years—not perniciously, but beneficially—not as a curse, but as a blessing. And posterity will bear testimony that I was right.

Document Set Eight
Life In Antebellum America

By 1850 a panorama view of America showed a nation on the verge of becoming a modern society. The North and the West were undergoing revolutions in their economies. These changes would draw them closer together as they began to reap the benefits of technological changes which would revolutionize every segment of their societies. The South never participated and found itself increasingly isolated from the rest of county.

Northern society leaped towards modernization as its economy shifted to the production of commodities in a factory environment. This economic transformation affected all aspects of its society. It laid the foundation for a 'New Industrial Order' that included urbanization, new modes of transportation and communication, and a new working class.

The first three documents examine unsettling aspects of industrialization for Northern society. Industrialization re-defined the role of the working class as production moved from the home to a workplace. Hours became longer and workers became more anonymous as they lost their identities as artisans and craftsmen. The first document, the Boston Carpenters' Strike of 1825, details the demands of the striking journeymen carpenters and the reaction to the strike by master carpenters. Students could compare the two points of view by noting the demands of the journeymen with the fears of the master carpenters. Over six hundred journeymen participated in the strike and demanded a ten hour work day. It failed because master carpenters were told by leading businessmen they would not be employed if they accepted the platform of the journeymen. Students could discuss why this tactic was successful and whether or not an organized labor movement could succeed during this period.

Lowell Massachusetts is considered the birth place of the American factory system. Its employment of young women in the production of textile was seen as a prototype for other industries. By 1836 the workplace environment had deteriorated. "The Abuse of Female Workers," document B described the conditions of its factory with "thirteen hour days and monotonous labor." Class discussion could focus on why women were willing to work in the conditions described in the document. What did the author mean in stating, "Far greater number of fortunes accumulated in the North in comparison with the South shows that hireling labor is more profitable for capital than slave labor?"

The 1840s brought a new wave of immigrants to the American shores. The devastation of the potato famine in Ireland forced thousands of Irish-Catholics to flee to the United States. They arrived poor and were forced to remain in Eastern seaboard cities like Boston. Many Americans feared them and believed the Irish would bring harm to American society. This nativist reaction often led to violence against the Irish community. In 1834, after a series of riots, a mob attacked a convent school in Boston believing that unspeakable acts were occurring within the school. Document C is an editorial by the *Boston Atlas* condemning the riots. Students should note the description of the anger and violence of the mobs. Why would people be driven to such actions at that time? Why do Americans react negatively to non-traditional immigrants? Are the fears and concern justified? Have there been similar incidents in modern America?

While Northern society wrestled with its internal changes, the South perpetuated its plantation society. Turning its back on the dynamic alterations occurring every where else in the country, it held onto its agrarian slave labor system. Slavery impacted all aspects of its society and therefore left little opportunity for change. Southerners perpetuated the image of itself as a "Plantation Society." Unfortunately the image sometimes sharply contrasted with reality. In 1831 a major slave revolt broke out in Southampton County Virginia. While revolts were few and far between, this one modified white Southerner views on the institution. The revolt was led by Nat Turner, an educated slave who believed he had been sent on a divine mission. In Document D, after his capture, Turner described this mission. Unlike many slaves, he had the opportunity to learn to read and write. Why would planters fear an educated slave? As an exercise, students can analyze Turner from his words and decide what purpose the revolt had for him?

The last set of documents concentrates on the reform movements of Northern society. One of the most vocal was the abolitionist movement. The stronger their attacks became, the more entrenched became the white South in defending and protecting their way of life. One of the leading Southern apologist was George Fitzhugh. A prolific writer, Fitzhugh used every opportunity he could to defend and justify slavery. In Document E, "The Blessings of Slavery," students have an opportunity to read his argument. They should note the comparisons by him of Northern and Southern societies. According to this thesis, which was more preferable? What historical evidence does he rely on to support Southern Slavery? Was he correct in claiming the North was more prejudice than the South? In a class exercise, the students could be divided into pro and anti slavery groups and then asked to present the arguments given by white Southerners like Fitzhugh and Northern abolitionists such as Garrison.

Questions for Document Set Eight

1. Compare the arguments of the Master Carpenters and Journeymen. What were the concerns of each group and why couldn't they agree?

2. What did the author mean in writing the following about the women in the Lowell factories, "hireling labor is more profitable than slave labor?"

3. Why were 6,000 women willing to work in the conditions of the Lowell factory?

4. According to the Boston Atlas editorial why was the attack on the convent school horrifying? What other alternatives did it suggest for the mob?

5. Did the editorial believe the concerns of the mob were wrong? Can evidence be found in the editorial to support nativist fears?

6. What was Nat Turner's Divine Mission?

7. How different was Nat Turner from most slaves of this period?

8. What arguments does Fitzhugh use to justify Southern slaver?

9. Explain his statement, "...capital supports and protects domestic slave; taxes, oppresses and persecutes the free laborer."

Document A
The Boston Carpenters' Strike, 1825

I. Resolutions of Journeymen Carpenters

Notice to house carpenters and housewrights in the country. An advertisement having appeared in the papers of this city, giving information that there is at this time a great demand for workmen in this branch of mechanical business in this city, it is considered a duty to state for the benefit of our brethren of the trade that we are not aware of any considerable demand fro labor in this business, as there is, at this time, a very considerable number of journeymen carpenters who are out of employ, and the probable inducement which led to the communication refereed to arises from a disposition manifested on the part of the builders in this city to make their own terms as to the price of labor and the number of hours labor which shall hereafter constitute a day's work. It being a well-known fact that the most unreasonable requirements have been hitherto extracted with regard to the terms of labor of journeymen mechanics in this city; and it is further well known that in the cities of New York, Philadelphia, Baltimore, and most of the other cities of much more liberal and equitable course of policy has been adopted by the master-builders, on this subject, giving to their journeymen that fair and liberal support to which they are unquestionably entitled. It is an undoubted fact that , on the present system, it is impossible for a journeyman housewright and house carpenter to maintain a family at the present time with the wages which are now usually given to the journeymen house carpenters in this city.

April 16

II. Resolutions of Master-Carpenters

Resolved, That we learn with surprise and regret that a large number of those who are employed as journeymen in this city have entered into a combination for the purpose of altering the time of commencing and terminating their daily labor from that which has been customary from time immemorial, thereby lessening the amount of labor each day in a very considerable degree.

Resolved, That we consider such a combination as unworthy of that useful and industrious class of the community who are engaged in it; that it is fraught with numerous and pernicious evils, not only as respect their employers but the public at large, and especially themselves; for all journeymen of good character and of skill may expect very soon to become masters and, like us, the employers of others; and by the measure which they are now inclined to adopt they will entail upon themselves the inconvenience to which they seem desirous that we should not be exposed?

Resolved, That we consider the measure proposed, as calculated to exert a very unhappy influence on our apprentices--by seducing them from that course of industry and economy of time to which we are anxious to inure them. That it will expose the journeymen themselves to many temptations and improvident practices from which they are happily secure; while they attend to that wise and salutary maxim of mechanics, "Mind your business." That we consider idleness as the most deadly bane to usefulness and honorable living; and knowing (such is human nature that, where there is no necessity, there is no exertion, we fear and dread the consequences of such a measure upon the morals and well-being of society.)

Resolved, That we cannot believe this project to have originated with many of the faithful and industrious sons of New England but are compelled to consider it an evil of foreign growth, and one which, we hope and trust, will not take root in the favored soil of Massachusetts. And especially that our city, the early rising and industry of whose inhabitants are universally proverbial, may not be infested with the unnatural production.

Resolved, That if such a measure were ever to be proper and necessary, the time has not yet arrived when it is so; if it would ever be just, it cannot be at a time like the present, when builders have generally made their engagements and contracts for the season, having predicated their estimats and prices upon the original state of things in reference to journey men.   And we appeal therefore to the good sense, the honesty, and justice of all who are engaged in this combination, and ask them to review their doings, contemplate their consequences, and then act as becomes men of sober sense and of prudence.

Resolved, finally, That we will make no alteration in the manner of employing journeymen as respects the time of commencing and leaving work and that we will employ no man who persists in adhering to the project of which we complain.

Document B
The Abuse of Female Workers of Lowell, 1836

We have lately visited the cities of Lowell [Mass.] and Manchester [N.H.] and have had an opportunity of examining the factory system more closely than before. We had distrusted the accounts which we had heard from persons engaged in the labor reform now beginning to agitate New England. We could scarcely credit the statements made in relation to the exhausting nature of the labor in the mills, and to the manner in which the young women—the operatives—lived in their boardinghouses, six sleeping in a room, poorly ventilated.

We went through many of the mills, talked particularly to a large number of the operatives, and ate at their boardinghouses, on purpose to ascertain by personal inspection the facts of the case. We assure our readers that very little information is possessed, and no correct judgments formed, by the public at large, of our factory system, which is the first germ of the industrial or commercial feudalism that is to spread over our land....

In Lowell live between seven and eight thousand young women, who are generally daughters of farmers of the different states of New England. Some of them are members of families that were rich in the generation before....

The operative work thirteen hours a day in the summer time, and from daylight to dark in the winter. At half past four in the morning the factory bell rings, and at five the girls must be in the mills. A clerk, placed as a watch, observes those who are a few minutes behind the time, and effectual means are taken to stimulate to punctuality. This is the morning commencement of the industrial discipline (should we not rather say industrial tyranny?) which is established in these associations of this moral and Christian community.

At seven the girls are allowed thirty minutes for breakfast, and at noon thirty minutes more for dinner, except during the first quarter of the year, when the time is extended to forty-five minutes. But within this time they must hurry to their boardinghouses and return to the factory, and that through the hot sun or the rain or the cold. A meal eaten under such circumstances must be quite unfavorable to digestion and health, as any medical man will inform us. After seven o'clock in the evening the factory bell sounds the close of the day's work.

Thus thirteen hours per day of close attention and monotonous labor are extracted from the young women in these manufactories....So fatigued—we should say, exhausted and worn out, but we wish to speak of the system in the simplest language—are numbers of girls that they go to bed soon after their evening meal, and endeavor by a comparatively long sleep to resuscitate their weakened frames for the toil of the coming day.

When capital has got thirteen hours of labor daily out of a being, it can get nothing more. It would be a poor speculation in an industrial point of view to own the operative; for the trouble and expense of providing for times of sickness and old age would more than counterbalance the difference between the price of wages and the expenses of board and clothing. The far greater number of fortunes accumulated by the North in comparison with the South shows that hireling labor is more profitable for capital than slave labor.

Now let us examine the nature of the labor itself, and the conditions under which it is performed. Enter with us into the large rooms, when the looms are at work. The largest that we saw is in the Amoskeag Mills at Manchester....The din and clatter of these five hundred looms, under full operation, struck us on first entering as something frightful and infernal, for it seemed such an atrocious violation of one of the faculties of the human soul, the sense of hearing. After a while we became somewhat used to it, and by speaking quite close to the ear of an operative and quite loud, we could hold a conversation and make the inquiries we wished.

The girls attended upon an average three looms; many attended four, but this requires a very active person, and the most unremitting care. However, a great many do it. Attention to two is as much as should be demanded of an operative. This gives us some idea of the application required during the thirteen hours of daily labor. The atmosphere of such a room cannot of course be pure; on the contrary, it is charged with cotton filaments and dust, which, we are told, are very injurious to the lungs.

On entering the room, although the day was warm, we remarked that the windows were down. We asked the reason, and a young woman answered very naively, and without seeming to be in the least aware that this privation of fresh air was anything else than perfectly natural, that "when the wind blew, the threads did not work well." After we had been in the room for fifteen or twenty minutes, we found ourselves, as did the persons who accompanied us, in quite a perspiration, produced by a certain moisture which we observed in the air, as well as by the heat....

The young women sleep upon an average six in a room, three beds to a room. There is no privacy, no retirement, here. It is almost impossible to read or write alone,, as the parlor is full and so many sleep in the same chamber. A young woman remarked to us that if she had a letter to write, she did it on the head of a bandbox, sitting on a trunk, as there was no space for a table.

So live and toil the young women of our country in the boardinghouses and manufactories which the rich an influential of our land have built for them.

Document C
The Burning of a Convent School, 1834

From all we can learn, the violence was utterly without cause. The institution was in its very nature unpopular, and a strong feeling existed against it. But there was nothing in the vague rumors that have been idly circulating to authorize or account for any the least act of violence. We should state, perhaps, that during the violent scenes that were taking place before the convent—while the mob were breaking the windows and staving in the doors of the institution—and while the fire was blazing upon the hill as a signal to the mob—one or two muskets were discharged from the windows of the nunnery, or some of the buildings in the vicinity.

What a scene must this midnight conflagration have exhibited—lighting up the inflamed countenances of an infuriated mob of demons—attacking a convent of women, a seminary for the instruction of young females; and turning them out of their beds half naked in the hurry of their flight, and half dead with confusion and terror. And this drama, too, to be enacted on the very soil that afforded one of the earliest places of refuge to the Puritans of New England—themselves flying from religious persecution in the Old World—that their descendants might wax strong and mighty, and in their turn be guilty of the same persecution in the New?

We remember no parallel to this outrage in the whole course of history. Turn to the bloodiest incidents of the French Revolution...and point us to its equal in unprovoked violence, in brutal outrage, in unthwarted iniquity. It is in vain that we search for it. In times of civil commotion and general excitement...there was some palliation for violence and outrage—in the tremendously excited state of the public mind. But here there was no such palliation. The courts of justice where open to receive complaints of any improper confinement, or unauthorized coercion. The civil magistrates were, or ought to be, on the alert to detect any illegal restraint, and bring its authors to the punishment they deserve. But nothing of the kind was detected. The whole matter was a cool, deliberate, systematized piece of brutality—unprovoked—under the most provoking circumstances totally unjustifiable—and visiting the citizens of the town, and most particularly its magistrates and civil officers, with indelible disgrace.

Document D
Nat Turner's Divine Mission

...To a mind like mine, restless, inquisitive and observant of every thing that was passing, it is easy to suppose that religion was the subject to which it would be directed, and although this subject principally occupied my thoughts—there was nothing that I saw or heard of to which my attention was not directed—The manner in which I learned to read and write, not only had great influence on my own mind, as I acquired it with the most perfect ease, so much so, that I have no recollection whatever of learning the alphabet—but to the astonishment of the family, one day, when a book was shewn to me to keep me from crying, I began spelling the names of different objects—this was a source of wonder to all in the neighborhood, particularly the blacks—and this learning was constantly improved at all opportunities—when I got large enough to go to work, while employed, I was reflecting on many things that would present themselves to my imagination, and whenever an opportunity occurred of looking at a book, when the school children were getting their lessons, I would find many things that the fertility of my own imagination had depicted to me before; all my time, not devoted to my master's service, was spent either in prayer, or in making experiments in casting different things in moulds made of earth, in attempting to make paper, gun-powder, and many other experiments, that although I could not perfect, yet convinced me of its practicability if I had the means. I was not addicted to stealing in my youth, nor have ever been—Yet such was the confidence of the negroes in the neighborhood, even at this early period of my life, in my superior judgment, that they would often carry me with them when they were going on any roguery, to plan for them. Growing up among them, with this confidence in my superior judgment, and when this, in their opinions, was perfected by Divine inspiration, from the circumstances already alluded to in my infancy, and which belief was ever afterwards zealously inculcated by the austerity of my life and manners, which became the subject of remark by white and black.—Having soon discovered to be great, I must appear so, and therefore studiously avoided mixing in society, and wrapped myself in mystery, devoting my time to fasting and prayer--by this time, having arrived to man's estate, and hearing the scriptures commented on at meetings, I was struck with that particular passage which says: "Seek ye the kingdom of Heaven and all things shall be added unto you." I reflected much on this passage, and prayed daily for light on this subject—As I was praying one day at my plough, the spirit spoke to me, saying "Seek ye the kingdom of Heaven and all things shall be added unto you." Question—what do you mean by the Spirit? Ans. The Spirit that spoke to the prophets in former days—and I was greatly astonished, and for two years prayed continually, whenever my duty would permit—and then again I had the same revelation, which fully confirmed me in the impression that I was ordained for some great purpose in the hands of the Almighty. Several years rolled round, in which many events occurred to strengthen me in this my belief. At this time I reverted in my mind to the remarks made of me in my childhood, and the things that had been shewn me—and as it had been said of me in my childhood by those by whom I had been taught to pray, both white and black, and in whom I had the greatest confidence, that I had too much sense to be raised, and if I was, I would never be of any use to any one as a slave. Now finding I had arrived to man's estate, and was a slave, and these revelations being made known to me, I began to direct my attention to this great object, to fulfill the purpose for which , by this time, I felt assured I was intended. Knowing the influence I had obtained over the minds of my fellow servants, (not by the means of conjuring and such like tricks—for to them I always spoke of such things with contempt) but by the communion of the Spirit whose revelations I often communicated to them, and they believed and said my wisdom came from God. I now began to prepare them for my purpose, by telling them something was about to happen that would terminate in fulfilling the great promise that had been made to me—....

Document E
George Fitzhugh: The Blessings of Slavery, 1856

Until the lands of America are appropriated by a few, population becomes dense, competition among laborers active, employment uncertain, and wages low, the personal liberty of all the whites will continue to be a blessing. We have vast unsettled territories; population may cease to increase slowly, as in most countries, and many centuries may elapse before the question will be practically suggested, whether slavery to capital be preferable to slavery to human masters. But the negro has neither energy nor enterprise, and, even in our sparser populations, finds with his improvident habits, that his liberty is a curse to himself, and a greater curse to the society around him. These considerations, and others equally obvious, have induced the South to attempt to defend negro slavery as an exceptional institution, admitting, nay asserting, that slavery, in the general or in the abstract, is morally wrong, and against common right. With singular inconsistency, after making this admission, which admits away the authority of the Bible, of profane history, and of the almost universal practice of mankind—they turn around and attempt to bolster up the cause of negro slavery by these very exploded authorities. If we mean not to repudiate all divine, and almost all human authority in favor of slavery, we must vindicate that institution in the abstract.

To insist that a status of society, which has been almost universal, and which is expressly and continually justified by Holy Wit, is its natural, normal, and necessary status, under the ordinary circumstances, is on its face a plausible and probable proposition. To insist on less, is to yield our cause, and to give up our religion; for if white slavery be morally wrong, be a violation of natural rights, the Bible cannot be true. Human and divine authority do seem in the general to concur, in establishing the expediency of having masters and slaves of different races. In very man nations of antiquity, and in some of modern times, the law has permitted the native citizens to become slaves to each other. But few take advantage of such laws; and the infrequency of the practice establishes the general truth that master and slave should be of different national descent. In some respects the wider the difference the better, as the slave will feel less mortified by his position. In other respects, it may be that too wide a difference hardens the hearts and brutalizes the feeling of both master and slave. The civilized man hates the savage, and the savage return the hatred with interest. Hence West India slavery of newly caught negroes is not a very humane, affectionate, or civilizing institution. Virginia negroes have become moral an intelligent. They love their master and his family, and the attachment is reciprocated. Still, we like the idle, but intelligent house-servants, better than the hard-used, but stupid outhands; and we like the mulatto better than the negro; yet the negro is generally more affectionate, contented and faithful.

The world at large looks on negro slavery as much the worst form of slavery; because it is only acquainted with West India slavery.

But our Southern slavery has become a benign and protective institution, and our negroes are confessedly better off than any free laboring population in the world.

How can we contend that white slavery is wrong, whilst all the great body of free laborers are starving; and slaves, white or black, throughout the world, are enjoying comfort?

We write in the cause of Truth and Humanity, and will not play the advocate for master or for slave.

The aversion to negroes, the antipathy of race, is much greater at the North than at the South; and it is very probable that this antipathy to the person of the negro, is confounded with or generates hatred of the institution with which he is usually connected. hatred to slavery is very generally little more than hatred of negroes.

There is one strong argument in favor of negro slavery over all other slavery; that he, being unfitted for the mechanic arts, for trade, and all skillful pursuits, leaves those pursuits to be carried on by the whites; and does not bring all industry into disrepute, as in Greece and Rome, where the slaves were not only the artists and mechanics, but also the merchants.

Whilst, as a general and abstract question, negro slavery has no other claims over other forms of slavery, except that from inferiority, or rather peculiarity, of race, almost all negroes require masters, whilst only the children, the women, and the very weak, poor, and ignorant, &c., among the whites, need some protective and governing relation of this kind; yet as a subject of temporary, but worldwide importance, negro slavery has become the most necessary of all human institutions.

The African slave trade to America commenced three centuries and a half since. By the time of the American Revolution,, the supply of slaves had exceeded the demand for slave labor, and the slaveholders, to get rid of a burden, and to prevent the increase of a nuisance, became violent opponents of the slave trade, and many of them abolitionists. New England, Bristol, and Liverpool, who reaped the profits of the trade, without suffering from the nuisance, stood out for a long time against its abolition. Finally, laws and treaties were made, and fleets fitted out to abolish it; and after a while, the slaves of most of South America, of the West Indies, and of Mexico were liberated. In the meantime, cotton, rice, sugar, coffee, tobacco, and other products of slave labor, came into universal use as necessaries of life. The population of Western Europe, sustained and stimulated by those products ,was trebled ,and that of the North increased tenfold. The products of slave labor became scarce and dear, and famines frequent. Now, it is obvious, that to emancipate all the negroes would be to starve Western Europe and our North. Not to extend and increase negro slaver, pari passu, with the extension and multiplication of free society, will produce much suffering. If all South America, Mexico, the West Indies, and our Union south of Mason and Dixon's line, of the Ohio and Missouri, were slaveholding, slave products would be abundant and cheap in free society; and their market for their merchandise, manufactures, commerce, &c., illimitable. Free white laborers might live in comfort and luxury on light work, but for the exacting and greedy landlords, bosses and other capitalists.

We must confess, that overstock the world as you will with comforts and with luxuries, we do not see how to make capital relax its monopoly—how to do aught but tantalize the hireling. Capital, irresponsible capital, begets, and ever will beget, the immedicabile vulnus of so-called Free Society. It invades every recess of domestic life, infects its food, its clothing, its drink, its very atmosphere, and pursues the hireling, from the hovel to the poor-house, the prison and the grave. Do what he will, go where he will, capital pursues and persecutes him. "Haeret lateri lethalis arundo!"

Capital supports and protects the domestic slave; taxes, oppresses and persecutes the free laborer.

Document Set Nine
Manifest Destiny and Its Consequences

Westward expansion was an integral part of the creation of the United States. From the first settlers of the 1600s, Americans assumped it was their destiny to move across the continent. By the 1830s this ideology influenced the policies and actions of the national government. During the next twenty years, through peace and war, the government would follow a course of action to fill in the continental borders of the nation.

The long term effects of Manifest Destiny were positive, helping to create a powerful industrial world power in the late nineteenth and twentieth centuries. However, in the context of the antebellum period, it was a driving force in fueling the sectional tensions of the North and the South. Each new territorial acquisition brought debate over whether or not it should be free or slave territory. Some Americans sought a compromise through popular sovereignty which allowed the residents of a territory to determine their status.

This set of documents looks at Manifest Destiny and its effect on the American nation. It begins with the author of the term Manifest Destiny, John L. O'Sullivan. In Document A, "The Great Nation of Futurity," O'Sullivan proposes to the American public that they are "a nation...destined to be the great nation of futurity." He glorifies America as a nation connected to the future and not the past. O'Sullivan used his magazine, The United States Magazine and Democratic Review to capture the attention of Americans and remind them that, "America is destined for better deeds." Students should find the article interesting and it can help them better understand how the rhetoric of this period helped to drive the expansion movement. They could be asked to cite specific examples from the speech of extreme nationalism. How could the national government use O'Sullivan's arguments to justify territorial expansion? Was the United States really beginning a new history and political system which was connected to the future rather than the past?

For many Americans the Mexican War represents the pinnacle of Manifest Destiny. Westward expansion had led to an inevitable conflict with Mexico. First in Texas, and later California, American settlers believed that these territories belonged within the borders of the United States. After losing Texas, it was understandable that Mexico had little interest in selling California and the New Mexico territory to President Polk in 1846. A border dispute in Texas provided the opportunity for the United States to send the military to the region and war broke out. Though it appeared to be a popular war with most Americans, some feared the consequences of the war for American society. Abraham Lincoln, a Whig Congressman, introduced a resolution demanding to know the exact spot at which American troops had been fired on. In Document B, Thomas Corwin, a Whig Senator from Ohio, argues that the war would heighten the tensions between pro and anti slavery groups in the United States. He fears that this external war will lead to a civil war. After reading Corwin's arguments, students could be asked to write an essay in which they take sides on the issue. Their essay could be focused to defend or argue against the thesis of Corwin. Were there other alternatives to achieve Manifest Destiny? Could the Civil War have been prevented if the Mexican War had not occurred?

In the third document of this set, students have an opportunity to analyze the effect of Manifest Destiny on native Americans. In 1846 the United States and Great Britain agreed to end their joint occupation of the Pacific Northwest. The treaty gave the United States the lands south of the 48th parallel. Chief Seattle was the leader of six native American tribes in this region. He had been told in 1854 by the territorial governor that the United States government wanted to buy his lands and establish reservations for his people. Document C, "Chief Seattle's Oration," is his reply to this offer. Unlike other tribes during this time Chief Seattle accepts the offer and acknowledges that a war would be horrific for his people. Class discussion would center on his comparisons of American and native American societies. Why was he willing to acquiesce to the demands of the government? Is his comparison of the two societies correct? What warning does he give to Americans about their future?

Questions for Document Set Nine

1. According to John L. O'Sullivan, what are the characteristics of the American nation which determine its future? How is the United States different from other nations?

2. What does Corwin fear will be the consequence of a war with Mexico? How correct was his perception and why?

3. What are the major differences between native American and white societies? Why was Chief Seattle willing to accept the government's offer.

Document A
John L. O'Sullivan
The Great Nation of Futurity

The American people having derived their origin from many other nations, and the Declaration of National Independence being entirely based on the great principle of human equality, these facts demonstrate at once our disconnected position as regards any other nation; that we have, in reality, but little connection with the past history of any of them and still less with all antiquity, its glories, or its crimes. On the contrary, our national birth was the beginning of a new history, the formation and progress of an untried political system, which separates us from the past and connects us with the future only; and so far as regards the entire development of the natural rights of man, in moral, political, and national life, we may confidently assume that our country is destined to be the great nation of futurity.

It is so destined, because the principle upon which a nation is organized fixes its destiny, and that of equality is perfect, is universal. It presides in all the operations of the physical world, and it is also the conscious law of the soul—the self-evident dictate of morality, which accurately defines the duty of man to man, and consequently man's rights as man. Besides, the truthful annals of any nation furnish abundant evidence that its happiness, its greatness, its duration, were always proportionate to the democratic equality in its system of government.

How many nations have had their decline and fall because the equal rights of the minority were trampled on by the despotism of the majority; or the interests of the many sacrificed to the aristocracy of the few; or the rights and interests of all given up to the monarchy of one? These three kinds of government have figured so frequently and so largely in the ages that have passed away that their history, through all time to come, can only furnish a resemblance. Like causes produce like effects, and the true philosopher of history will easily discern the principle of equality, or of privilege, working out its inevitable result. The first is regenerative, because it is natural and right; and the latter is destructive to society, because it is unnatural and wrong.

What friend of human liberty, civilization, and refinement can cast his view over the past history of the monarchies and aristocracies of antiquity, and not deplore that they ever existed? What philanthropist can contemplate the oppressions, the cruelties, and injustice inflicted by them on the masses of mankind and not turn with moral horror from the retrospect?

America is destined for better deeds. It is our unparalleled glory that we have no reminiscences of battlefields, but in defense of humanity, of the oppressed of all nations, of the rights of conscience, the rights of personal enfranchisement. Our annals describe no scenes of horrid carnage, where men were led on by hundreds of thousands to slay one another, dupes and victims to emperors, kings, nobles, demons in the human form called heroes. We have had patriots to defend our homes, our liberties, but no aspirants to crowns or thrones; nor have the American people ever suffered themselves to be led on by wicked ambition to depopulate the land, to spread desolation far and wide, that a human being might be placed on a seat of supremacy.

We have no interest in the scenes of antiquity, only as lessons of avoidance of nearly all their examples. The expansive future is our arena and for our history. We are entering on its untrodden space with the truths of God in our minds, beneficent objects in our hearts, and with a clear conscience unsullied by the past. We are the nation of human progress, and who will, what can, set limits to our onward march? Providence is with us, and no earthly power can. We point to the everlasting truth on the first page of our national declaration, and we proclaim to the millions of other lands that "the gates of hell"—the powers of aristocracy and monarchy—"shall not prevail against it."

The far-reaching, the boundless future, will be the era of American greatness. In its magnificent domain of space and time, the nation of many nations is destined to manifest to mankind the excellence of divine principles; to establish on earth the noblest temple ever dedicated to the worship of the Most High the- Sacred and the True. Its floor shall be a hemispheres- roof the firmament of the star-studded heavens, and its congregation of Union of many Republics, comprising hundreds of happy millions, calling owning no man master, but governed by God's natural and moral law of equality, the law of brotherhood—of "peace and good will amongst men."

Yes, we are the nation of progress, of individual freedom, of universal enfranchisement. Equality of rights is the cynosure of our union of states, the grand exemplar of the correlative equality of individuals; and, while truth sheds its effulgence, we cannot retrograde without dissolving the one and subverting the other. We must onward to the fulfillment of our mission—to the entire development of the principle of our organization—freedom of conscience, freedom of person, freedom of trade and business pursuits, universality of freedom and equality. This is our high destiny, and in nature's eternal, inevitable decree of cause and effect we must accomplish it. All this will be our future history, to establish on earth the moral dignity and salvation of man—the immutable truth and beneficence of God. For this blessed mission to the nations of the world, which are shut out from the lifegiving light of truth, has America been chosen; and her high example shall smite unto death the tyranny of kings, hierarchs, and oligarchs and carry the glad tidings of peace and good will where myriads now endure in existence scarcely more enviable than that of beasts of the field. Who, then, can doubt that our country is destined to be the great nation of futurity?

Document B
Thomas Corwin Against the Mexican War

What is the territory, Mr. President, which you propose to wrest from Mexico? It is consecrated to the heart of the Mexican by many a well-fought battle with his old Castilian master. His Bunker Hills, and Saratogas, and Yorktowns are there! The Mexican can say, "There I bled for liberty! and shall I surrender that consecrated home of my affections to the Anglo-Saxon invaders? What do they want with it? They have Texas already. They have possessed themselves of the territory between the Nueces and the Rio Grande. What else do they want? To what shall I point my children as memorials of that independence which I bequeath to them, when those battlefields shall have passed from my possession?"

Sir, had one come and demanded Bunker Hill of the people of Massachusetts, had England's lion ever showed himself there, is there a man over thirteen and under ninety who would not have been ready to meet him? Is there a river on this continent that would not have run red with blood? Is there a field but would have been piled high with the unburied bones of slaughtered Americans before these consecrated battlefields of liberty should have been wrested from us? But this same American goes into a sister republic, and says to poor, weak Mexico, "Give up your territory, you are unworthy to possess it; I have got one half already, and all I ask of you is to give up the other!"....

Sir, look at this pretense of want of room. With twenty millions of people, you have about one thousand millions of acres of land, inviting settlement by every conceivable argument, bringing them down to a quarter of a dollar an acre, and allowing every man to squat where the pleases....

There is one topic connected with this subject which I tremble when I approach, and yet I cannot forbear to notice it. It meets you in every step you take; it threatens you which way soever you go in the prosecution of this war. I allude to the question of slavery. Opposition to its further extension, it must be obvious to everyone, is a deeply rooted determination with men of all parties in what we call the nonslaveholding states. New York, Pennsylvania, and Ohio, three of the most powerful, have already sent their legislative instructions here. So it will be, I doubt not, in all the rest. It is vain now to speculate about the reasons for this. Gentlemen of the South may call it prejudice, passion, hypocrisy, fanaticism. I shall not dispute with them now on that point. You and I cannot alter or change this opinion, if we would. These people only say we will not, cannot consent that you shall carry slavery where it does not already exist. They do not seek to disturb you in that institution as it exists in your states. Enjoy it if you will and as you will. This is their language; this their determination. How is it in the South? Can it be expected that they should expend in common their blood and their treasure in the acquisition of immense territory, and then willingly forgo the right to carry thither their slaves, and inhabit the conquered country if they please to do so? Sir, I know the feelings and opinions of the South too well to calculate on this. Nay, I believe they would even contend to any extremity for the mere right, had they no wish to exert it. I believe (and I confess I tremble when the conviction presses upon me) that there is equal obstinacy on both sides of this fearful question.

If, then, we persist in war, which, if it terminates in anything short of a mere wanton waste of blood as well as money, must end (as this bill proposes) in the acquisition of territory, to which at once this controversy must attach—this bill would seem to be nothing less than a bill to produce internal commotion. Should we prosecute this war another moment, or expend one dollar in the purchase or conquest of a single acre of Mexican land, the North and the South are brought into collision on a point where neither will yield. Who can foresee or foretell the result! Who so bold or reckless as to look such a conflict in the face unmoved! I do not envy the heart of him who can realize the possibility of such a conflict without emotions too painful to be endured. Why, then, shall we, the representatives of the sovereign states of the Union—the chosen guardians of this confederated Republic, why should we precipitate this fearful struggle, by continuing a war the result of which must be to force us at once upon a civil conflict? Sir, rightly considered, this is treason, treason to the Union, treason to the dearest interests, the loftiest aspirations, the most cherished hopes of our constituents. It is a crime to risk the possibility of such a contest. It is a crime of such infernal hue that every other in the catalogue of iniquity, when compared with it, whitens into virtue....Let us abandon all idea of acquiring further territory and by consequence cease at once to prosecute this war. Let us call home our armies, and bring them at once within our own acknowledged limits. Show Mexico that you are sincere when you say you desire nothing by conquest. She has learned that she cannot encounter you in war, and if she had not, she is too weak to disturb you here. Tender her peace, and , my life on it, she will then accept it. But whether she shall or not, you will have peace without her consent. It is your invasion that has made war; your retreat will restore peace. Let us then close forever the approaches of internal feud, and so return to the ancient concord and the old ways of national prosperity and permanent glory. Let us here, in this temple consecrated to the Union, perform a solemn lustration; let us wash Mexican blood from our hands, and on these altars, and in the presence of that image of the Father of his Country that looks down upon us, swear to preserve honorable peace with all the world and eternal brotherhood with each other.

Document C
Chief Seattle's Oration

...Yonder sky that has wept tears of compassion upon my people for centuries untold, and which to us appears changeless and eternal, may change. Today is fair. Tomorrow it may be overcast with clouds. My words are like the stars that never change. Whatever Seattle says the great chief at Washington can rely upon with as much certainty as he can upon the return of the sun or the seasons. The White Chief says that Big Chief at Washington sends us greetings of friendship and goodwill. This is kind of him for we know he has little need of our friendship in return. His people are many. They are like the grass that covers vast prairies. My people are few. They resemble the scattering trees of a storm-swept plain. The great, and I presume—good White Chief sends us word that he wishes to buy our lands but is willing to allow us enough to live comfortably. This indeed appears just, even generous, for the Red Man no longer has rights that he need respect, and the offer may be wise also, as we are no longer in need of an extensive country.

There was a time when our people covered the land as the waves of a wind-ruffled sea cover its shell paved floor, but that time long since passed away with the greatness of tribes that are now but a mournful memory. I will not dwell on nor mourn over, our untimely decay, nor reproach my paleface brothers with hastening it as we too may have been somewhat to blame.

Youth is impulsive. When our young men grow angry at some real or imaginary wrong, and disfigure their faces with black paint, it denotes that their hearts are black, and that they are often cruel and relentless, and our old men and old women are unable to restrain them. Thus has ever been. Thus it was when the white men first began to push our forefathers further westward. But let us hope that the hostilities between us may never return. We would have everything to lose and nothing to gain. Revenge by young men is considered gain, even at the cost of their own lives, but old men who stay at home in times of war, and mothers who have sons to lose, know better.

Our good father at Washington—for I presume he is now our father as well as yours...sends us word that if we do as he desires he will protect us. His brave warriors will be to us a bristling wall of strength, and his wonderful ships of war will fill our harbors so that our ancient enemies far to the northward—the Hydas and Tsimpsians, will cease to frighten our women, children, and old men. Then in reality will he be our father and we his children. But can that ever be? Your God is not our God! Your God loves your people and hates mine. He folds his strong protecting arms lovingly about the pale face and leads him by the hand as a father leads his infant son- but He has forsaken His red children—if they really are his. Our God, the Great Spirit, seems also to have forsaken us. Your God makes your people wax strong every day. Soon they will fill all the land. Our people are ebbing away like a rapidly receding tide that will never return. The white man's God cannot love our people or He would protect them. They seem to be orphans who can look nowhere for help. How then can we be brothers? How can your God become our God and renew our prosperity and awaken in us dreams of returning greatness. If we have a common heavenly father He must be partial—for He came to His paleface children. We never saw him. He gave you laws but had no word for his red children whose teeming multitudes once filled this vast continent as stars fill the firmament. No; we are two distinct races with separate origins and separate destinies. There is little in common between us.

To us the ashes of our ancestors are sacred and their resting place is hallowed ground. You wander far from the graves of your ancestors and seemingly without regret. Your religion was written upon tables of stone by the iron finger of your God so that you could not forget. The Red Man could never comprehend nor remember it. Our religion is the traditions of our ancestors—the dreams of our old men, given them in solemn hours of night by the Great Spirit; and the visions of our sachems, and is written in the hearts of our people.

Your dead cease to love you and the land of their nativity as soon as they pass the portals of the tomb and wander away beyond the stars. They are soon forgotten and never return. Our dead never forget the beautiful world that gave them being. They still love its verdant valleys, its murmuring rivers, its magnificent mountains, sequestered vales and verdant lined lakes and bays, and even yearn in tender, fond affection over the lonely heartened living, and often return from the Happy Hunting Ground to visit, guide, console and comfort them.

Day an night cannot dwell together. The Red Man has ever fled the approach of the White Man, as the morning mist flees before the morning sun.

However, your proposition seems fair and I think that my people will accept it and will retire to the reservation you offer them. Then we will dwell apart in peace....

It matters little where we pass the remnant of our days. They will not be many. The Indians' night promises to be dark. Not a single star of hope hovers above his horizon. Sad-voiced winds moan in the distance. Grim fate seems to be on the Red Man's Trail, and wherever he goes he will hear the approaching footsteps of his fell destroyer and prepare stolidly to meet his doom, as does the wounded doe that hears the approaching footsteps of the hunter.

...But why would I mourn at the untimely fate of my people? Tribe follows tribe, and nation follows nation, like the waves of the sea. It is the order of nature, and regret is useless. Your time of decay may be distant, but it will surely come, for even the White Man whose God walked and talked with him as friend with friend, cannot be exempt from the common destiny. We may be brothers after all. We will see.

We will ponder your proposition and when we decide we will let you know. But should we accept it, I here and now make this condition that we will not be denied the privilege without molestation of visiting at any time the tombs of our ancestors, friends, and children....

And when the last Red Man shall have perished, and the memory of my tribe shall have become a myth among the White Men, these shores will swarm with the invisible dead of my tribe, and when your children's children think themselves alone in the field, the store, the ship, upon the highway, or in the silence of the pathless woods, they will not be alone. In all the earth there is no place dedicated to solitude. At night when the streets of your cities and villages are silent and you think them deserted, they will throng with the returning hosts that once filled them and still love this beautiful land. The White Man will never be alone.

Let him be just and deal kindly with my people, for the dead are not powerless. Dead, did I say? There is no death, only a change of worlds.

Document Set Ten
A Road to War

The 1850s was a decade of crisis as the last hope for peace between the sections were shattered. The last hope had been the Compromise of 1850 which quickly proved to be a failure. As the years progressed the political system became deadlocked and was unable to deal with the growing divisions between the sections. It was a time where each day seemed to bring another occasion for Northerners and Southerners to become hardened in their stands. By the end of the decade most knew that a Civil War was a "fait accompli."

This set of documents provides examples of some of the events which inflamed sectional differences. During the Civil War Abraham Lincoln introduced Harriet Beecher Stowe as, "The little lady who started the Civil War." In the first document students have an opportunity to read a selection from her novel, *Uncle Tom's Cabin*. Many of them are familiar with the book and why it had such a dramatic impact on Northern society. The novel served as a platform for Stowe and other Northern abolitionists about slavery and Southern society. Students can analyze the two main characters of the selection; Tom and Simon Legree. Were most slaves as "saintly" as Tom and were most planters as evil as Legree? How does Stowes description of slavery as an institution compare with the one described in the selection by Fitzhugh? Was Lincoln correct in his analysis of the impact of the novel on American society?

Until 1857 the United States Supreme Court had not been directly involved in the sectional conflict. However, a case on appeal from the Circuit Court afforded the Supreme Court the opportunity to finally render a decision which they believed could resolve the issue of slavery in the territories. The Dred Scott decision did not resolve the issue and, in fact, further fueled the sectional fires of the era. Led by Roger Taney, a Southern Democrat, the Court's decision supported the Southern argument that slaves were property. After reading the Court's decision in Document B, students could debate its main thesis concerning the role of the Constitution in protecting slavery anywhere in the nation. What in the Constitution would the Court have cited to support this argument? Was the Court correct in declaring the Missouri Compromise unconstitutional? Was this part of the decision an issue in the original case? The actions of the Supreme Court in this case can be used to show students how the Supreme Court can make national policies through its decisions.

During the 1850s there were few national political figures. Stephen Douglas, the Democratic Senator from Illinois, because of his role in the Compromise of 1850 and the Kansas-Nebraska Act was in the national limelight throughout most of this period. His support of popular sovereignty made him seem a moderate in a time of political extremism. Many believed that Douglas could win the Presidential election of 1860. In 1858 Douglas sought reelection and his Republic opponent was Abraham Lincoln. Douglas was re-elected but the campaign brought Lincoln national attention. Document C, "A House Divided," was Lincoln's acceptance of the nomination. Students should note Lincoln's reference to policies which have led to, "A House Divided." To what policies was Lincoln referring? After reading the speech they could decide whether or not Lincoln believed a Civil War was inevitable? Given the time frame, why would Lincoln believe it had come to an all or nothing?

Questions for Document Set Ten

1. Describe how Uncle Tom's Cabin fostered Northern abolitionist beliefs.

2. How correct was Stowe's characterization of Southern plantation life?

3. Cite the section of the Constitution which supports the Dred Scott decision.

4. How did the Dred Scott decision heighten sectional tensions?

5. According to Abraham Lincoln what crises must the nation reach and pass in order to survive?

Document A
Uncle Tom's Cabin

"And now," said Legree, "come here, you Tom. You see, I telled ye I didn't buy ye jest for the common work. I mean to promote ye, and make a driver of ye; and tonight ye may jest as well begin to get ye hand in. Now, ye jest take this yer gal and flog her; ye've seen enough on't [of it] to know how." "I beg Mas'r' pardon," said Tom; "hopes Mas'r won't set me at that. It's what I an't used to—never did—and can't do, no way possible."

"Ye'll larn a pretty smart chance of things ye never did know, before I've done with ye!" said Legree, taking up a cowhide and striking Tom a heavy blow across the cheek, and following up the infliction by a shower of blows. "There!" he said, as he stopped to rest; "now, will ye tell me ye can't do it?"

"Yes, Mas'r," said Tom, putting up his hand, to wipe the blood that trickled down his face. "I'm willin' to work, night and day, and work while there's life and breath in me. But this yer thing I can't feel it right to do; and, Mas'r, I never shall do it—never!"

Tom had a remarkably smooth, soft voice, and a habitually respectful manner that had given Legree an idea that he would be cowardly and easily subdued. When he spoke these last words, a thrill of amazement went through everyone. The poor woman clasped her hands and said, "O Lord!" and everyone involuntarily looked at each other and drew in their breath, as if to prepare for the storm that was about to burst.

Legree looked stupefied and confounded; but at last burst forth: "What!" ye blasted black beast! tell me ye don't think it right to do what I tell ye! What have any of you cussed cattle to do with thinking what's right? I'll put a stop to it! Why, what do ye think ye are? May be ye think ye're a gentleman, master Tom, to be a telling your master what's right, and what an't! So you pretend it's wrong to flog the gal!"

"I think so, Mas'r, said Tom; "the poor crittur's sick and feeble; 'twould be downright cruel, and it's what I never will do, nor begin to. Mas'r, if you mean to kill me, kill me; but, as to my raising my hand again any one here, I never shall—I'll die first!"

Tom spoke in a mild voice, but with a decision that could not be mistaken. Legree shook with anger; his greenish eyes glared fiercely, and his very whiskers seemed to curl with passioin. But, like some ferocious beast, that plays with its victim before he devours it, he kept back his strong impulse to proceed to immediate violence, and broke out into bitterly raillery.

"Well, here's a pious dog, at last, let down among us sinner—a saint, a gentleman, and no less, to talk to us sinners about our sins! Powerful holy crittur, he must be! Here, you rascal, you make believe to be so pious—didn't you never hear, out of yer Bible, 'Servants, obey yer masters'? An't I yer master? Didn't I pay down twelve hundred dollars, cash, for all there is inside yer old cussed black shell? An't yer mine, now, body and soul?" he said, giving Tom a violent kick with his heavy boot; "tell me!"

In the very depth of physical suffering, bowed by brutal oppression, this question shot a gleam of joy an triumph through Tom's soul. He suddenly stretched himself up, and, looking earnestly to heaven, while the tears and blood that flowed down his face mingled, he exclaimed," No! no! no! my soul an't yours, Mas'r! You haven't bought it—ye can't buy it! It's been bought and paid for by One that is able to keep it. No matter, no matter, you can't harm me!"

"I can't!" said Legree, with a sneer; "we'll see-we'll see! Here Sambo, Quimbo, give this dog such a breakin' in as he won't get over this month!"

The two gigantic Negroes that now laid hold of Tom, with fiendish exultation in their faces, might have formed no unapt personification of powers of darkness. The poor woman screamed with apprehension, and all rose, as by a general impulse, while they drageed him unresisting from the place.

Document B
The Dred Scott Decision

Now...the right of property in a salve is distinctly and expressly affirmed in the Constitution. The right to traffic in it, like an ordinary article of merchandise and property, was guaranteed to the citizens of the United States, in every state that might desire it, for twenty years. And the government in express terms is pledged to protect it in all future time, if the slave escapes from his owner. This is done in plain words—too plain to be misunderstood. And no word can be found in the Constitution which gives Congress a greater power over slave property, or which entitles property of that kind to less protection, than property of any other description. The only power conferred is the power coupled with the duty of guarding and protecting the owner in his rights.

Upon these considerations, it is the opinion of the Court that the Act of Congress [Missouri Compromise] which prohibited a citizen from holding and owning property of this kind in the territory of the United States north of the line [of 36 30'] therein mentioned is not warranted by the Constitution, and is therefore void; and that neither Dred Scott himself, nor any of his family, were made free by being carried into this territory; even if they had been carried there by the owner with the intention of becoming a permanent resident....

Upon the whole, therefore, it is the judgment of this Court that it appears by the record before us that the plaintiff in error [Dred Scott] is not a citizen of Missouri, in the sense in which that word is used in the Constitution; and that the Circuit Court of the United States for that reason had no jurisdiction in the case, and could give no judgment in it.

Document C
The House Divided

Mr. President and Gentlemen of the Convention:

If we could first know where we are, and whither we are tending, we could better judge what to do and how to do it. We are now far into the fifth year since a policy was initiated with the avowed object, and confident promise, of putting an end to slavery agitation. Under the operation of that policy, that agitation has not only not ceased but has constantly augmented. In my opinion, it will not cease until a crisis shall have been reached and passed. "A house divided against itself cannot stand." I believe this government cannot endure permanently half-slave and half-free. I do not expect the Union to be dissolved—I do not expect the house to fall-but I do expect it will cease to be divided. It will become all one thing or all the other. Either the opponents of slavery will arrest the further spread of it and place it where the public mind shall rest in the belief that it is in the course of ultimate extinction or its advocates will push it forward, till it shall become alike lawful in all the states, old as well as new—North as well as South.

Document Set Eleven
The World Turned Upside Down

The American Civil War began over the question of which form of political sovereignty would determine the course of the nation. The South believed that the union was a compact of states and therefore they could chose whether or not to remain as part of the union. Lincoln believed the war was fought to preserve the union and to maintain the sovereignty of the federal government. Though political issues framed the war, its reality meant dividing a nation and forcing it to fight itself. The costs would be high for both sides with 600,000 lives lost.

In this set of documents students have an opportunity to see the war through the eyes of the people. Document A, "Clara Barton: Medical Life at the Battlefield," is a poignant description of the consequences of war. Clara Barton is a name associated with nursing and war. Nicknamed the "Angel of the Battlefield," her speeches and writing depicted the conditions under which medicine worked in 19th century war conditions. In this selection students can sense the amount of death and dying that was associated with working in a Civil War field hospital. Barton implies that the supplies at hand were too few for the massive task expected of them with "...3000 suffering men crowded upon the few acres within our reach." Given the large number of casualties could adequate medical attention have been provided? How different is this picture of war from the speeches given by the politicians of the time?

The most important battle of the Civil War was fought at Gettysburg, Pennsylvania in July of 1863. Over three days, the carnage would mount and when it was finished, the South would never again mount an offense into northern territory The following November Lincoln came to the town to dedicate a memorial cemetery. In Document B, "The Gettysburg Address," students have an opportunity to read his well-known speech. They should pay careful attention to the thesis of this short discourse. What did Lincoln mean in "that these dead shall not have died in vain, that this nation...shall have a new birth of freedom?" Is it evident, from the speech, what were his goals in winning the war? Why has the speech become so important in the literature of American History?

The issue of slavery was not specifically part of the dynamics of the early part of the war. Most Northerners believed the war was being fought to preserve the union and not over the question of the emancipation of slaves. However, from the beginning of the war, blacks attempted to participate in the war effort. By its end, over 186,000 African Americans had served in the Union military. Unfortunately, they received lower pay, had poorer supplies and equipment and were led by white officers. Document C, "A Black Soldier Writes to President Lincoln, 1863," highlights some of these problems. As the author points out, the General Officers, "were prejudiced against Us." Having not received their pay for over a month, he compares their situation to that of fugitive slaves who worked as laborers for the war effort. From reading the letter what conclusions could students reach about the participation of African Americans in the Civil War. What did the author mean in stating, "the Black man laid his life at the altar of the Nation, and he was refused?"... Were Northerners opposed to African American participation in the war effort? It is important to point out the letter was written after the Emancipation Proclamation was issued.

Questions for Document Set Eleven

1. Given Clara Barton's description of field hospitals, what conclusions can be made about the treatment of the wounded during the Civil War?

2. Why would Clara Barton's narration change nursing and medicine after the war was over?

3. Why is the Gettysburg Address one of the great symbols of the Civil War and American History?

4. According to the Address why was the Civil War being fought?

5. How were African American soldiers treated during the Civil War?

6. What specific grievances did the author of the letter have against the Union army and Northern society?

Document A
Clara Barton: Medical Life at the Battlefield

...Our coaches were not elegant or commodious; they had no dows, no seats, no platforms, no steps, a slide door on the side the only entrance, and this higher than my head. For my man attaining my elevated position, I must beg of you to draw on your imaginations and spare me the labor of reproducing the boxes, boards, and rails, which in those days, seemed to help me up and down the world. We did not criticize the unsightly helpers and were thankful that the stiff springs did not quite jostle us out. This need not be limited too this particular trip or train, but will for all that I have known in Army life. This is the kind of conveyance which your tons of generous gifts have reached the field with the freights. These trains through day and night, sunshine an heat and cold, have thundered over heights, across plains, the ravines, and over hastily built army bridges 90 feet across the stream beneath.

At 10 o'clock Sunday (August 31) our train drew up at Fairfax Station. The ground, for acres, was a thinly wooded slope-and among the trees on the leaves and grass, were laid the wounded who pouring in by scores of wagon loads, as picked up on the field the flag of truce. All day they came and the whole hillside was red. Bales of hay were broken open and scattered over the ground littering of cattle, and the sore, famishing men were laid upon it.

And when the night shut in, in the mist and darkness about us, we knew that standing apart from the world of anxious hearts, throbbing over the whole country, we were a little band of almost empty handed workers literally by ourselves in the wild woods of Virginia, with 3000 suffering men crowded upon the few acres within our reach.

After gathering up every available implement or convenience for our work, our domestic inventory stood 2 water buckets, 5 tin cups, 1 camp kettle, 1 stew pan, 2 lanterns, 4 bread knives, 3 plates, and a 2-quart tin dish, and 3000 guest to serve.

You will perceive by this, that I had not yet learned to equip myself, for I was no Pallas, ready armed, but grew into my work by hard thinking and sad experience. It may serve to relieve your apprehension for the future of my labors if I assure you that I was never caught so again.

But the most fearful scene was reserved for the night. I have said that the ground was littered with dry hay and that we had only two lanterns, but there were plenty of candles. The wounded were laid so close that it was impossible to move about in the dark. The slightest misstep brought a torrent of groans from some poor mangled fellow in your path.

Consequently here were seen persons of all grades from the careful man of God who walked with a prayer upon his lips to the careless driver hunting for his lost whip, - each wandering about among this hay with an open flaming candle in his hands.

The slightest accident, the mere dropping of a light could have enveloped in flames this whole mass of helpless men.

How we watched and pleaded and cautioned as we worked and wept that night! How we put socks and slippers upon their cold feet, wrapped your blankets and quilts about them, and when we no longer these to give, how we covered them in the hay and left them to their rest!"...

The slight, naked chest of a fair-haired lad caught my eye, dropping down beside him, I bent low to draw the remnant of his blouse about him, when with a quick cry he threw his left arm across my neck and, burying his face in the folds of my dress, wept like a child at his mother's knee. I took his head in my hands and held it until great burst of grief passed away. "And do you know me?" he asked at length, "I am Charley Hamilton, we used to carry your satchel home from school.!" My faithful pupil, poor Charley. That mangled right hand would never carry a satchel again.

About three o'clock in the morning I observed a surgeon with a little flickering candle in hand approaching me with cautious step up in the wood. "Lady," he said as he drew near, "will you go with me? Out on the hills is a poor distressed lad, mortally wounded, and dying. His piteous cries for his sister have touched all our hearts none of us can relieve him but rather seem to distress him by presence."

By this time I was following him back over the bloody track, with great beseeching eyes of anguish on every side looking up into our faces, saying so plainly, "Don't step on us."

This finds us shortly after daylight Monday morning. The train of cars were rushing on for the wounded and hundreds of wagons were bringing them in from the field still held by the enemy, where poor sufferers had lain three days with no visible means of . If immediately placed upon the trains an not detained, at least four hours must elapse before they could be in the hospital and nourished. They were already famishing, weak an sinking from loss of blood and they could ill afford a further fast of twenty-four hours. I felt confident that unless nourished at once, all the weaker must be past recovery before reaching the hospitals of Washington. Once taken from the wagons and laid with those already cared for would be overlooked and perish on the way.

Document B
Gettysburg Address, November 19, 1863
by Abraham Lincoln

Fourscore and seven years ago our fathers brought forth on this continent a new nation, conceived in liberty, and dedicated to the proposition that all men are created equal.

Now we are engaged in a great civil war, testing whether that nation, or any nation so conceived and so dedicated, can long endure. We are met on a great battlefield of that war. We have come to dedicate a portion of that field as a final resting-place for those who here gave their lives that nation might live. It is altogether fitting and proper that we should do this.

But, in a larger sense, we cannot dedicate—we cannot consecrate-we cannot hallow—this ground. The brave men, living and dead, who struggled here, have consecrated it far above our poor power to add or detract. The world will little note nor long remember what we say here, but it can never forget what they did here. It is for us, the living, rather, to be dedicated here to the unfinished work which they who fought here have thus far so nobly advanced. It is rather for us to be here dedicated to the great task remaining before us—that from these honored dead we take increased devotion to that cause for which they gave the last full measure of devotion; that we here highly resolve that these dead shall not have died in vain; that this nation, under God, shall have a new birth of freedom; and that government of the people, by the people, for the people, shall not perish from the earth.

Document C
The Way We Lived
A Black Soldier Writes to President Lincoln, 1863

Morris Island, S.C.

September 28, 1863

Your Excellency, Abraham Lincoln:

Your Excellency will pardon the presumption of an humble individual like myself, in addressing you, but the earnest solicitation of my comrades in arms besides the genuine interest felt by myself in the matter is my excuse, for placing before the Executive head of the Nation our Common Grievance.

On the 6th of the last Month, the Paymaster of the Department informed us, that if we would decide to receive the sum of $10 (ten dollars) per month, he would come and pay us that sum, but that, on the sitting of Congress, the Regt. [regiment] would, in his opinion, be allowed the other 3 (three). He did not give us any guarantee that this would be, as he hoped; certainly he had no authority for making any such guarantee, and we cannot suppose him acting in any way interested.

Now the main question is, are we Soldiers, or are we Laborers? We are fully armed, and equipped, have done all the various duties pertaining to a Soldier's life, have conducted ourselves to the complete satisfaction of General Officers, who were, if anything, prejudiced against us, but who now accord us all the encouragement and honors due us; have shared the perils an labor of reducing the first strong-hold that flaunted a Traitor Flag; and more, Mr. President, to-day the Anglo-Saxon Mother, Wife, or Sister are not alone in tears for departed Sons, Husbands and Brothers. The patient, trusting descendant of Afric's Clime have dyed the ground with blood, in defence of the Union, and Democracy. Men, too, your Excellency, who know in a measure the cruelties of the iron heel of oppression, which in years gone by, the very power their blood is now being spilled to maintain, ever ground them in the dust.

But when the war trumpet sounded o'er the land, when men knew not the Friend from the Traitor, the Black man laid his life at the altar of the Nation,—and he was refused. When the arms of the Union were beaten, in the first year of the war, and the Executive called for more food for its ravenous maw, again the black man begged the privilege of aiding his country in her need, to be again refused.

And now he is in the War, and how has he conducted himself? Let their dusky forms rise up, out of the mires of James Island, and give the answer. Let the rich mould around Wagner's parapet be upturned, and there will be found an eloquent answer. Obedient and patient and solid as a wall are they. All we lack is a paler hue and a better acquaintance with the alphabet.

Now your Excellency, we have done a Soldier's duty. Why can't we have a Soldier's pay? You caution the Rebel chieftain, that the United States knows no distinction in her soldiers. She insists on having all her soldiers of whatever creed or color, to be treated according to the usages of War. Now if the United States exacts uniformity of treatment of her soldiers from the insurgents, would it not be well and consistent to set the example herself by paying all her soldiers alike?

We of this Regt. were not enlisted under any "contraband" act. But we do not wish to be understood as rating our service of more value to the Government than the service of the ex-salve. Their service is undoubtedly worth much to the Nation, but Congress made express provision touching their case, as slaves freed by military necessity, and assuming the Government to be their temporary Guardian. Not so with us. Freemen by birth and consequently having the advantage of thinking and acting for ourselves so far as the Laws would allow us, we do not consider ourselves fit subjects for the Contraband act.

We appeal to you, Sir, as the Executive of the Nation, to have us justly dealt with. The Regt. do pray that they be assured their service will be fairly appreciated by paying them as American Soldiers, not as menial hirelings. Blackmen, you may well know, are poor; three dollars per month, for a year, will supply their needy wives and little ones with fuel. If you, as Chief Magistrate of the Nation, will assure us of our whole pay, we are content. Our Patriotism, our enthusiasm will have a new impetus, to exert our energy more and more to aid our Country. Not that our hearts ever flagged in devotion, spite the evident apathy displayed in our behalf, but we feel as though our country spurned us, now we are sworn to serve her. Please give this a moment's attention.

Document Set Twelve
To Heal The Nation's Wounds

With the end of the Civil War the most pressing question for the nation was how to devise a plan to reconstruct the Union. Among the issues to be resolved were how to treat the South, what to do with the newly emancipated slaves and whether or not to allow the white South to return to its place of prominence in the region. While these issues were debated on the national level, the South quickly attempted to find solutions for the economic and social disruptions which had occurred as a result of the war.

As an agrarian economy, the South had depended on land and labor for its wealth. The war had destroyed much of the land and had eliminated the institution of slavery. In the first years, after the war ended, the white power structure devised new political and economic arrangements to revive the economy. The Black Codes were instituted to define the relationship of the white and black South. Throughout the region, state legislatures codified the role of the freedmen in Southern society. Document A, "Mississippi Black Codes," is an example of the way in which the old order could be maintained while acknowledging the changes the war had made for the section. Class discussion could focus on a comparison of the privileges and restrictions which were given to freedmen. How was the relationship of white and black societies defined by these codes? The Congress reacted very strongly to the codes and they were a factor in why the Radical Republicans took Reconstruction away from Andrew Johnson. What sections of the code would these Congressmen find offensive and why?

The continued dependence on an agricultural economy and the loss of dependable labor through the institution of slavery forced the South to look for a replacement. The freedmen did not have the necessary capital to develop an independent farming system. As a result, many replaced legal slavery with an economic bondage known as sharecropping. Document B is a typical contractual agreement between a landowner and sharecropper. Students should pay careful attention to what the owner furnished the farmer. After analyzing the document, they should consider the reasons why this system insured that the sharecropper remained poor and in debt to the owner. What would be the effect of, "The sale of every cropper's part of the cotton to be made by me when and where I choose to sell?"... Would it be possible for any sharecropper to ever become an independent farmer?

The Radical Republicans reacted quickly to the legal and economic changes being made in the South. Unlike the executive branch, who believed a quick and expedient re-union was possible, these legislators thought the white South was unrepentant for the war. They quickly took over the reigns of power and began to institute their own plan for reconstruction which issued federal protection of the freedmen. Document C, "The Fourteenth Amendment to the Constitution," was intended to guarantee the political rights of the freedmen and punish Southerners who had actively participated in the war. It threatened the South with no national representation if freedmen were denied the right to vote. Students should consider how the Fourteenth Amendment became a tool to enhance federal power. Could it change the political power structure of the South. What would be the effect of the amendment on black/white relationship in the region?

During the period in which the Federal government controlled the South, some white Southerners sought extra legal ways to maintain control. Among the organizations which developed was the Ku Klux Klan, an organization dedicated to using violence to intimidate and influence the political actions of the freedmen. Document D is a set of statements made by former slaves about their experiences with the Klan. Pierce Harper recalls that if freedmen, "...made good money an' had a good farm de Ku Klux'd come and murder you." Students could decide how this fear might overwhelm and threaten the community into submission. Did the actions of the Klan establish a pattern which would dominate race relations in the South until the 1960's? They should consider the unwillingness of the federal government to provide protection from this violence.

Questions for Document Set Twelve

1. How was the relationship between white and black societies defined by the Black Codes?

2. What privileges did freedmen gain and lose in the Black Codes?

3. Did the freedmen have any alternative to the sharecropping system?

4. Under the sharecropping system had the freedmen replaced economic slavery for legal slavery?

5. Why didn't the Fourteenth Amendment insure the political enfranchisement of the freedmen?

6. According to the testimony of the former slaver how did the Ku Klux Klan intimidate and threaten their existence?

Document A
Mississippi Black Code, 1865

The Civil Rights of Freedmen in Mississippi

Section 1. Be it enacted by the legislature of the State of Mississippi, That all freedmen, free Negroes, and mulattoes may sue an be sued, impleaded and be impleaded in all the courts of law and equity of this state, and may acquire personal property and choses in action, by descent or purchase, any may dispose of the same, in the same manner, and to the same extent that white persons may: Provided that the provisions of this section shall not be so construed as to allow any freedman, free Negro, or mulatto to rent or lease any lands or tenements, except in incorporated town or cities in which places the corporate authorities shall control the same.

Sec. 2. Be it further enacted, That all freedmen, free Negroes, and mulattoes may intermarry with each other, in the same manner and under the same regulations that are provided by law for white persons: Provided, that the clerk of probate shall keep separate records of the same.

Sec. 3. Be it further enacted, That all freedmen, free Negroes, and mulattoes, who do now and have heretofore lived and cohabited together as husband and wife shall be taken and held in law as legally married, and the issue shall be taken and held as legitimate for all purposes. That it shall not be lawful for any freedman, free Negro, or mulatto to intermarry with any white person; nor for any white person to intermarry with any freedman, free Negro, or mulatto; any person who shall so intermarry shall be deemed guilty of felony and, on conviction thereof, shall be confined in the state penitentiary for life; and those shall be deemed freedmen, free Negroes, and mulattoes who are of pure Negro blood, and those descended from a Negro to the third generation inclusive, though one ancestor of each generation may have been a white person.

Sec. 4. Be it further enacted, That in addition to cases in which freedmen, free Negroes, and mulattoes are now by law competent witnesses, freedmen, free Negroes, or mulattoes shall be competent in civil cases when a party or parties to the suit, either plaintiff or plaintiffs, defendant or defendants, also in cases where freedmen, free Negroes, and mulattoes is or are either plaintiff or plaintiffs, defendant or defendants, and a white person or white persons is or are the opposing party or parties, plaintiff or plaintiffs, defendant or defendants. They shall also be competent witnesses in all criminal prosecutions where the crime charged is alleged to have been committed by a white person upon or against the person or property of a freedman, free Negro, or mulatto: Provided that in all cases said witnesses shall be examined in open court on the stand, except, however, they may be examined before the grand jury, and shall in all cases be subject to the rules and tests of the common law as to competency and credibility.

Sec. 5. Be it further enacted, That every freedman, free Negro, and mulatto shall, on the second Monday of January, one thousand eight hundred and sixty-six, and annually thereafter, have a lawful home or employment....

Sec. 6. Be it further enacted, That all contracts for labor made with freedmen, free Negroes, and mulattoes for a longer period than one month shall be in writing and in duplicate, attested and read to said freedman, free Negro, or mulatto, by a beat, city or county officers, or two disinterested white persons of the country in which the labor is to be performed, of which each party shall have one; and said contracts shall be taken and held as entire contracts, and if the laborer shall quit the service of the employer, before expiration of his term of service, without good cause, he shall forfeit his wages for that year, up to the time of quitting.

Sec. 7. Be it further enacted, That every civil officer shall, and every person may, arrest and carry back to his or her legal employer any freedman, free Negro, or mulatto who shall have quit the service of his or her employer before the expiration of his or her term of service without good cause, and said officer and person shall be entitled to receive for arresting and carrying back every deserting employee aforesaid, the sum of five dollars, and ten cents per mile from the place of arrest to the place of delivery, and the same shall be paid by the employer, and held as a set-off for so much against the wages of said deserting employee.

Sec. 8. Be it further enacted, That upon affidavit made by the employer of any freedman, free Negro, or mulatto, or other credible person, before any justice of the peace or member of the board of police, that any freedman, free Negro, or mulatto, legally employed by said employer, has illegally deserted said employment, such justice of the peace or member of the board of police shall issue his warrant or warrants, returnable before himself, or other such officer, directed to any sheriff, constable, or special deputy, commanding him to arrest said deserter and return him or her to said employer, and the like proceedings shall be had as provided in the preceding section....

Sec. 9. Be it further enacted, That if any person shall persuade or attempt to persuade, entice, or cause any freedman, free Negro, or mulatto to desert from the legal employment of any person, before the expiration of his or her term of service, or shall knowingly employ any such deserting freedman, free Negro, or mulatto, or shall knowingly give or sell to any such deserting freedman, free Negro, or mulatto, any food, raiment, or other thing, he or she shall be guilty of a misdemeanor and, upon conviction, shall be fined not less than twenty-five dollars and not more then two hundred dollars and the costs, and, if said fine and costs shall not be immediately paid, the court shall sentence said convict to not exceeding two months' imprisonment in the county jail, and he or she shall moreover be liable to the party injured in damages:....

Sec. 10. Be it further enacted, That it shall be lawful for any freedman, free Negro, or mulatto to charge any white person, freedman, free Negro, or mulatto, by affidavit, with any criminal offense against his or her person or property and upon such affidavit the proper process shall be issued and executed as if said affidavit was made by a white person, and it shall be lawful for any freedman, free Negro, or mulatto, in any action, suit, or controversy pending, or about to be instituted, in any court of law or equity of this state, to make all needful and lawful affidavits, as shall be necessary for the institution, prosecution, or defense of such suit or controversy.

Sec. 11. Be it further enacted, That the penal laws of this state, in all cases not otherwise specially provided for, shall apply and extend to all freedmen, free Negroes, and mulattoes....

Approved November 25, 1865

Document B
A Sharecrop Contract

To every one applying to rent land upon shares, the following conditions must be read, and agreed to.

To every 30 and 35 acres, I agree to furnish the team, plow, and farming implements, except cotton planters, and I do not agree to furnish a cart to every cropper. The croppers are to have half of the cotton, corn and fodder (and peas and pumpkins and potatoes if any are planted) if the following conditions are complied with, but—if not—they are to have only two fifths (2/5). Croppers are to have no part or interest in the cotton seed raised from the crop planted and worked by them. No vine crops of any description, that is, no watermelons, muskmelons,...squashes or anything of that kind, except peas and pumpkins, and potatoes, are to be planted in the cotton or corn. All must work under my direction. All plantation work to be done by the croppers. My part of the crop to be housed by them, and the fodder and oats to be hauled and put in the house. All the cotton must be topped about 1st August. If any cropper fails from any cause to save all the fodder from his crop, I am to have enough fodder to make it equal to one half of the whole if the whole amount of fodder had been saved.

For every mule or horse furnished by me there must be 1000 good sized rails...hauled, and the fence repaired as far as they will go, the fence to be torn down and put up from the bottom if I so direct. All croppers to haul rails and work on fence whenever I may order. Rails to be split when I may say. Each cropper to clean out every ditch in his crop, and where a ditch runs between two croppers, the cleaning out of that ditch is to be divided equally between them. Every ditch bank in the crop must be shrubbed down and cleaned off before the crop is planted and must be cut down every time the land is worked with his hoe and when the crop is "laid by," the ditch banks must be left clean of bushes, weeds, and seeds. The cleaning out of all ditches must be done by the first of October. The rails must be split and the fence repaired before corn is planted.

Each cropper must keep in good repair all bridges in his crop or over ditches that he has to clean out and when a bridge needs repairing that is outside of all their crops, then any one that I call on must repair it.

Fence jams to be done as ditch banks. If any cotton is planted on the land outside of the plantation fence, I am to have three fourths of all the cotton made in those patches, that is to say, no cotton must be planted by croppers in their home patches.

All croppers must clean out stable and fill them with straw, and haul straw in front of stable whenever I direct. All the cotton must be manured, and enough fertilizer must be brought to manure each crop highly, the croppers to pay for one half of all manure bought, the quantity to be purchased for each crop must be left to me.

No cropper to work off the plantation when there is any work to be done on the land he has rented, or when his work is needed by me or other croppers. Trees to be cut down on Orchard, house field & Evanson fences, leaving such as I may designate.

Road field to be planted from the very edge of the ditch to the fence, and all the land to be planted close up to the ditches and fences. No stock of any kind belonging to croppers to run in the plantation after crops are gathered. If the fence should be blown down, or if trees should fall on the fence outside of the land planted by any of the croppers, any one or all that I may call upon must put it up an repair it. Every cropper must feed or have fed, the team he works, Saturday nights, Sundays, and every morning before going to work, beginning to feed his team (morning, noon, and night every day in the week) on the day he rents and feeding it to including the 31st day of December. If any cropper shall from any cause fail to repair his fence as far as 1000 rails will go, or shall fail to clean out any part of his ditches, or shall fail to leave his ditch banks, any part of them, well shrubbed and clean when his crop is laid by, or shall fail to clean out stables, fill them up and haul straw in front of them whenever he is told, he shall have only two-fifths (2/5) of the cotton, corn, fodder, peas and pumpkins made on the land he cultivates.

If any cropper shall fail to feed his team Saturday nights, all day Sunday and all the rest of the week, morning/noon, and night, for every time he so fails he must pay me five cents.

No corn or cotton stalks must be burned, but must be cut down, cut up and plowed in. Nothing must be burned off the land except when it is impossible to plow it in.

Every cropper must be responsible for all gear and farming implements placed in his hands, and if not returned must be paid for unless it is worn out by use.

Croppers must sow & plow in oats and haul them to the crib, but must have no part of them. Nothing to be sold from their crops, nor fodder nor corn to be carried out of the fields until my rent is all paid, and all amounts they owe me and for which I am responsible are paid in full.

I am to gin & pack all the cotton and charge every cropper an eighteenth of his part, the cropper to furnish his part of the bagging, ties, & twine.

The sale of every cropper's part of the cotton to be made by me when and where I choose to sell, and after deducting all they owe me and all sums that I may be responsible for on their accounts, to pay them their half of the net proceeds. Work of every description, particularly the work on fences and ditches, to be done to my satisfaction, and must be done over until I am satisfied that it is done as it should be.

No wood to burn, nor light wood, nor poles, nor timber for boards, nor wood for any purpose whatever must be gotten above the house occupied by Henry Beasley—nor must any trees be cut down nor any wood used for any purpose, except for firewood, without my permission.

Document C
The Fourteenth Amendment, 1868

Sec. 1. All persons born or naturalized in the United States, and subject to the jurisdiction thereof, are citizens of the United States and of the State wherein they reside. No State shall make or enforce any law which shall abridge the privileges or immunities of citizens of the United States; nor shall any State deprive any person of life, liberty, or property, without due process of law; nor deny to any person within its jurisdiction the equal protection of the laws.

Sec. 2. Representatives shall be apportioned among the several States according to their respective numbers, counting the whole number of persons in each State, excluding Indians not taxed. But when the right to vote at any election for the choice of electors for President and Vice President of the United States, Representatives in Congress, the Executive and Judicial officers of a State, or the members of the Legislature thereof, is denied to any of the male inhabitants of such State, being twenty-one years of age, and citizens of the United States, or in any way abridged, except for participation in rebellion, or other crime, the basis of representation therein shall be reduced in the proportion which the number of such male citizens shall bear to the whole number of male citizens twenty-one years of age in such State.

Sec. 3. No person shall be a Senator or Representative in Congress, or elector of President and Vice President, or hold any office, civil or military, under the United States, or under any State, who, having previously taken an oath, as a member of Congress, or as an officer of the United States, or as a member of any State legislature, or as an executive or judicial officer of any State, to support the Constitution of the United States, shall have engaged in insurrection or rebellion against the same, or given aid or comfort to the enemies thereof. But Congress may by a vote of two-thirds of each House, remove such disability.

Sec. 4. The validity of the public debt of the United States, authorized by law, including debts incurred for payment of pensions and bounties for services in suppressing insurrection or rebellion, shall not be questioned. But neither the United States nor any State shall assume or pay any debt or obligation incurred in aid of insurrection or rebellion against the united States, or any claim for the loss or emancipation of any slave; but all such debts, obligations and claims shall be held illegal and void.

Sec. 5. The Congress shall have power to enforce, by appropriate legislation, the provisions of this article.

Document D
The Victims of Ku Klux Klan

Pierce Harper

After de colored people was considered free an' turned loose de Klu Klux broke out. Some of de colored people commenced to farming like I tol' you an' all de ol' stock dey could pick up after de Yankees left dey took an' took care of. If you got so you made good money an' had a good farm de Klu Klux'd come an' murder you. De gov'ment built de colored people school houses an' de Klu Klux went to work an' burn 'em down. Dey'd go to de jails an' take de colored men out an' knock der brains out an' break der necks an' throw 'em in de river.

Der was a man dat dey taken, his name was Jim Freeman. Dey taken him an' destroyed his stuff an' him 'cause he was making some money. Hung him on a tree in his front yard, right in front of his cabin. Der was some young men who went to de schools de gov'ment opened for de colored folks. some white widder woman said someone had stole something she own', so dey put these young fellers in jail 'cause dey suspicioned 'em. De Klu Kluxes went to de jail an' took 'em out an' kill 'em. Dat happened de second year after de War.

After de Klu Kluxes got so strong de colored men got together an' made a complaint before de law. De Gov'nor told de law to give 'em de ol' guns in de commissary what de Southern soldiers had use, so dey issued de colred men old muskets an' told 'em to protect theirselves.

De colored men got together an' organized the 'Malicy {Militia}. Dey had leaders like regular soldiers, men dat led 'em right on. Dye didn't meet 'cept when dey heard de Klu Kluxes was coming to get some of de colored folks. Den de one who knowed dat tol' de leader an' he went 'round an' told de others when an' where dey's meet. Den dey was ready for 'em. Dey's hide in de cabins an' when de Klu Kluxes come dere dey was. Den's when dey found out who a lot of de Klu Kluxes was, 'cause a lot of 'em was killed. Dey wore dem long sheets an' you couldn't tell who dey was. Dey even covered der horses up so you couldn't tell who dey belong to. Men you thought was your friend was Klu Kluxes. You deal wit' em in de stores in de day time an' at night dey come out to your house an' kill you.

Sue Craft

My teacher's name Dunlap—a white teacher teachin' de cullud. De Ku Klux whupped him fo' teachin' us. I saw de Ku Klux ridin' a heap dem days. Dey had hoods pulled ovah der faces. One time dey come to our house twict. Fus' time dey come quiet. It was right 'fore de 'lection o' Grant jus' after slavery. It was fus' time cullud people 'lowed t' vote. Dey ast my father was he goint to vote for Grant. He tell 'em he don' know he goin' vote. After 'lection day come back, whoopin' an' hollerin. Dey shoot out de winder lights. It wa 'cause my father voted for Grant. Dey broke de do' open. My father was a settn' on de bed. I 'member he had a shot gun in his han'. Well, de broke de do' down, an' then father he shoot, an' dey scattered all ovah de fence.

Morgan Ray

...I heard a lot about the Klu Klux, but it warn't till long afterwards dat I evah see 'em. It was one night after de work of de day was done and I was takin' a walk near where I worked. Suddenly I heard the hoof beats of horses and I natcherly wuz curious and waited beside the road to see what was coming'. I saw a company of men hooded and wearin' what looked like sheets. Dey had a young cullud man as der prisoner. I wuz too skairt to say anything or ask any questions. I just went on my sweet way. Later I found out dey acclaimed de prisoner had assulted a white woman. Dey strung him up when he wouldn't confess, and shot him full of holes and threw his body in de pond."

Document Set Thirteen
The Wealth of A Nation

The last quarter of the nineteenth century experienced an explosion of economic growth. Much of the change was due to the expansion of America's industrial base which led to a dramatic reshaping of American society. By the end of the century the United States had become the number one industrial power in the world. It had left behind its agrarian, homogeneous lifestyle and developed into an urban, industrial heterogeneous world power.

The new America brought prosperity and progress for some citizens, while others never reaped the rewards of change. This set of documents looks at both sides of the transformation of American society. It portrays the winners and losers of industrialization.

Mark Twain, one of the leading novelist of the times, viewed Industrial American with disdain and despair. Many of his works re-affirmed America's agrarian past and harshly criticized the new American society. In Document A, "The Gilded Age," students have an opportunity to read a selection from a novel which portrayed America as a harsh, materialistic world. Its main character, Colonial Beriah Sellers, represents the typical get rich quick speculator from this time period. In the piece selected, a young engineer Harry Brierly discovers the monetary relationship between the company and the government.

As students analyze this document they can assess how closely this piece mirrors the values and morals of the time period. They should note the underlying assumption that it was "business as usual" in the financial arrangements between business and government. Was Twain exaggerating or does the document reflect what was actually occurring during this period?

During this period a group of capitalists rose to prominence and directed the path of industrialization. They created industrial machines which efficiently combined the resources of the nation to make the United States the number one industrial power in the world. In the second document, "The Gospel of Wealth," Andrew Carnegie, one of the leading industrialists of the time, provides a rationale for the accumulation and distribution of wealth amassed by these entrepreneurs. Written in 1889 in The New American Review, this piece not only justified their fortunes but also provided a model for the distribution of their wealth. It is an interesting piece as Carnegie is able to support the laissez-faire economics and, at the same time, acknowledge the social responsibilities of the upper class. Discussion could focus on how Carnegie supports the new industrial economy. What is his assessment of capitalism and its effect on the nation? Who will benefit from the disposal of this "surplus wealth?" Was Carnegie correct in believing that his was the correct way to improve society?

Westward expansion was an integral part of the changes of the late nineteenth century. With the closing of the frontier in 1890 the nation truly was an integrated functional economic unit. It also forced the national government to develop a final policy concerning native Americans. Pushed westward after 1830, native tribes were once again seen as a barrier to national needs. While many had been placed on reservations, it was not clear that this was the best policy for them. Helen Hunt Jackson in her book, *A Century of Dishonor*, drew national attention to the conditions of native Americans. Published in 1881 it led to the passage of the Dawes Act, an attempt to provide native Americans with a stable lifestyle. In Document C students have an opportunity to read the conclusion of the book. Its description of native tribes and their conditions reminds students of the cost that can be paid for progress. Why did she use the phrase, "dark stain," in describing the relationship between native Americans and the United States government? Is Jackson correct in her assessment of national government policies for native Americans?

Document D, "Wounded Knee," compliments the Jackson selection. Written from the observations of a participant in that massacre, it is a detailed account of what happened at Wounded Knee. Students should consider the reasons why the American government feared the Ghost Dancers. Were Sitting Bull and Big Foot really a threat to society? If the tribes were returning to the reservation why did the army open fire?

Questions for Document Set Thirteen

1. After reading the Gilded Age selection assess who would bear the cost of the relationship between business and government?

2. Was Twain correct in his analysis of the time period?

3. Does the Gospel of Wealth reinforce the concepts of Social Darwinism?

4. Do you agree with Carnegie that the nation was better off because of the new economic order?

5. Was there an alternative to the Gospel of Wealth philosophy?

6. Why would A Century of Dishonor stir national reform about native Americans?

7. Analyze the statement of Black Elk, "...I was not sorry for the women and children. It was better for them to be happy in the other world, and I wanted to be there."

Document A
The Gilded Age

He called, with official importance in his mien, at No. – Wall Street, where a great gilt sign betokened the presence of the headquarters of the "Columbus River Slackwater Navigation Company." He entered and gave a dressy porter his card, and was requested to wait a moment in a sort of anteroom. The porter returned in a minute, and asked whom he would like to see?
"The president of the company, of course."
"He is busy with some gentlemen, sir; says he will be done with them directly."
That a copper-plate card with "Engineer- Chief" on it should be received with such tranquillity as this, annoyed Mr. Brierly not a little.
"Good morning, sir; take a seat–take a seat."
"Thank you, sir," said Harry, throwing as much chill into his manner as his ruffled dignity prompted.
"We perceive by your reports and the reports of the chief superintendent, that you have been making gratifying progress with the work. We are all very much pleased."
"Indeed?" We did not discover it from your letters–which we have not received; nor by the treatment our drafts have met with–which were not honored; nor by the reception of any part of the appropriation, no part of it having come to hand."
"Why, my dear Mr. Brierly, there must be some mistake. I am sure we wrote you and also Mr. Sellers, recently–when my clerk comes he will show copies–letters informing you of the ten per cent. assessment."
"Oh, certainly, we got those letters. But what we wanted was money to carry on the work–money to pay the men.
"Certainly, certainly–true enough–but we credited you both for a large part of your assessments–I am sure that was in our letters."
"Of course that was in–I remember that."
"Ah, very well, then. Now we begin to understand each other."
"Well, I don't see that we do. There's two months' wages due the men, and–"
"How? Haven't you paid the men?"
"Paid them! How are we going to pay them when you don't honor our drafts?"
"Why, my dear sir, I cannot see how you can find an fault with us. I am sure we have acted in a perfectly straightforward business way. Now let us look at the thing a moment. You subscribed for one hundred shares of the capital stock, at one thousand dollars a share, I believe?"
"Yes, sir, I did."
"And Mr. Sellers took a like amount?"
"Yes, sir."
"Very well. No concern can get along without money. We levied a ten per cent. assessment. It was the original understanding that you and Mr. Sellers were to have the positions you now hold, with salaries of six hundred dollars a month each, while in active service. You were duly elected to these places, and you accepted them.
"Certainly."
"Very well. You were given your instructions and put to work. By your reports it appears that you have expended the sum of $9,640 upon the said work. Two months' salary to you two officers amounts altogether to $2,400–about one-eighth of your ten per cent. assessment, you see; which leaves you in debt to the company for the other seven-eighths of the assessment–viz., something over $8,000 apiece. Now, instead of requiring you to forward this aggregate of $16,000 or $17,000 to New York, the company voted unanimously to let you pay it over to the contractors, laborers from time to time, and give you credit on the books for it. And they did it without a murmur, too, for they were pleased with the progress you had made, and were glad to pay you that little compliment–and a very neat one it was, too, I am sure. The work you did fell short of $10,000, a trifle. Let me see–$9,640 from $20,000–salary $2,400 added–ah, yes, the balance due the company from yourself and Mr. Sellers is $7,960, which I will take the responsibility of allowing to stand for the present, unless you prefer to draw a check now, and thus–"
"Confound it, do you mean to say that instead of the company owing us $2,400, we owe the company $7,960?"

Document B
The Gospel of Wealth

The problem of our age is the proper administration of wealth, that the ties of brotherhood may still bind together the rich and poor in harmonious relationship. The conditions of human life have not only been changed, but revolutionized, within the past few hundred years. In former days there was little difference between the dwelling, dress, food, and environment of the chief and those of his retainers....The contrast between the palace of the millionaire and the cottage of the laborer with us to-day measures the change which has come with civilization. This change, however, is not to be deplored, but welcomed as highly beneficial. It is well, say, essential, for the progress of the race that the houses of some should be homes for all that is highest and best in literature and the arts, and for all the refinements of civilization, rather than that none should be so. Much better this great irregularity than universal squalor. Without wealth there can be no Meccenas.

...to-day the world obtains commodities of excellent quality at prices which even the preceding generation would have deemed incredible. In the commercial world similar causes have produced similar results, and the race is benefited thereby. The poor enjoy what the rich could not before afford. What were the luxuries have become the necessaries of life....

Objections to the foundations upon which society is based are not in order, because the condition of the race is better with these than it has been with any other which has been tried.....No evil, but good, has come to the race from the accumulation of wealth by those who have had the ability and energy to produce it....

We start, then, with a condition of affairs under which the best interests of the race are promoted, but which inevitably gives wealth to the few....What is the proper mode of administering wealth after the laws upon which civilization is founded have thrown it into the hands of the few?....

There are but three modes in which surplus wealth can be disposed of. It can be left to the families of the decedents; or it can be bequeathed for public purposes; or, finally, it can be administered by its possessors during their lives....

There remains, then, only one mode of suing great fortunes; but in this we have the true antidote for the temporary unequal distribution of wealth, the reconciliation of the rich and the poor–a reign of harmony, another ideal, differing, indeed, from that of the Communist in requiring only the further evolution of existing conditions, not the total overthrow of our civilization. It is founded upon the most intense Individualism....Under its sway we shall have an ideal State, in which the surplus wealth of the few will become, in the best sense, property of the many, because administering for the common good; and this wealth, passes through the hands of the few, can be made much more potent force for the elevation of our race than if distributed in small sums to the people themselves. Even the poorest can be made to see this, and to agree that great sums gathered by some of their fellow-citizens–spent for public purposes, from which masses reap the principal benefit, are more valuable to them than if scattered among themselves in trifling amounts through the course of many years.

If we consider the results which flow from the Cooper Institute, for instance...., and compare these with those who would have ensured for the good of the man form an equal sum distributed by Mr. Cooper in his lifetime in the form of wages, which the highest form of distributing, being work done and not for charity,, we can estimate of the possibilities for the improvement of the race which lie embedded in the present law of the accumulation of wealth....

This, then, is held to be the duty of the man of wealth: To set an example of modest, unostentatious living, shunning display or extravagance; to provide moderately for the legitimate wants of those dependent upon him; and, after doing so, to consider all surplus revenues which come to him simply as trust funds, which he is called upon to administer, and strictly bound as a matter of duty to administer in the manner which, in his judgment, is best calculated to produce the most beneficial results for the community–the man of wealth thus becoming the mere trustee and agent for his poorer brethren, bringing to their service his superior wisdom, experience, and ability to administer, doing for them better than they would or could do for them selves....

In bestowing charity, the main consideration should be to help those who will help themselves; to provide part of the means by which those who desire to improve may do so; to give those who desire to rise the aids by which they may rise; to assist, but rarely or never to do all. Neither the individual nor the race is improved by alms giving. Those worthy of assistance, except in rare cases, seldom require assistance....

The rich man is thus almost restricted to following the examples of Peter Cooper, Enoch Pratt of Baltimore, Mr. Pratt of Brooklyn, Senator Stanford, and others, who know that the best means of benefiting the community is to place within its reach the ladders upon which the aspiring can rise–free libraries, parks, and means of recreation, by which men are helped in body and mind; works of art, certain to give pleasure and improve the general condition of the people; in this manner returning their surplus wealth to the mass of their fellows in the forms best calculated to do them lasting good.

Thus is the problem of rich and poor to be solved. The laws of accumulation will be left free, the laws of distribution free. Individualism will continue, but the millionaire will be but a trustee for the poor, intrusted for a season with a great part of the increased wealth of the community, but administering it for the community far better than if could or would have done for itself. The best minds will thus have reached a stage in the development of the race in which it is clearly seen that there is no mode of disposing of surplus wealth creditable to thoughtful and earnest men into whose hands it flows, save by using it year by year for the general good....

Such, in my opinion, is the true gospel concerning wealth, obedience to which is destined some day to solve the problem of the rich and the poor,, and to bring "Peace on earth, among men good will."

Document C
A Century of Dishonor

There are within the limits of the United States between two hundred and fifty and three hundred thousand Indians, exclusive of those in Alaska. The names of the different tribes and bands, as entered in the statistical table so the Indian Office Reports, number nearly three hundred. One of the most careful estimates which have been made of their numbers and localities gives them as follows: "In Minnesota and States east of the Mississippi, about 32,500; in Nebraska, Kansas, and the Indian Territory, 70,650; in the Territories of Dakota, Montana, Wyoming, and Idaho, 65,000; in Nevada and the Territories of Colorado, New Mexico, Utah, and Arizona, 84,000; and on the Pacific slope, 48,000."

Of these, 130,000 are self-supporting on their own reservations, "receiving nothing from the Government except interest on their own moneys, or annuities granted them in consideration of the cession of their lands to the United States."

...Of the remainder, 84,000 are partially supported by the Government—the interest money due them and their annuities, as provided by treaty, being inadequate to their subsistence on the reservations where they are confined....

There are about 55,000 who never visit an agency, over whom the Government does not pretend to have either control or care. These 55,000 "subsist by hunting, fishing, on roots, nuts,, berries, etc., and by begging and stealing"; and this also seems to dispose of the accusation that the Indian will not "work for a living." There remains a small portion, about 31,000, that are entirely subsisted by the Government.

There is not among these three hundred bands of Indians one which has not suffered cruelly at the hands either of the Government or of white settlers. The poorer, the more insignificant, the more helpless the band, the more certain the cruelty and outrage to which they have been subjected. This is especially true of the bands on the Pacific slope. These Indians found themselves of a sudden surrounded by and caught up in the great influx of gold-seeking settlers, as helpless creatures on a shore are caught up in a tidal wave. There was not time for the Government to make treaties; not even time for communities to make laws. The tale of the wrongs, the oppressions, the murders of the Pacific-slope Indians in the last thirty years would be a volume by itself, and is too monstrous to be believed.

It makes little difference, however, where one opens the record of the history of the Indians; every page and every year has its dark stain. The story of one tribe is the story of all, varied only differences of time and place; but neither time nor place makes any difference in the main facts. Colorado is as greedy and unjust in 1880 as was Georgia in 1830, and Ohio in 1795; and the United States Government breaks promises now as deftly as then, and with an added ingenuity from long practice.

One of its strongest supports in so doing is the wide-spread sentiment among the people of dislike to the Indian, of impatience with his presence as a "barrier to civilization" and distrust of it as a possible danger. The old tales of the frontier life, with its horrors of Indian warfare, have gradually, by two or three generations' telling, produced in the average mind something like an hereditary instinct of questioning and unreasoning aversion which it is almost impossible to dislodge or soften....

President after president has appointed commission after commission to inquire into and report upon Indian affairs, and to make suggestions as to the best methods of managing them. The reports are filled with eloquent statements of wrongs done to the Indians, of perfidies on the part of the Government; they counsel, as earnestly as words can, a trial of the simple and unperplexing expedients of telling truth, keeping promises, making fair bargains, dealing justly in all ways and all things. These reports are bound up with the Government's Annual Reports, and that is the end of them....

"The history of the Government connections with the Indians is a shameful record of broken treaties and unfulfilled promises. The history of the border white man's connection with the Indians is a sickening record of murder, outrage, robbery, and wrongs committed by the former, as the rule, and occasional savage outbreaks and unspeakably barbarous deeds of retaliation by the latter, as the exception.

Taught by the Government that they had rights entitled to respect, when those rights have been assailed by the rapacity of the white man, the arm which should have been raised to protect them has ever been ready to sustain the aggressor.

The testimony of some of the highest military officers of the United States is on record to the effect that, in our Indian wars, almost without exception, the first aggressions have been made by the white man....Every crime committed by a white man against an Indian is concealed and palliated. Every offence committed by an Indian against a white man is borne on the wings of the post or the telegraph to the remotest corner of the land, clothed with all the horrors which the reality or imagination can throw around it. Against such influences as these are the people of the United States need to be warned."

To assume that it would be easy, or by any one sudden stroke of legislative policy possible, to undo the mischief and hurt of the long past, set the Indian policy of the country right for the future, and make the Indians at once safe and happy, is the blunder of a hasty and uninformed judgment. The notion which seems to be growing more prevalent, that simply to make all Indians at once citizens of the United States would be a sovereign and instantaneous panacea for all their ills and all the Government's perplexities, is a very inconsiderate one. To administer complete citizenship of a sudden, all round, to all Indians, barbarous and civilized alike, would be as grotesque a blunder as to dose them all round with any one medicine, irrespective of the symptoms and needs of their diseases. It would kill more than it would cure. Nevertheless, it is true, as was well stated by one of the superintendents of Indian Affairs in 1857, that, "so long as they are not citizens of the United States, their rights of property must remain insecure against invasion. The doors of the federal tribunals being barred against them while wards and dependents, they can only partially exercise the rights of free government, or give to those who make, execute, and construe the few laws they are allowed to enact, dignity sufficient to make them respectable. While they continue individually to gather the crumbs that fall from the table of the united States, idleness, improvidence, and indebtedness will be the rule, and industry, thrift, and freedom from debt the exception. The utter absence of individual title to particular lands deprives every one among them of the chief incentive to labor and exertion–the very mainspring on which the prosperity of a people depends."

All judicious plans and measures for their safety and salvation must embody provisions for their becoming citizens as fast as they are fit, and must protect them till then in every right and particular in which our laws protect other "persons" who are not citizens....

However great perplexity and difficulty there may be in the details of any and every plan possible for doing at this late day anything like justice to the Indian, however, hard it may be for good statesmen and good men to agree upon the things that ought to be done, there certainly is, or ought to be , no perplexity whatever, on difficulty whatever, in agreeing upon certain things that ought not to be done, and which must cease to be done before the first steps can be taken toward righting the wrongs, curing the ills, and wiping out the disgrace to us of the present conditions of our Indians.

Cheating robbing breaking promises-these three are clearly things which must cease to be done. One more thing, also, and that is the refusal of the protection of the law to the Indian's rights of property, "of life, liberty, and the pursuit of happiness."

When these four things have ceased to be done, time, statesmanship, philanthropy, and Christianity can slowly and surely do the rest. Till these four things have ceased to be done, statesmanship and philanthropy alike must work in vain, and even Christianity can reap but small harvest.

Document Set D
Account of the Wounded Knee Massacre, 1890

Black Elk

It was about this time that bad news came to us from the north. We heard that some policemen from Standing Rock had gone to arrest Sitting Bull on Grand River, and that he would not let them take him; so there was a fight, and they killed him.

It was now near the end of the Moon of Popping Trees, and I was twenty-seven years old [December, 1890]. We heard that Big Foot was coming down from the Badlands with nearly four hundred people. Some of these were from Sitting Bull's band. They had run away when Sitting Bull was killed, and joined Big Foot on Good River. There were only about a hundred warriors in this band, and all the others were women and children and some old men. They were all starving and freezing, and Big foot was so sick that they had to bring him along in a pony drag. They had all run away to hide in the Badlands, and they were coming in now because they were starving and freezing. Soldiers were over there looking for them. The soldiers had everything and were not freezing an starving. Near Porcupine Butte the soldiers came up to the Big Foots, and they surrendered and went along with the soldiers to Wounded Knee Creek.

It was in the evening when we heard that the Big Foots were camped over there with the soldiers, about fifteen miles by the old road from where we were. It was the next morning [December 29, 1890] that something terrible happened.

That evening before it happened, I went in to Pine Ridge and heard these things, and while I was there, soldiers started for where the Big Foots were. These made about five hundred soldiers that were there next morning. When I saw them starting I felt that something terrible was going to happen. That night I could hardly sleep at all. I walked around most of the night.

In the morning I went out after my horses, and while I was out I heard shooting off toward the east, and I knew from the sound that it must be wagon-guns [cannon] going off. The sounds went right through my body, and I felt that something terrible would happen. [He donned his ghost shirt, and armed only with a bow, mounted his pony and rode in the direction of the shooting, and was joined on the way by others.]

In a little while we had come to the top of the ridge where, looking to the east, you can see for the first time the monument and the burying ground on the little hill where the church is. That is where the terrible thing started. Just south of the burying ground on the little hill a deep dry gulch runs about east and west, very crooked, and it rises westward to nearly the top of the ridge where we were. It had no name, but the Wasichus [white men] sometimes called Battle Creek now. We stopped on the ridge not far from the head of the dry gulch. Wagon guns were still going off over there on the little hill, and they were going off again where they hit among the gulch. There was much shooting down yonder, and there were many cries, and we could see calvarymen scattered over the hills ahead of us. Calvarymen were riding along the gulch and shooting into it, where the women and children were running away and trying to hide in the gullies and the stunted pines....

We followed down along the dry gulch, and what we saw was terrible. Dead and wounded women and children and little babies were scattered all along there where they had been trying to run away. The soldiers had followed along the gulch, as they ran, and murdered them in there. Sometimes they were in heaps because they had huddled together, and some were scattered all along. sometimes bunches of them had been killed and torn to pieces where the wagon guns hit them. I saw a little baby trying to suck its mother, but she was bloody and dead.

There were two little boys as one place in this gulch. They had guns and they had been killing soldiers all by themselves. We could see the soldiers they had killed. The boys were all alone there, and they were not hurt. These were very brave little boys.

When we drove the soldiers back, they dug themselves in, and we were not enough people to drive them out from there. In the evening they marched off up Wounded Knee Creek, and then we saw all that they had done there.

Men and women and children were heaped and scattered all over the flat at the bottom of the little hill where the soldiers had their wagon-guns, and westward up the dry gulch all the way to the high ridge, the dead women and children and babies were scattered.

When I saw this I wished that I had died too, but I was not sorry for the women and children. It was better for them to be happy in the other world, and I wanted to be there too. But before I went there I wanted to have revenge. I thought there might be a day, and we should have revenge.

In the morning the soldiers began to take all the guns away from the Big Foots, who were camped in the flat below the little hill where the monument and burying ground are now. The people had stacked most of their guns, and even their knives, by the teepee where Big Foot was lying sick. Soldiers were on the little hill and all around, and there were soldiers across the dry gulch to the south and over east along Wounded Knee Creek too. The people were nearly surrounded, and the wagon-guns were point at them.

It was a good winter day when all this happened. The sun was shining. But after the soldiers marched away from their dirty work, a heavy snow began to fall. The wind came up in the night. There was a big blizzard, and it grew very cold. The snow drifted deep in the crooked gulch, and it was one long grave of butchered women and children and babies, who had never done any harm and were only trying to run away.

Report on Wounded Knee Massacre and the Decrease in Indian Land Acreage, 1891

President Benjamin Harrison

The first was necessary to protect the settlers; the second is progressing well the president announced in his third annual message, December 9, 1891, excerpted below.

The outbreak among the Sioux which occurred in December last is as to its causes and incidents fully reported upon by the War Department and the Department of the Interior. That these Indians had some just complaints, especially in the matter of the reduction of the appropriation for rations and in the delays attending the enactment of laws to enable the Department to perform the engagements entered into with them, is probably true; but the Sioux tribes are naturally warlike and turbulent, and their warriors were excited by their medicine men and chiefs, who preached the coming of an Indian messiah who was to give them power to destroy their enemies. In view of the alarm that prevailed among the white settlers near the reservation and of the fatal consequences that would have resulted from an Indian incursion, I placed at the disposal of General Miles, commanding the Division of the Missouri, all such forces as we thought by him to be required. He is entitled to the credit of having given thorough protection to the settlers and of bringing the hostiles into subjection with the least possible loss of life....

Since March 4, 1889, about 23,000,000 acres have been separated from Indian reservations and added to the public domain for the use of those who desired to secure free homes under our beneficent laws. It is difficult to estimate the increase of wealth which will result from the conversion of these waste lands into farms, but it is more difficult to estimate the betterment which will result to the families that have found renewed hope and courage in the ownership of a home and the assurance of a comfortable subsistence under free and healthful conditions. It is also gratifying to be able to feel, as we may, that this work has proceeded upon lines of justice toward the Indian, and that he may now, if he will, secure to himself the good influences of a settled habitation, the fruits of industry, and the security of citizenship.

Document Set Fourteen
Huddled Masses

To insure success, Industrialization needed cheap unskilled labor. The consequence of this demand was the final transformation of the American worker and the working class. Work became impersonal, conditions were poor and wages were low. For many families economic survival meant the entire household working. One result of this need was the dramatic increase in the number of children in the workforce.

The first selection, "Children In The Coal Mines," depicts the life of child miners. Written by John Spargo in 1906, it describes the hazards for children who were paid 60 cents and worked ten hour days in untenable working conditions. The document should raise a number of questions for the students. Why were children used in the mines? Did their families have any other alternatives? How does Saprgo perceive the role of state governments in supervising the situation?

The largest source for an adequate labor supply came from Eastern and Southern immigrants. From 1880-1910 the United States experienced the greatest number of immigrants in its history. The experience would create a truly heterogeneous society. The transition for many of them was difficult and it took them a generation before they found "their place." The next two documents portray some of these problems. The Daily Forward was the major Yiddish newspaper read in the United States. It had its own version of Dear Abbey in a column called 'A Bintel Brief." In each issue it published a series of letters from readers about the types of problems they faced. Document B gives three examples of the letters, and advice, which were often to be found in the newspaper. Students can discuss how the letters reflect the difficulty immigrants had in assimilating into American society.

Chinese immigrants faced the most difficulty in assimilating into the American culture. In Document D students have an opportunity to read the experiences of one Chinese immigrant as he faced life in the United States. Why was he willing to immigrate? Was his pattern of success typical of most immigrants? According to his account, were the Chinese treated differently than other immigrants?

For many Americans these new immigrants posed a threat to them and the American way of life. By the 1880s a wave of nativism swept the nation as Americans voiced their fears and pressured for restrictions on immigrants. The American Protective Association gained widespread popularity in its anti-Catholic, anti-immigrant stance. Document D is the secret oath of the members of this organization. Students should consider why it expressed a strong fear of Catholics and wanted to prohibit them from holding political office. How rational were the fears of the American public concerning these new immigrants? What underlying concerns motivated their vocal disdain for these groups?

Questions for Document Set Fourteen

1. After reading Spargo's account assess the long term consequences for these children who worked in the mines?

2. Why weren't there stronger child labor laws?

3. According to the letters to "The Bintel Brief" what difficulties did Jewish immigrants face in the New World?

4. Compare the experiences of the Jewish and Chinese immigrants? What similarities and differences were there?

5. Why did the American Protective Association fear Catholic immigrants?

Document A
Children in the Coal Mines

Work in the coal breakers is exceedingly hard and dangerous. Crouched over the chutes, the boys sit hour after hour, picking out the pieces of slate and other refuse from the coal as it rushes past to the washers. From the cramped position they have to assume, most of them become more or less deformed and bent-backed like old men. When a boy has been working for some time and begins to get round-shouldered, his fellows say that "He's got his boy to carry around whenever he goes."

The coal is hard, and accidents to the hands, such as cut, broken, or crushed fingers, are common among the boys. Sometimes there is a worse accident: a terrified shriek is heard, and a boy is mangled and torn in the machinery, or disappears in the chute to be picked out later smothered and dead. Clouds of dust fill the breakers and are inhaled by the boys, laying the foundations for asthma and miners' consumption.

I once stood in a breaker for half an hour and tried to do the work a twelve-year-old boy was doing day after day, for ten hours at a stretch, for sixty cents a day. The gloom of the breaker appalled me. Outside the sun shone brightly, the air was pellucid, and the birds sang in chorus with the trees and the rivers. Within the breaker there was blackness, clouds of deadly dust enfolded everything, the harsh, grinding roar of the machinery and the ceaseless rushing of coal through the chutes filled the ears. I tried to pick out the pieces of slate from the hurrying stream of coal, often missing them; my hands were bruised and cut in a few minutes; I was covered from head to foot with coal dust, and for many hours afterwards I was expectorating some of the small particles of anthracite I had swallowed.

I could not do that work and live, but there were boys of ten and twelve years of age doing it for fifty and sixty cents a day. Some of them had never been inside of a school; few of them could read a child's primer. True, some of them attended the night schools, but after working ten hours in the breaker the educational results from attending school were practically nil. "We goes fer a good time, an' we keeps de guys wot's dere hoppin' all de time," said little Owen Jones, whose work I had been trying to do....

As I stood in that breaker I thought of the reply of the small boy to Robert Owen [British social reformer]. Visiting an English coal mine one day, Owen asked a twelve-year-old if he knew God. The boy stared vacantly at his questioner: "God?" he said, "God? No, I don't. He must work in some other mine." It was hard to realize amid the danger and din and blackness of that Pennsylvania breaker that such a thing as belief in a great All-good God existed.

From the breakers the boys graduate to the mine depths, where they become door tenders, switch boys, or mule drivers. Here, far below the surface, work is still more dangerous. At fourteen and fifteen the boys assume the same risks as the men, and are surrounded by the same perils. Nor is it in Pennsylvania only that these conditions exist. In the bituminous mines of West Virginia, boys of nine or ten are frequently employed. I met one little fellow ten years old in Mt. Carbon, W. Va., last year, who was employed as a "trap boy." Think of what it means to be a trap boy at ten years of age. It means to sit alone in a dark mine passage hour after hour, with no human soul near; to see no living creature except the mules as they pass with their loads, or a rat or two seeking to share one's meal; to stand in water or mud that covers the ankles, chilled to the marrow by the cold draughts that rush in when you open the trap door for the mules to pass through; to work for fourteen hours–waiting–opening and shutting a door–then waiting again–for sixty cents; to reach the surface when all is wrapped in the mantle of night, and to fall to the earth exhausted and have to be carried away to the nearest "shack" to be revived before it is possible to walk to the farther shack called "home." Boys twelve years of age may be legally employed in the mines of West Virginia, by day or by night, and for as many hours as the employers care to make them toil or their bodies will stand the strain. Where the disregard of child life is such that this may be done openly and with legal sanction, it is easy to believe what miners have again and again told me–that there are hundreds of little boys of nine and ten years of age employed in the coal mines of this state.

Document B
Letters to the *Jewish Daily Forward* (1906-1907)

Dear Editor,

I am a Russian revolutionist and a freethinker. Here in America I became acquainted with a girl who is also a freethinker. We decided to marry, but the problem is that she has Orthodox parents, and for their sake we must have a religious ceremony. If we refuse the ceremony we will be cut off from them forever. Her parents also want me to go to the synagogue with them before the wedding, and I don't know what to do. Therefore I ask you to advise me how to act.

Respectfully, J.B.

ANSWER:

The advice is that there are times when it pays to give in to old parents and not grieve them. It depends on the circumstances. When one can get along with kindness it is better not to break off relations with the parents.

Worthy Editor,

Allow me a little space in your newspaper and, I beg you, give me some advice as to what to do.

There are seven people in our family -- parents and five children. I am the oldest child, and a fourteen-year-old girl. We have been in the country two years and my father, who is a frail man, is the only one working to support the whole family.

I go to school, where I do very well. But since times are hard now and my father earned only five dollars this week, I began to talk about giving up my studies and going to work in order to help my father as much as possible. But my mother didn't ever want to hear of it. She wants me to continue my education. She even went out and spent ten dollars on winter clothes for me. But I didn't enjoy the clothes, because I think I am doing the wrong thing. Instead of bringing something into the house, my parents have to spend money on me.

I have a lot of compassion for my parents. My mother is now pregnant, but she still has to take care of the three boarders we have in the house. Mother and Father work very hard and they want to keep me in school.

I am writing to you without their knowledge, and I beg you to tell me how to act. Hoping you can advise me, I remain,
Your reader,

ANSWER:

The advice to the girl is that she should obey her parents and further her education, because in that way she will be able to give them greater satisfaction than if she went out to work.

Worthy Editor,

I was born in America and my parents gave me a good education. I...finished high school, completed a course in bookkeeping and got a good job. I have many friends, and several boys have already proposed to me. Recently I went to visit my parents' home town in Russian Poland. My mother's family in Europe had invited my parents to a wedding, but instead of going themselves, they sent me....I had a good time. Our European family, like my parents, are quite well off and they treated me well. The indulged me in everything and I stayed with them six months.

It was lively in the town....they all accepted me warmly, looked up to me -- after all, I was a citizen of the free land, America. Among the social leaders of the community was an intelligent young man, a friend of my uncle's, who took me to various gatherings and affairs.

He was very attentive, and after a short while he declared his love for me in a long letter....

As my love for him grew, however, I wrote to my parents about him, and then we became officially engaged.

A few months later we both went to my parents in the States and they received him like their own son. My bridegroom immediately began to learn English and tried to adjust to the new life. Yet when I introduced him to my friends they looked at him with disappointment. "This 'greenhorn' is your fiancee?" they asked. I told them what a big role he played in his town, how everyone respected him, but they looked at me as if I were crazy and scoffed at my words.

At first I thought, Let them laugh, when they get better acquainted with him they'll talk differently. In time, though, I was affected by their talk and began to think, like them, that he really was a "greenhorn" and acted like one.

In short, my love for him is cooling off gradually. I'm suffering terribly because my feelings for him are changing. In Europe, where everyone admired him and all the girls envied me, he looked different. But, here, I see before me another person.

I haven't the courage to tell him, and I can't even talk about it to my parents. He still loves me with all his heart, and I don't know what to do. I choke it all up inside myself, and I beg you to help me with advice in my desperate situation.

Respectfully,

A Worried Reader

ANSWER:

The writer would make a grave mistake if she were to separate from her bridegroom now. She must not lose her common sense and be influenced by the foolish opinions of her friends who divided the world into "greenhorns" and real Americans.

We can assure the writer that her bridegroom will learn English quickly. He will know American history and literature as well as her friends do, and be a better American than they. She should be proud of his love and laugh at those who call him "greenhorn."

Document C
Life of a Chinese Immigrant

The village where I was born is situated in the province of Canton, on one of the banks of the Si-Kiang River. It is called a village, altho it is really as big as a city, for there are about 5,000 men in it over eighteen years of age–women and children and even youths are not counted in our villages....

...I heard about the American foreign devils, that they were false, having made a treaty by which it was agreed that they could freely come to China, and the Chinese as freely go to their country. After this treaty was made China opened its doors to them and then they broke the treaty that they had asked for by shutting the Chinese out of their country....

The man had gone away from our village a poor boy. Now he returned with unlimited wealth, which he had obtained in the country of the American wizards. After many amazing adventures he had become a merchant in a city called Mott Street, so it was said....

Having made his wealth among the barbarians this man had faithfully returned to pour it out among his tribesmen, and he is living in our village now very happy, and a pillar of strength to the poor.

The wealth of this man filled my mind with the idea that I, too, would like to go to the country of the wizards and gain some of their wealth, and after a long time my father consented, and gave me his blessing, and my mother took leave of me with tears, while my grandfather laid his hand upon my head and told me to remember and live up to the admonitions of the Sages, to avoid gambling, bad women and men of evil minds, and so to govern my conduct that when I died my ancestors might rejoice to welcome me as a guest on high.

My father gave me $100, and I went to Hong Kong with five other boys from our place and we got steerage passage on a steamer, paying $50 each....

...Of the great power of these people I saw many signs. The engines that moved the ship were wonderful monsters, strong enough to lift mountains. When I got to San Francisco, which was before the passage of the Exclusion act, I was half starved, because I was afraid to eat the provisions of the barbarians, but a few days' living in the Chinese quarter made me happy again....

The Chinese laundryman does not learn his trade in China; there are no laundries in China....All the Chinese laundrymen here were taught in the first place by American women just as I was taught.

When I went to work for that American family I could not speak a word of English, and I did not know anything about house work. The family consisted of husband, wife and two children. They were very good to me and paid me $3.50 a week, of which I could save $3.....

In six months I had learned how to do the work of our house quite well, and I was getting $5 a week and board, and putting away about $4.25 a week. I had also learned some English, and by going to a Sunday school I learned more English and something about Jesus, who was a great Sage, and whose precepts are like those of Kong-foo-tsze.

It was twenty years ago when I came to this country, and I worked for two years as a servant, getting at least $35 a month. I sent money home to comfort my parents....

When I first opened a laundry it was in company with a partner, who had been in the business for some years. We went to a town about 500 miles inland, where a railroad was building. We got a board shanty and worked for the men employed by the railroads....

We were three years with the railroad, and then went to the mines, where we made plenty of money in gold dust, but had a hard time, for many of the miners were wild men who carried revolvers and after drinking would come into our place to shoot and steel shirts, for which we had to pay. One of these men hit his head hard against a flat iron and all the miners came and broke our laundry, chasing us out of town. They were going to hang us. We lost all our property and $365 in money, which member of the mob must have found.

Luckily most of our money was in the hands of Chinese bankers in San Francisco. I drew $500 and went East to Chicago, where I had a laundry for three years, during which I increased my capital to $2,500. After that I was four years in Detroit. I went home to China in 1897, but returned in 1898, and began a laundry business in Buffalo.

The ordinary laundry shop is generally divided into three rooms. In front is the room where the customers are received, behind that a bedroom and in the back the work shop, which is also the dining room and kitchen. The stove and cooking utensils are the same as those of the Americans.....

I have found out, during my residence in this country, that much of the Chinese prejudice against Americans is unfounded, and I no longer put faith in the wild tales that were told about them in our village, tho some of the Chinese, who have been here twenty years and who are learned men, still believe that there is no marriage in this country, that the land is infested with demons and that all the people are given over to general wickedness.

I know better. Americans are not all bad, nor are they wicked wizards. Still, they have their faults, and their treatment of us is outrageous....

The reason why so many Chines go into the laundry business in this country is because it requires little capital and is one of the few opportunities that are open....

There is no reason for the prejudice against the Chinese. The cheap labor cry was always a falsehood. Their labor was never cheap, and is not chap now. It has always commanded the highest market price. But the trouble is that the Chinese are such excellent and faithful workers that bosses will have no others when they can get them. If you look at men working on the street you will find an overseer for every four or five of them. That watching is not necessary for Chinese. They work as well when left to themselves as they do when some one is looking at them.....

Document D
The Secret Oath of American Protective Association

I do most solemnly promise and swear that I will always, to the utmost of my ability, labor, plead, and wage a continuous warfare against ignorance and fanaticism; that I will use my utmost power to strike the shackles and chains of blind obedience to the Roman Catholic Church from the hampered and bound consciences of a priest-ridden and church-oppressed people; that I will never allow anyone, a member of the Roman Catholic Church, to become a member of this order, I knowing him to be such; that I will use my influence to promote the interest of all Protestants everywhere in the world that I may be; that I will not employ a Roman Catholic in any capacity, if I can procure the services of a Protestant.

I furthermore promise and swear that I will not aid in building or maintaining, by my resources, any Roman Catholic church or institution of their sect or creed whatsoever, but will do all in my power to retard and break down the power of the Pope, in this country or any other; that I will not enter into any controversy with a Roman Catholic upon the subject of this order, nor will I enter into any agreement with a Roman Catholic to strike or create a disturbance whereby the Catholic employees may undermine and substitute their Protestant co-workers; that in all grievances I will seek only Protestants, and counsel with them to the exclusion of all Roman Catholics, and will not make known to them anything of any nature matured at such conferences.

I furthermore promise and swear that I will not countenance the nomination, in any caucus or convention, of a Roman Catholic for any office in the gift of the American people, and that I will not vote for, or counsel others to vote for, any Roman Catholic, but will vote only for a Protestant, so far as may lie in my power (should there be two Roman Catholics in opposite tickets, I will erase the name on the ticket I vote); that I will at all times endeavor to place the political positions of this government in the hands of Protestants, to the entire exclusion of the Roman Catholic Church, of the members thereof, and the mandate of the Pope.

To all of which I do most solemnly promise and swear, so help me God.

Amen.

Document Set Fifteen
City Life

The late nineteenth century saw American cities transformed into large urban environments. Urbanization meant the creation of environments stretched beyond the traditional borders of a city. Revolutions in modes of transportation allowed the development of new residential areas known as the suburbs. Unlike the pre Civil War era, neighborhoods were segregated and the rich and poor no longer lived side by side. The population growth of these urban centers presented many problems for its inhabitants. The poor were locked into sub-standard housing with high rates of crime and disease.

There were dramatic changes in the lifestyle of urban dwellers of the late nineteenth century. Technology helped create an infrastructure which made this urban environment very different from the cities of the pre Civil War period. This set of documents looks at the positive and negative aspects of urban living in the late nineteenth century.

Document A, "The Life of the Urban Poor," is a selection from a book written in 1872, *The Dangerous Classes Of New York and Twenty Years Among Them*. The author, Charles Loring Brace, was the founder of the Children's Aide Society. He hoped the publication would create public awareness about the problems of the urban slums. After reading the selection, students can assess why these problems developed. Did urbanization occur too quickly for the political system of these cities? While Brace believed the book would lead to public outcry for change, how else might the piece have been interpreted by the middle and upper classes?

Twenty years later George Waring a New York City Commissioner wrote about the sanitary conditions in New York (Document B). Unlike Brace, Waring's piece is more positive as he is able to show the progress that the City of New York made in dealing with the problems of sanitation. His before and after picture of life in New York depicts to students the positive effects for the citizens of a healthy environment. They should pay careful attention to the reasons why it had been so difficult to clean up the New York streets.

Life was very different in the new urban centers of industrial America. The next two sets of documents provide examples of new forms of entertainment which developed during this period. Large populations, more leisure time, new modes of transportation were all factors in the creation of entertainment centers like Coney Island in New York. A proto type for other cities, Coney Island provided an array of ways for people to enjoy themselves in an inexpensive fashion. "Bathing At Coney Island" (Document C) is a selection from *Coney Island Frolics: How New York's Gay Girls and Jolly Boys Enjoy Themselves By The Sea* written in 1883. The monograph could help explain appropriate behavior at the shore. Why was this type of monograph popular during this era? Was there any relationship to the huge influx of immigrants into New York? Careful analysis of the selection could help students understand the morals and values of this period.

The traveling medicine show provided American town with entertainment and home remedies. In Document D., "Doc Porter's Kickapoo Indian Medicine Show," William Naylor describes his experience as part of this traveling group. Why were these shows so popular at the turn of the century? Did they represent rural or urban America? Would they have been as popular in major cities as they were in small towns?

Questions for Document Set Fifteen

1. After reading the piece by Brace, what rationale would Social Darwinists give for these conditions?

2. Why did the conditions described in the Brace piece occur? Was urbanization the cause of these problems?

3. Who does Waring blame for the sanitary conditions in New York prior to 1895?

4. How are women depicted in the "Bathing At Coney Island" document?

5. Why were traveling medicine shows important to Americans at the turn of the century?

Document A
The Life of the Urban Poor

...The intensity of the American temperament is felt in every fibre of these children of poverty and vice. Their crimes have the unrestrained and sanguinary character of a race accustomed to overcome all obstacles. They rifle a bank, where English thieves pick a pocket; they murder, where European proletaires cudgel or fight with fists; in a riot, they begin what seems about to be the sacking of a city, where English rioters would merely batter policemen, or smash lamps. The "dangerous classes" of New York are mainly American-born, but the children of Irish and German immigrants.....

There are thousands on thousands in New York who have no assignable home, and "flirt" from attic to attic, and cellar to cellar; there are other thousands more or less connected with criminal enterprises; and still other tens of thousands, poor, hard-pressed, and depending for daily bread on the day's earnings, swarming in tenement-houses, who behold the gilded rewards of toil all about them, but are never permitted to touch them.

All these great masses of destitute, miserable, and criminal persons believe that for ages the rich have had all the good things of life, while to them have been left the evil things. Capital to them is the tyrant.

Let but Law lift its hand from them for a season, or let the civilizing influences of American life fail to reach them, and, if the opportunity offered, we should see an explosion from this class which might leave this city in ashes and blood.

Seventeen year ago, my attention had been called to the extraordinarily degraded condition of the children in a district lying on the west side of the city, between Seventeenth and Nineteenth Streets, and the Seventh and Tenth Avenues. A certain block, called "Misery Row," in Tenth Avenue, was the main seed-bed of crime and poverty in the quarter, and was also invariably a "fever-nest." Here the poor obtained wretched rooms at a comparatively low rent; these they sub-let, and thus, in little, crowded, close tenements, were herded men, women and children of all ages. The parents were invariably given to hard drinking, and the children were sent out to beg or to steal. Besides them, other children, who were orphans, or who had run away from drunkards' homes, or had been working on the canal-boats that discharged on the docks near by, drifted into the quarter, as if attracted by the atmosphere of crime and laziness that prevailed in the neighborhood. These slept around the breweries of the ward, or on the hay-barges, or in the old sheds of Eighteenth and Nineteenth Streets. They were mere children, and kept life together by all sorts of street-jobs—helping the brewery laborers, blackening boots, sweeping sidewalks, "smashing baggages" (as they called it), and the like. Herding together, they soon began too form an unconscious society for vagrancy and idleness. Finding that work brought but poor pay, they tried shorter roads to getting money by petty [sic] thefts, in which they were very adroit. Even if they earned a considerable sum by a lucky day's job, they quickly spent it in gambling, or for some folly.

The police soon knew them as "street-rats;" but, like the rats, they were too quick and cunning to be often caught in their petty plunderings, so they gnawed away at the foundations of society undisturbed.

Document B
Sanitary Conditions in New York

Before 1895 the streets were almost universally in a filthy state. In wet weather they were covered with slime, and in dry weather the air was filled with dust. Artificial sprinkling in summer converted the dust into mud, and the drying winds changed the mud to powder. Rubbish of all kinds, garbage, and ashes lay neglected in the streets, and in the hot weather the city stank with the emanations of putrefying organic matter. It was not always possible to see the pavement, because of the dirt that covered it. One expert, a former contractor of street-cleaning, told me that West Broadway could not be cleaned, because it was so coated with grease from wagon-axles; it was really coated with slimy mud. The sewer inlets were clogged with refuse. Dirty paper was prevalent everywhere, and black rottenness was seen and smelled on every hand.

The practice of standing unharnessed trucks and wagons in the public streets was well-nigh universal in all except the main thoroughfares and the better residence districts. The Board of Health made an enumeration of vehicles so standing on Sunday, counting twenty-five thousand on a portion of one side of the city; they reached the conclusion that there were in all more than sixty thousand. These trucks not only restricted traffic and made complete street-cleaning practically impossible, but they were harbors of vice and crime. Thieves and highwaymen made them their dens, toughs caroused in them, both sexes resorted to them, and they were used for the vilest purposes, until they became, both figuratively and literally, a stench in the nostrils of the people. In the crowded districts they were a veritable nocturnal hell. Against all this the poor people were powerless to get relief. The highest city officials, after feeble attempts at removal, declared that New York was so peculiarly constructed (having no alleys through which the rear of the lots could be reached) that its commerce could not be carried on unless this privilege were given to its truckmen; in short, the removal of the trucks was "an impossibility...."

The condition of the streets, of the force, and of the stock was the fault of no man and of no set of men. It was the fault of the system. The department was throttled by partizan control—so throttled it could neither do good work, command its own respect and that of the pubic, nor maintain its material in good order. It was run as an adjunct of a political organization. In that capacity it was a marked success. It paid fat tribute; it fed thousands of voters, and it gave power and influence to hundreds of political leaders. It had this appointed function, and it performed it well....

New York is now thoroughly clean in every part, the empty vehicles are gone...."Clean streets" means much more than the casual observer is apt to think It has justly been said that "cleanliness is catching," and clean streets are leading to clean hallways and stair cases and cleaner living-rooms....

Few realize the many minor ways in which the work of the department has benefited the people at large. For example, there is far less injury from dust to clothing, to furniture, and to goods in shops; mud is not tracked from the streets on to the sidewalks, and thence into the houses; boots require far less cleaning; the wearing of overshoes has been largely abandoned; wet feet and bedraggled skirts are mainly things of the past; and children now make free use of a playground of streets which were formerly impossible to them. "Scratches," a skin disease of horses due to mud and slush, used to entail very serious cost on truckmen and liverymen. It is now almost unknown. Horses used to "pick up a nail" with alarming frequency, and this caused great loss of service, and, like scratches made the bill of the veterinary surgeon a serious matter. There are practically no nails now to be found in the streets.

The great, the almost inestimable, beneficial effect of the work of the department is showing the large reduction of the death-rate and in the less keenly realized but still more important reduction in the sick-rate. As compared with the average death-rate of 26.78 of 1882-94, that of 1895 was 23.10, that of 1896 was 21.52, and that of the first half of 1897 was 19.63. If this latter figure is maintained throughout the year, there will have been fifteen thousand fewer deaths than there would have been had the average rate of the thirteen previous years prevailed.

The report of the Board of Health for 1896, basing its calculations on diarrheal diseases July, August, and September, in the filthiest wards, in the most crowded wards, and in the remainder of the city, shows a very marked reduction in all, and the largest reduction in the first two classes.

Document C
Bathing at Coney Island

There are various ways of bathing at Coney Island. You can go in at the West End, where they give you a tumbledown closet like a sentry box stuck up in the sand, or at the great hotels where more or less approach to genuine comfort is afforded. The pier, too, is fitted up with extensive bathing houses, and altogether no one who wants a dip in the briny and has a quarter to pay for it need to go without it.

If a man is troubled with illusions concerning the female form divine and wishes to be rid of those illusions he should go to Coney Island and closely watch the thousands of women who bathe there every Sunday.

A woman, or at least most women, in bathing undergoes a transformation that is really wonderful. They waltz into the bathingrooms clad in all the paraphernalia that most gladdens the feminine heart. The hair is gracefully dressed, and appears most abundant; the face is decorated with all that elaborate detail which defies description by one uninitiated in the mysteries of the boudoir; the form is moulded by the milliner to distracting elegance of proportion, and the feet appear aristocratically slender and are arched in French boots.

Thus they appear as they sail past the gaping crowds of men, who make Coney Island a loafing place on Sundays. They seek out their individual dressing-rooms and disappear. Somewhere inside of an hour, they make their appearance ready for the briny surf. If it were not for the men who accompany them it would be impossible to recognize them as the same persons who but a little while ago entered those diminutive rooms....

The broad amphitheatre at Manhattan Beach built at the water's edge is often filled with spectators. Many pay admission fees to witness the feats of swimmers, the clumsiness of beginners and the ludicrous mishaps of the never-absent stout persons. Under the bathinghouse is a sixty horse-power engine. It rinses and washes the suits for the bathers, and its steady puffing is an odd accompaniment to the merry shouts of the bathers and the noise of the shifting crowd ashore....

A person who intends to bathe at Manhattan or Brighton Beach first buys a ticket and deposits it in a box such as is placed in every elevated railroad station. If he carries valuables he may have them deposited without extra charge in a safe that weighs seven tons and has one thousand compartments. He encloses them in an envelope and seals it. Then he writes his name partly on the flap of the envelope and partly on the envelope itself. For this envelope he receives a metal check attached to an elastic string, in order that he may wear it about his neck while bathing. This check has been taken from one of the compartments of the safe which bears the same number as the check. Into the same compartment the sealed envelope is put. When the bather returns from the surf he must return the check and must write his name on a piece of paper. This signature is compared with the one on the envelope. Should the bather report that his check has been lost or stolen his signature is deemed a sufficient warrant for the return of the valuables. The safe has double doors in front and behind. Each drawer may be drawn out from either side. When the throng presses six men may be employed at this safe.

Document D
The Medicine Show

I was born in New York City on the West Side, but when I was just a baby my people moved up to the Bronx. Our chief diversion on Sundays was to go to Coney Island and ride our bicycles out there. I suppose I always had a flair for the kind of entertainment Coney Island offered. There was a kind of fascination to me in the excitement and glamour of the carnival spirit.

Eventually, when I was about nineteen years old, I joined DOC PORTER'S KICKAPOO INDIAN MEDICINE SHOW.....

I stayed with Doc Portrer for six years, singing "Poor Mourner, You Shall Be Free," "Kansas," and some of the popular songs like "Two Little Girls in Blue," "Down Went M'Ginty," and "After the Ball." All my work was black-face, and I imagined I was just as good as most vaudeville performers on stages in theaters. We traveled in covered hacks and spring wagons and all our shows were given out of doors. Our lights were gasoline flares on each side of the stage, which was a platform at the back end of the wagon. We traveled all over the small circuits of upper New York, part of Pennsylvania, New Jersey, and as far south as Virginia. In the days of the medicine show there were not so many laws regulating the practice of medicine or the sale of drugs and not so many licenses and restrictions as now. This was especially true in the backwoods towns we'd usually shown in—often towns without railroads and where other shows didn't come.

So Doc Porter didn't have to do anything but drive into a town, pick out a vacant spot somewhere, and set up our pitch there. Everybody would know as soon as we got into a town, but Doc usually hunted up the newspaper office if there was a paper and gave the editor an ad telling where our show was located. That got him on the good side of the editor, and the editor in those backwoods places was an important person. He would call on the marshall, and if there was a mayor he would visit him too....

Once we hit a place back in the hill country of Virginia called Rocky Comfort. It wasn't really a town. There was a water-power grist mill, a store, a blacksmith shop, and about a quarter of a mile up the little valley there was a meeting house, where traveling preachers would sometimes hold revivals, which were called camp meetings.

Doc Porter stopped there to have the horses shod, and it happened there was a camp meeting going on. It looked like a pretty busy place. The natives from miles around had come, brought their families, their hound dogs, and their rifles and were camped out in the grove around the meeting house. Doc got the idea that our Medicine Show would add to the general entertainment and we could give shows between religious services. It worked. Doc was diplomatic and didn't try to compete with the preaching but sort of helped it out and never gave a show while preaching was going on. Instead we'd all attend the services. That put us in solid with the brethren and we sold a lot of medicine.

Doc Porter's medicines were all made up by himself, and he was jealous of the "ancient Kickapoo formulas" he used. They were all made "from roots and barks and the tender succulent foliage of healing, life-giving herbs the Great Manitou of Nature planted in the forests, on the hills, and in the valleys to give his children, the noble tribe of Kickapoos, those priceless secrets of Life and health and Happiness; they were handed down from father to son and from generation to generation—cherished and guarded with the very lives of their possessors? Then when my great-great grandfather saved the life of the Chief Medicine Man of the Kickapoo Tribe, the 'Bounding Cougar,' that great Chief showed his gratitude by giving my noble pioneer ancestor their marvelous formulas and he bade him go forth and give his White Brethren the blessing the Great Manitou had bestowed upon his Red Children."

Doc Porter sure had a great string of palaver, and though I heard it a thousand times I never got tired of listening to his lecture.

One of the tricks Doc Porter used to stimulate sales of his Kickapoo Indian remedies was the psychology of suggestion. Doc had it down fine. He would always wind up his lecture with a detailed description of the symptoms of all the diseases the Kickapoo Indian medicines were supposed to cure. The way he described those diseases—how anybody would feel when they were getting them, or had them or were about to have them—was enough to make anybody shiver. By the time Doc got through describing symptoms, practically everybody in the neighborhood would be imagining they felt at least some of them. Why, I used to sit and listen to Doc's horror stories of diseases till I'd get to feeling the symptoms myself! Doc was a foxy old bird and I guess he wasn't far off base when he'd say, "Most diseases people get are just imagination, anyhow!"...

Doc Porter was versatile alright, and nothing ever seemed to stump him. He used to say: "It ain't what anybody knows for certain, but what they think they know for certain that counts, and if people buy Kickapoo Indian Medicine and think it'll cure them, it's darn near sure to cure them. And so they haven't been cheated!"

Which shows that Doc was sincere in believing that the stuff he mixed up out of wild cherry bark, senna leaves, slippery elm bark, sassafras roots, and other "Indian Herbs"—all of which he fortified with about sixty percent of good raw whisky—were genuinely beneficial medicines and that he was a human benefactor. One thing I'm sure of is the tour old Medicine Show gave a lot of people who otherwise didn't have very much entertainment a chance to see and hear something different and be amused.

That's the way a carnival man is. He don't give them anything, yet he gives them something—entertainment, experience, or amusement for the chicken feed he takes away from them at his rack or wheel or ringboard. And if he has a run of "mud-luck," he always finds a way to get out somehow, raise a stake, or climb back into the game. You don't see any genuine old-time carnival birds working the street for a dime, or picking up crumbs from a kitchen back door. They're independent; and even if they're down to the last two bits, you'd never know it by looking at them, or hear it from their own lips. They might do a lot of cussing in private, but never a hard-luck story to outsiders. They've always got some kind of idea tucked back in their head that they can pull out and turn into ham-and-egg money somehow. Even if the show goes flat, they'll raise tickets to the next burg someway. And they'll raise it on the square, according to the ethics of the profession: "Give the suckers nothing for their money—but when you give them nothing, you give them something!"

Document Sixteen
The American Flag Around the Globe

For the first three decades after the Civil War American energy was devoted to national economic and social changes. Little attention was paid to foreign policy and there was not much interest in developments occurring beyond the American shores. This attitude began to change as the nation realized the benefits of an active expansionist world policy. This set of documents provides an overview of the arguments which developed over this change in policy.

Several factors were catalysts for this shift in policy. Business groups were concerned that rapid industrialization would result in a saturation of domestic markets. They sought a foreign policy which would support American business interests abroad. Leading political figures of the time expressed concern that if the United States did not revise its policies, leading European powers would dominate around the globe.

For some Americans, it was the nation's responsibility and duty to disseminate our way of life to non-Western cultures. This first document, "Our Country," was written by one of the leading proponents of this theory. Joshia Strong was a Christian minister who believed that because the Anglo-Saxon race was superior, it was the duty of the American government to develop an aggressive foreign policy. Students should note his rationale for an expansionist policy. Why did he believe it was, "the white man's burden," to command an influence over the world's future? How closely tied were his arguments to the concepts of Social Darwinism?

The Spanish American war was a "splendid little war" for the United States. It allowed the United States to emerge as a major world power. It was a popular war for most Americans who believed that they were fighting to liberate Cube from tyrannical Spanish rule. The passage of the Tellar Amendment assured Cuba its independence. American victory, however, brought other responsibilities that were not as easily resolved. Decisions had to be made concerning the other Spanish territories, Puerto Rico, Guam and the Philippines. The next three sets of documents present both sides of this controversy and its final resolution.

In Document B, "The March of the Flag," Albert Beveridge provides one of the strongest arguments for keeping the Philippines. As the leading spokesman for a strong expansionist foreign policy, Beveridge cites how the superiority of American institutions must, "...broaden their blessed reign..." Were his argument a logical extension of Manifest Destiny? What comparisons can be made with the arguments of Strong? What similarities can be found in both pieces? What assumptions did both authors make about the fate of non-Western groups if they were not governed by the United States? Were their arguments racist?

William Graham Sumner in "On Empire and the Philippines," (Document C) presents the other side of this argument. Using the same set of theories, this group believed that acquiring colonies was anti-American and that it could do great harm to society. Unlike the expansionists, Sumner did not believe the Filipinos wanted our way of life. He warns that, "...we shall inherit from the Spaniards...the task of suppressing rebellions." As a leading advocate for Social Darwinism, is there evidence of his beliefs in this argument? Why was Sumner concerned about having the United States associated with European imperialism?

The final decision about the Philippines rested with President McKinley. The last document, "McKinley Decides On The Philippines," explains his reasons for keeping the Philippines. As McKinley notes, it was one of the most difficult decisions he had to make. He understood both sides of the argument and knew this decision would determine the path of American foreign policy in the twentieth century. Students should pay close attention to his rational for his decision. They should consider what were the strongest influences on him. Was he more concerned with Christian duty or the potential for American greatness?

Questions for Document Set Sixteen

1. According to Joshia Strong why must the United States become a world power?

2. Did Strong, Beveridge and Sumner rely upon the doctrine of Social Darwinism to support their arguments?

3. Who had the most convincing argument and why?

4. What other alternatives were there for the United States to become a world power?

5. Did William McKinley make the right decision? Explain.

Document A
Our Country

Every race which has deeply impressed itself on the human family has been the representative of some great idea—one or more—which had given direction to the nation's life and form to its civilization. Among the Egyptians this seminal idea was life, among the Persians it was light, among the Hebrews it was purity, among the Greeks it was beauty, among the Romans it was law. The Anglo-Saxon is the representative of two great ideas, which are closely related. One of them is that of civil liberty. Nearly all of the civil liberty in the world is enjoyed by Anglo-Saxons: the English, the British colonists, and the people of the United States....The noblest races have always been lovers of liberty. That love ran strong in early German blood, and has profoundly influenced the institutions of all the branches of the great German family; but it was left for the Anglo-Saxon branch fully to recognize the right of the individual to himself, and formally to declare it the foundation stone of government.

The other great idea of which the Anglo-Saxon is the exponent is that of a pure spiritual Christianity. It was no accident that the great reformation of the sixteenth century originated among a Teutonic, rather than a Latin people. It was the fire of liberty burning in the Saxon heart that flamed up against the absolutism of the Pope....

It is not necessary to argue to those for whom I write that the two great needs of mankind, that all men may be lifted up into the light of the highest Christian civilization, are, first, a pure, spiritual Christianity, and, second, civil liberty. Without controversy, these are the forces which, in the past, have contributed most to the elevation of the human race, and they must continue to be, in the future, the most efficient ministers to its progress. It follows, then, that the Anglo-Saxon, as the great representative of these two ideas, the depositary [sic] of these two greatest blessings, sustains peculiar relations to the world's future, is divinely commissioned to be, in a peculiar sense, his brother's keeper....

There can be no reasonable doubt that North America is to be the great home of the Anglo-Saxon, the principal seat of his power, the center of his life and influence. Not only does it constitute seven-elevenths of his possessions, but this empire is unsevered, while the remaining four-elevenths are fragmentary and scattered over the earth. Australia will have a great population; but its disadvantages, as compared with North America, are too manifest to need mention. Our continent has room and resources and climate, it lies in the pathway of the nations, it belongs to the zone of power, and already, among Anglo-Saxons, do we lead in population and wealth..

Mr. Darwin is not only disposed to see, in the superior vigor of our people, an illustration of his favorite theory of natural selection, but even intimates that the world's history thus far has been simply preparatory for our future, and tributary to it. He says: "There is apparently much truth in the belief that the wonderful progress of the United States, as well as the character of the people, are the results of natural selection; for the more energetic, restless, and courageous men from all parts of Europe have emigrated during the last ten or twelve generations to that great country, and have there succeeded best...."

...The time is coming when the pressure of population on the means of subsistence will be felt there as it is now felt in Europe and Asia. Then will the world enter upon a new stage of its history—the final competition of races, for which the Anglo-Saxon is being schooled. Long before the thousands millions are here, the mighty centrifugal tendency, inherent in this stock and strengthened in the United States, will assert itself. Then this race of unequaled energy, with all the majesty of numbers and the might of wealth behind it—the representative, let us hope, of the largest liberty, the purest Christianity, the highest civilization—having developed peculiarly aggressive traits calculated to impress its institutions upon mankind, will spread itself over the earth. If I read not amiss, this powerful race will move down upon Mexico, down upon Central and South America, out upon the islands of the sea, over upon Africa and beyond. And can anyone doubt that the result of this competition of races will be the "survival of the fittest"?.....

In my own mind, there is no doubt that the Anglo-Saxon is to exercise the commanding influence in the world's future; but the exact nature of that influence is, as yet, undetermined. How far his civilization will be materialistic and atheistic, and how long it will take thoroughly to Christianize and sweeten it, how rapidly he will hasten the coming of the kingdom wherein dwelleth righteousness, or how many ages he may retard it, is still uncertain; but it is now being swiftly determined....

Notwithstanding the great perils which threaten it, I cannot think our civilization will perish; but I believe it is fully in the hand of the Christians of the United States, during the next fifteen or twenty years, to hasten or retard the coming of Christ's kingdom in the world by hundreds, and perhaps thousands, of years. We of this generation and nation occupy the Gibraltar of the ages which command the world's future.

Document B
The March of the Flag

It is a noble land that God has given us; a land that can feed and clothe the world; a land whose coastlines would inclose half the countries of Europe; a land set like a sentinel between the two imperial oceans of the globe, a greater England with a nobler destiny.

It is a mighty people that He has planted on this soil; a people sprung from the most masterful blood of history; a people perpetually revitalized by the virile, man-producing working folk of all the earth; a people imperial by virtue of their power, by right of their institutions, by authority of their Heaven-directed purposes—the propagandists and not the misers of liberty.

It is a glorious history our God has bestowed upon His chosen people; a history heroic with faith in our mission and our future; a history of statesmen who flung the boundaries of the Republic out into unexplored lands and savage wilderness; a history of soldiers who carried the flag across blazing deserts and through the ranks of hostile mountains, even to the gates of sunset; a history of a multiplying people who overran a continent in half a century; a history of prophets who saw the consequences of evils inherited from the past and of martyrs who died to save us from them; a history divinely logical, in the process of whose tremendous seasoning we find ourselves to-day.

Therefore, in this campaign, the question is larger than a party question. It is an American question. It is a world question. Shall the American people continue their march toward the commercial supremacy of the world? Shall free institutions broaden their blessed reign as the children of liberty wax in strength, until the empire of our principles is established over the hearts of all mankind?

Have we no mission to perform, no duty to discharge to our fellowman? Has God endowed us with gifts beyond our deserts and marked us as the people of His peculiar favor, merely to rot in our own selfishness, as men and nations must, who take cowardice for their companion and self for their deity—as China has, as India has, as Egypt has?

Shall we be as the man who had one talent and hid it, or as he who had ten talents and use them until they grew to riches? And shall we reap the reward that waits on our discharge of our high duty; shall we occupy new markets for what our farmers raise, our factories make, our merchants sell—aye, and, please God, new markets for what our ships shall carry?

Hawaii is ours, Porto Rico is to be ours; at the prayer of her people Cuba finally will be ours; in the islands of the East, even to the gates of Asia, coaling stations are to be ours at the very least; the flag of a liberal government is to float over the Philippines, and may it be the banner that Taylor unfurled in Texas and Fremont carried to the coast.

The Opposition tells us that we ought not to govern a people without their consent. I answer, The rule of liberty that all just government derives its authority from the consent of the governed, applies only to those who are capable of self-government. We govern the Indians without their consent, we govern our territories without their consent, we govern our children without their consent. How do they know that our government would be without their consent? Would not the people of the Philippines prefer the just, human, civilizing government of this Republic to the savage, bloody rule of pillage and extortion from which we have rescued them?

And, regardless of this formula of words made only for enlightened, self-governing people, do we owe no duty to the world? Shall we turn these peoples back to the reeking hands from which we have taken them? Shall we abandon them, with Germany, England, Japan, hungering for them? Shall we save them from those nations, to give them a self-rule of tragedy?...Then, like men and not like children, let us on to our tasks, our mission, and our destiny.

Wonderfully has God guided us. Yonder at Bunker Hill and Yorktown His providence was above us. At New Orleans and on ensanguined seas His hand sustained us. Abraham Lincoln was His minister and His was the altar of freedom the Nation's soldiers set up on a hundred battle-fields. His power directed Dewey in the East and delivered the Spanish fleet into our hands, as He delivered the elder Armada into the hands of our English sires two centuries ago. The American people can not use a dishonest medium of exchange; it is ours to set the world its example of right and honor. We can not fly from our world duties; it is ours to execute the purpose of a fate that has driven us to be greater than our small intentions. we can not retreat from any soil where Providence has unfurled our banner; it is ours to save that soil for liberty and civilization.

Document C
On Empire and the Philippines

There is not a civilized nation that does not talk about its civilizing mission just as grandly as we do. The English, who really have more to boast of it in this respect than anybody else, talk least about it, but the Phariseeism with which they correct and instruct other people has made them hated all over the globe. The French believe themselves the guardians of the highest and purest culture, and that the eyes of all mankind are fixed on Paris, whence they expect oracles of thought and taste. The Germans regard themselves as charged with a mission, especially to us Americans, to save us from egoism and materialism. The Russians, in their books and newspapers, talk about the civilizing mission of Russian in language that might be translated from some of the finest paragraphs of our imperialistic newspapers.

The first principle of Mohammedanism is that we Christians are dogs and infidels, fit only to be enslaved or butchered by Moslems. It is a corollary that wherever Mohammedanism extends it carries, in the belief of its votaries, the highest blessings, and that the whole human race would be enormously elevated if Mohammedanism should supplant Christianity everywhere.

To come, last, to Spain, the Spaniards have, for centuries, considered themselves the most zealous and self-sacrificing Christians, especially charged by the Almighty, on this account, to spread the true religion and civilization over the globe. They think themselves free and noble, leaders in refinement and the sentiments of personal honor, and they despise us as sordid money-grabbers and heretics. I could bring you passages from peninsular authors of the first rank about the grand role of Spain and Portugal in spreading freedom and truth.

Now each nation laughs at all the others when it observes these manifestations of national vanity. You may rely upon it that they are all ridiculous by virtue of these pretensions, including ourselves. The point is that each of them repudiates the standards of the others, and the outlying nations, which are to be civilized, hate all the standards of civilized men.

We assume that what we like and practice, and what we think better, must come as a welcome blessing to Spanish-Americans an Filipinos. This is grossly and obviously untrue. They hate our ways. They are hostile to our ideas. Our religion, language, institutions, and manners offend them. They like their own ways, and if we appear amongst them as rulers, there will be social discord in all the great departments of social interest. The most important thing which we shall inherit from the Spaniards will be the task of suppressing rebellions.

If the United States takes out of the hands of Spain her mission, on the ground that Spain is not executing it well, and if this nation in its turn attempts to be schoolmistress to others, it will shrivel up into the same vanity and self-conceit of which Spain now presents an example. To read our current literature one would think that we were already well on the way to it.

Now, the great reason why all these enterprises which begin by saying to somebody else, "We know what is good for you better than you know yourself and we are going to make you do it," are false and wrong is that they violate liberty; or, to turn the same statement into other words, the reason why liberty, of which we Americans talk so much, is a good thing is that it means leaving people to live out their own lives in their own way, while we do the same.

If we believe in liberty, as an American principle, why do we not stand by it? Why are we going to throw it away to enter upon a Spanish policy of dominion and regulation?

Document D
McKinley Decides on Philippines

When next I realized that the Philippines had dropped into our laps, I confess I did not know what to do with them. I sought counsel from all sides—Democrats as well as Republicans—but got little help. I thought first we would take only Manila; then Luzon; then other islands, perhaps, also.

I walked the floor of the White House night after night until midnight; and I am not ashamed to tell you, gentlemen, that I went down on my knees and prayed Almighty God for light and guidance more than one night. And one night late it came to me this way—I don't know how it was, but it came:

(1) That we could not give them back to pain—that would be cowardly and dishonorable;

(2) That we could not turn them over to France or Germany, our commercial rivals in the Orient—that would be bad business and discreditable;

(3) That we could not leave them to themselves—they were unfit for self-government, and they would soon have anarchy and misrule worse then Spain's was; and

(4) That there was nothing left for us to do but to take them all, and to educate the Filipinos, and uplift and civilize and Christianize them and by God's grace do the very best we could by them, as our fellow men for whom Christ also died

And then I went to bed and went to sleep, and slept soundly, and the next morning I sent for the chief engineer of the War Department (our map-maker), and I told him to put the Philippines on the map of the United States (pointing to a large map on the wall of his office), and there they are and there they will stay while I am President!

Document Set Seventeen
The End and the Beginning of the American Political System

By the 1890s it was evident that change was occurring too quickly for the political system. In spite of increased voter interest in the political process, no level of government was able to address the important issues of the day. Officials were more concerned with staying in office than representing their constituents. The executive branch was relegated to a caretaker position, Congress was powerful, but undistinguished, and few effective pieces of legislation were passed.

No one better symbolized the Old Political Order than George Washington Plunkitt, a Tammy Hall ward boss. The urban political machines used political patronage to ensure its tenure in control of the cities. In Document A, Plunkitt describes how honest graft worked to enrich the members of these machines. Students should consider Plunkitt's argument. Can you distinguish between honest and dishonest graft? Who would suffer in this system? If these politicians were concerned with growing rich, how committed were they to the voters' needs? Given this situation, was it logical that urban politics was the first level of government to be reformed?

Farmers were one of the first groups to express their discontent with the failures of the political process. In Document B, Life on the Prairie, students have an opportunity to understand how difficult life was for farming families in the Midwest. The selection is taken from the novel *Giants In The Earth* by O. E. Rolvaag. Seen from the perspective of the wife, Beret, the isolation and desperation was particularly hard on the women of the family. Why were families willing to bear the hardships of this type of life in a, "...nameless, abandoned region?" How much more difficult were these hardships made by the environment?

By 1890 farm discontent had developed into political activism and a third party movement known as the Populist Party. Its main goal was to take back government from special interests and restore it to the people. Document C, "The Omaha Platform of the Populist Party," was written for the 1892 Presidential election. What problems does the party describe in the platform? Students should consider whether the concerns of the Populists were also concerns for the rest of the nation? Were the Populists reactionary or progressive in their thinking. How much of their platform would eventually be implemented? Why were the Populists feared by the two major political parties?

Ironically while the Populists were demanding greater participation in the political process, African Americans were being pushed out of the system. By the end of the century they had lost many of the political rights which had been granted at the end of the Civil War. The Jim Crow laws, passed throughout the South, legalized the separation of the races. In Document D students can read the landmark Supreme Court case that sanctified these laws. Plessy v Ferguson guaranteed that African Americans would become second class citizens for the next fifty years. Students should note how the court interpreted the 14th and 15th Amendments. According to the decision, on what terms can social equality between the races occur?

Given the tone of the period African Americans found themselves in a no man's land. With no support from the legal or political system there were few alternatives for them. Booker T. Washington, the most influential African American leader of the period, believed that the only path for the community was vocational training. Document E, "The Atlanta Compromise," delineates Washington's thesis. The speech was given to a predominantly white audience. Why was it received with overwhelming approval? Is he reaching out to both communities? Why were some members of the African American community angered by his speech? Was Washington realistic in his appraisal of the situation for African Americans?

Questions for Document Set Seventeen

1. According to George Washington Plunkitt who benefits from Tammy Hall being in power?

2. Given the hardships of life on the prairie, why did families continue to settle in the region?

3. Based on the Rolvaag selection, describe life on the prairie.

4. Analyze the following statement from the Populist platform, "wealth belongs to him who creates it."

5. Were the Populists idealistic in their party platform?

6. After analyzing the Plessy v Ferguson decision, did the Supreme Court believe that one race was inferior to the other?

7. Given the Court decision, could equality between the races occur?

8. Is Booker T. Washington placating white society in his speech?

Document A
George Washington Plunkitt

"Everybody is talkin' these days about Tammany men growin' rich on graft, but nobody thinks of drawin' the distinction between honest graft and dishonest graft. There's all the difference in the world between the two. Yes, many of our men have grown rich in politics. I have myself. I've made a big fortune out of the game, and I'm gettin' richer every day, but I've not gone in for dishonest graft—blackmailin' gamblers, saloon-keepers, disorderly people, etc.—and neither has any of the men who have made big fortunes in politics.

"There's an honest graft, and I'm an example of how it works. I might sum up the whole thing by sayin': 'I seen my opportunities and I took 'em.'

"Just let me explain my examples. My party's in power in the city, and it's goin' to undertake a lot of public improvements. Well, I'm tipped off, say, that they're going to layout a new park at a certain place.

"I see my opportunity and I take it. I go to that place and I buy up all the land I can in the neighborhood. Then the board of this or that makes its plan public, and there is a rush to get my land, which nobody cared particular for before.

"Ain't it perfectly honest to charge a good price and make a profit on my investment and foresight? Of course it is. Well, that's honest graft....

"...It's just like lookin' ahead in Wall Street or in the coffee or cotton market.

"...Now, let me tell you that most politicians who are accused of robbin the city get rich the same way.

"They didn't steal a dollar from the city treasury. They just seen their opportunities and took them. That is why, when a reform administration comes in and spends a half million dollars in tryin' to find the public robberies they talk about in the campaign, they don't find them.

"The books are always all right. The money in the city treasury is all right. Everything is all right All they can show is that the Tammany heads of departments looked after their friends, within the law, and gave them what opportunities they could to make honest graft....

"I've been readin' a book by Lincoln Steffens on *The Shame of the Cities*. Steffens means well but, like all reformers, he don't know how to make distinctions. He can't see no difference between honest graft and dishonest graft and, consequent, he gets things all mixed up. There's the biggest kind of a difference between political looters and politicians who make a fortune out of politics by keepin' their eyes wide open. The looter goes in for himself alone without considerin' his organization or his city. The politician looks after his own interests, the organization's interests, and the city's interests all at the same time....

Document B
Life on the Prairie

In a certain sense, she had to admit to herself, it was lovely up here. The broad expanse stretching away endlessly in every direction, seemed almost like the ocean—especially now, when darkness was falling. It reminded her strongly of the sea, and yet it was very different....This formless prairie had no heart that beat, no waves that sang, no soul that could be touched...or cared....

The infinitude surrounding her on every hand had might not have been so oppressive, might even have brought her a measure of peace, if it had not been for the deep silence, which lay heavier here than in a church. Indeed, what was there to break it? She had passed beyond the outposts of civilization; the nearest dwelling places of men were far away. Here no warbling of birds rose on the air, no buzzing of insects sounded; even the wind had died away; the waving blades of grass that trembled to the faintest breath now stood erect and quiet, as if listening, in the great hush of the evening....All along the way, coming out, she had noticed this strange thing; the stillness had grown deeper, the silence more depressing, the farther west they journeyed; it must have been over two weeks now since she had heard a bird sing! Had they travelled into some nameless, abandoned region? Could no living thing exist out here, in the empty, desolate, endless wastes of green and blue?...How could existence go on, she thought, desperately? If life is to thrive and endure, it must at least have something to hide behind!...

The Children were playing boisterously a little way off. What a terrible noise they made! But she had better let them keep on with their play, as long as they were happy....She sat perfectly quiet, thinking of the long, oh, so interminably long march that they would have to make, back to the place where human beings dwelt. It would be small hardship for her, of course, sitting in the wagon; but she pitied Per Hansa and the boys—and then the poor oxen!...He certainly would soon find out for himself that a home for men and women and children could never be established in this wilderness....And how could she bring new life into the world out here!...

Slowly her thoughts began to centre on her husband; they grew warm and tender as they dwelt on him. She trembled as they came....

But only for a brief while. As her eyes darted nervously here and there, flitting from object to object and trying to pierce the purple dimness that was steadily closing in, a sense of desolation so profound settled upon her that she seemed unable to think at all. It would not do to gaze any longer at the terror out there, where everything was turning to grim and awful darkness....She threw herself back in the grass and looked up into the heavens. But darkness and infinitude lay there, also—the sense of utter desolation still remained....Suddenly, for the first time, she realized the full extent of her loneliness, the dreadful nature of the fate that had overtaken her. Lying there on her back, and staring up into the quiet sky across which the shadows of night were imperceptibly creeping, she went over in her mind every step of their wanderings, every mile of the distance they had travelled since they had left home....

Winter was ever tightening its grip. The drifting snow flew wildly under a low sky, and stirred up the whole universe into a whirling mass; it swept the plain like the giant broom of a witch, churning up a flurry so thick that people could scarcely open their eyes.

As soon as the weather cleared icy gusts drove through every chink and cranny, leaving white frost behind; people's breaths hung frozen in the air the moment it was out of the mouth; if one touched iron, a piece of skin would be torn away.

At intervals a day of bright sunshine came. Then the whole vast plain flittered with the flashing brilliance of diamonds; the glare was so strong that it burnt the sight; the eyes saw blackness where there was nothing but shining white.....

But no sooner had they reached America than the west-fever had smitten the old settlements like a plague. Such a thing had never happened before in the history of mankind; people were intoxicated by bewildering visions; they spoke dazedly, as though under the force of a spell...."Go west!...Go west, folks!...The farther west, the better the land!" ...Men beheld in feverish dreams the endless plains, teeming with fruitfulness, glowing, out there where day sank into night—a Beulah Land of corn and wine!...She had never dreamed that the good Lord would let such folly loose among men. Were it only the young people who had been caught by the plague, she would not have wondered; but the old had been taken even worse...."Now we're bound west?" said the young...."Wait a minute—we're going along with you!" cried the old, and followed after....Human beings gathered together, in small companies and large—took whatever was movable along, and left the old homestead without as much as a sigh! Ever westward led the course, to where the sun glowed in matchless glory as it sank at night; people drifted about in a sort of delirium, like sea birds in mating time; then they flew toward the sunset, in small flocks, and large—always toward Sunset Land....Now she saw it clearly: here on the trackless plains, the thousand-year-old hunger of the poor after human happiness had been unloosed!

Document C
The Omaha Platform of the Populist Party

Preamble

The conditions which surround us best justify our cooperation; we meet in the midst of a nation brought to the verge of moral, political, and material ruin. Corruption dominates the ballot-box, the Legislatures, the Congress, and touches even the ermine of the bench. The people are demoralized; most of the States have been compelled to isolate the voters at the polling places to prevent universal intimidation and bribery. The newspapers are largely subsidized or muzzled, public opinion silenced, business prostrated, homes covered with mortgages, labor impoverished, and the land concentrating in the hands of capitalists. The urban workmen are denied the right to organize for self-protection, imported pauperized labor beats down their wages, a hireling standing army, unrecognized by our laws, is established to shoot them down, and they are rapidly degenerating into European conditions. The fruits of the toil of millions are boldly stolen to build up colossal fortunes for a few, unprecedented in the history of mankind and the possessors of these, in turn, despise the Republic and endanger liberty. From the same prolific womb of governmental injustice we breed the two great classes—tramps and millionaires....

Assembled on the anniversary of the birthday of the nation, and filled with the spirit of the grand general and chief who established our independence, we seek to restore the government of the Republic to the hands of the "plain people," with which class it originated. We assert our purposes to be identical with the purposes of the National Constitution; to form a more perfect union and establish justice, insure domestic tranquillity, provide for the common defence, promote the general welfare, and secure the blessings of liberty for ourselves and our posterity....

Platform

We declare, therefore—

First.—That the union of the labor forces of the United States this day consummated shall be permanent and perpetual; may its spirit enter into all hearts for the salvation of the Republic and the uplifting of mankind.

Second.—Wealth belongs to him who creates it, and every dollar taken from industry without an equivalent is robbery. "If any will not work, neither shall he eat." The interests of rural and civil labor are the same; their enemies are identical.

Third.—We believe that the time has come when the railroad corporations will either own the people or the people must own the railroads....

FINANCE.—We demand a national currency, safe, sound, and flexible issued by the general government only, a full legal tender for all debts, public and private....

1. We demand free and unlimited coinage of silver and gold at the present legal ration of 16 to 1.

2. We demand that the amount of circulating medium be speedily increased to not less than $50 per capita.

3. We demand a graduated income tax.

4. We believe that the money of the country should be kept as much as possible in the hands of the people, and hence we demand that all State and national revenues shall be limited to the necessary expenses of the government, economically and honestly administered.

5. We demand that postal savings banks be established by the government for the safe deposit of the earnings of the people and to facilitate exchange.

TRANSPORTATION.—Transportation being a means of exchange and a public necessity, the government should own and operate the railroads in the interest of the people. The telegraph and telephone, like the post-office system, being a necessity for the transmission of news, should be owned and operated by the government in the interest of the people.

LAND.—The land, including all the natural sources of wealth, is the heritage of the people, and should not be monopolized for speculative purposes, and alien ownership of land should be prohibited. All land now held by railroads and other corporations in excess of their actual needs, and all lands now owned by aliens should be reclaimed by the government and held for actual settlers only.

EXPRESSION OF SENTIMENTS

1. **RESOLVED,** That we demand a free ballot, and a fair count of all elections, and pledge ourselves to secure it to every legal voter without Federal intervention, through the adoption by the States of the unperverted Australian or secret ballot system.

2. **RESOLVED,** That the revenue derived from a graduated income tax should be applied to the reduction of the burden of taxation now levied upon the domestic industries of this country.

3. **RESOLVED,** That we pledge our support to fair and liberal pensions to ex-Union soldiers and sailors.

4. **RESOLVED,** That we condemn the fallacy of protecting American labor under the present system, which opens our ports to the pauper and criminal classes of the world and crowds out our wage-earners; and we denounce the present ineffective laws against contract labor, and demand the further restriction of undesirable emigration.

5. **RESOLVED,** That we cordially sympathize with the efforts of organized workingmen to shorten the hours of labor, and demand a rigid enforcement of the existing eight-our law on Government work, and ask that a penalty clause be added to the said law.

6. **RESOLVED,** That we regard the maintenance of a large standing army of mercenaries, known as the Pinkerton system, as a menace to our liberties, and we demand its abolition....

7. **RESOLVED,** That we commend to the favorable consideration of the people and the reform press the legislative system known as the initiative and referendum.

8. **RESOLVED,** That we favor a constitutional provision limiting the office of President and Vice-president to one term, and providing for the election of Senators of the United States by a direct vote of the people.

9. **RESOLVED,** That we oppose any subsidy or national aid to any private corporation for any purpose.

Document D
Plessy v. Ferguson

This case turns upon the constitutionality of an act of the general assembly of the state of Louisiana, passed in 1890, providing for separate railway carriages for the white and colored races....

The constitutionality of this act is attacked upon the ground that it conflicts both with the 13th Amendment of the Constitution, abolishing slavery, and the 14th Amendment, which prohibits certain restrictive legislation on the part of the states.

1. That it does not conflict with the 13th Amendment, which abolished slavery and involuntary servitude, except as a punishment for crime, is too clear for argument....Indeed, we do not understand that the 13th Amendment is strenuously relied upon by the plaintiff....

The object of the [14th] amendment was undoubtedly to enforce the absolute equality of the two races before the law, but in the nature of things it could not have been intended to abolish distinctions based upon color, or to enforce social, as distinguished from political, equality, or a commingling of the two races upon terms unsatisfactory to either. Laws permitting, and even requiring their separation in places where they are liable to be brought into contact do not necessarily imply the inferiority of either race to the other, and have been generally, if not universally, recognized as within the competency of the state legislatures in the exercise of their police power....

We consider the underlying fallacy of the plaintiff's argument to consist in the assumption that the enforced separation of the two races stamps the colored race with a badge of inferiority. If this be so, it is not by reason of anything found in the act, but solely because the colored race chooses to put that construction upon it....

The argument also assumes that social prejudice may be overcome by legislation, and that equal rights cannot be secured to the Negro except by an enforced commingling of the two races. We cannot accept this proposition. If the two races are to meet on terms of social equality, it must be the result of natural affinities, a mutual appreciation of each other's merits and a voluntary consent of individuals....Legislation is powerless to eradicate racial instincts or abolish distinctions based upon physical differences and the attempt to do so can only result in accentuating the difficulties of the present situation. If the civil and political right of both races be equal, one cannot be inferior (552) to the other civilly or politically. If one race be inferior to the other socially, the Constitution of the United States cannot put them upon the same plane.

Document E
The Atlanta Compromise

...Ignorant and inexperienced, it is not strange that in the first years of our new life we began at the top instead of at the bottom; that a seat in Congress or the state legislature was more sought than real estate or industrial skill; that the political convention or stump speaking had more attractions than starting a dairy farm or a truck garden.

A ship lost at sea for many days suddenly sighted a friendly vessel. From the mast of the unfortunate vessel was seen a signal, "Water, water; we die of thirst!" The answer from the friendly vessel at once came back, "Cast down your bucket where you are."...The captain of the distressed vessel, at least heeding the injunction, cast down his bucket, and it came up full of fresh, sparkling water...To those of my race who underestimate the importance of cultivating friendly relations with the Southern white man, who is their next-door neighbor, I would say: "Cast down your bucket where you are" — cast it down in making friends in every manly way of the people of all races by whom we are surrounded.

Cast it down in agriculture, mechanics, in commerce, in domestic service, and in the professions....Our greatest danger is that in the great leap from slavery to freedom we may overlook the fact that the masses of us are to live by the productions of our hands, and fail to keep in mind that we shall prosper in proportion as we learn to dignify and glorify common labour, and put brains and skill into the common occupations of life...No race can prosper till it learns that there is as much dignity in tilling a field as in writing a poem. It is at the bottom of life we must begin, and not at the top.

To those of the white race who look to the incoming of those of foreign birth and strange tongue and habits for the prosperity of the South, were I permitted I would repeat what I say to my own race, "Cast down your bucket where you are." Cast it down among the eight millions of Negroes whose habits you know, whose fidelity and love you have tested in days when to have proved treacherous meant the ruin of your firesides. Cast down your bucket among these people who have, without strikes and labour wars, tilled your fields, cleared your forests, built your railroads and cities, and brought forth treasures from the bowels of the earth...Casting down your bucket among my people...you waste places in your fields, and run your factories. While doing this, you can be sure in the future, as in the past, that you are law-abiding, and unresentful people that the world has seen....In all things that are purely social we can be as separate as the finders, yet one as the hand in all things essential to mutual progress....

The wisest among my race understand that the agitation of questions of social equality is the extremist folly, and that progress in the enjoyment of all the privileges that will come to us must be the result of severe and constant struggle rather than of artificial forcing. No race that has anything to contribute to the markets of the world is long in any degree ostracized. It is important and right that all privileges of the law be ours, but it is vastly more important that we be prepared for the exercise of these privileges. The opportunity to earn a dollar in a factory just now is worth infinitely more than the opportunity to spend a dollar in an opera-house.

Document Set Eighteen
Reforming American Society

As the first major reform movement of the twentieth century, the Progressive Movement established the framework for American liberalism. It changed the relationship between government and society, making it the agency of change to improve the quality of life for Americans. Using terms like "regulate," "bring order," and "make more efficient" its agenda supported progress and focused on solutions for problems created by the new economic order.

The first call for action occurred on the local level as Progressives analyzed the conditions of the new urban environment. The Triangle Fire highlighted for many Americans the plight of the workers. Only after 146 young girls died did the city of New York create a Bureau of Fire Prevention. Document A is an account by Pauline Newman of the conditions in the factory. She describes how the owners exploited the workers for in "...a world of greed; the human being didn't mean anything." Why were workers willing to accept this type of work environment? Why weren't conditions regulated by the government until after the fire?

The ascendancy of Theodore Roosevelt to the Presidency catapulted the Progressive Movement onto the national political scene. His strong support for the movement brought it popularity and publicity. By the 1912 election two of the candidates for the office presented progressive platforms. Students should read both Roosevelt's "New Nationalism" (Document B) and Woodrow Wilson's "New Freedom" (Document C). They can contrast the ideas of the two men. Which philosophy was more realistic for the nation? Why did Wilson attack Roosevelt on the issue of trusts? Students should note the tone of the discussion, did the candidates have different visions for the nation? Could both platforms be considered Progressive?

Questions for Document Set Eighteen

1. Given the description of the Triangle Factory, why were workers willing to work under those conditions?

2. Why did it take a tragedy in order to initiate reform?

3. Compare the visions of New Nationalism and New Freedom?

4. Which philosophy was more realistic for twentieth century America?

Document A
The Triangle Factory

I'd like to tell you about the kind of world we lived in 75 years ago because all of you probably weren't born then. Seventy-five years is a long time, but I'd like to give you at least a glimpse of that world because it has no resemblance to the world we live in today, in any respect.

That world 75 years ago was a world of incredible exploitation of men, women, and children. I went to work for the Triangle Shirtwaist Company in 1901. The corner of a shop would resemble a kindergarten because we were young, eight, nine, ten years old. It was a world of greed; the human being didn't mean anything. The hours were from 7:30 in the morning to 6:30 at night when it wasn't busy. When the season was on we worked until 9 o'clock. No overtime pay, not even supper money. There was a bakery in the garment center that produced little apple pies the size of this ashtray {holding up ashtray for group to see] and that was what we got for our overtime instead of money.

My wages as a youngster were $1.50 for a seven-day week. I know it sounds exaggerated, but it isn't; it's true. If you worked there long enough and you were satisfactory you got 50 cents a week increase every year. So by the time I left the Triangle Waist Company in 1909, my wages went up to $5.50, and that was quite a wage in those days.

All shops were as bad as the Triangle Waist Company. When you were told Saturday afternoon, through a sign on the elevator, "If you don't come in on Sunday, you needn't come in on Monday," what choice did you have? You had no choice.

I worked on the 9th floor with a lot of youngsters like myself. Our work was not difficult. When the operators were through with sewing shirtwaists, there was a little thread left, and we youngsters would get a little scissors and trim the threads off.

And when the inspectors came around, do you know that happened? The supervisors made all the children climb into one of those crates that they ship material in, and they covered us over with finished shirtwaists until the inspector had left, because of course we were too young to be working in the factory legally.

The Triangle Waist Company was a family affair, all relatives of the owner running the place, watching to see that you did your work, watching when you went to the toilet. And if you were two or three minutes longer than foremen or foreladies thought you should be, it was deducted from your pay. If you came five minutes late in the morning because the freight elevator didn't come down to take you up in time, you were sent home for half a day without pay.

Rubber heels came into use around that time and our employers were the first to use them; you never knew when they would sneak up on you, spying, to be sure you did not talk to each other during working hours.

Most of the women rarely took more than $6.00 a week home, most less. The early sweatshops were usually so dark that gas jets (for light) burned day and night. There was no insulation in the winter, only a pot-bellied stove in the middle of the factory. If you were a finisher and could take your work with you (finishing is a hand operation) you could sit next to the stove in winter. But if you were an operator or a trimmer it was very cold indeed. Of course in the summer you suffocated with practically no ventilation.

There was no drinking water, maybe a tap in the hall, warm, dirty. What were you going to do? Drink this water or none at all. Well, in those days there were vendors who came in with bottles of pop for 2 cents, and much as you disliked to spend the two pennies you got the pop instead of the filthy water in the hall.

The condition was no better and no worse than the tenements where we lived. You got out of the workshop, dark and cold in the winter, hot in summer, dirty unswept floors, no ventilation, and you would go home. What kind of home did you go to? You won't find the tenements we lived in. Some of the rooms didn't have any windows. I lived in a two-room tenement with my mother and two sisters and the bedroom had no windows, the facilities were down in the yard, but that's the way it was in the factories too. In the summer the sidewalk, fire escapes, and the roof of the tenements became bedrooms just to get a breath of air.

We wore cheap clothes, lived in cheap tenements, ate cheap food. There was nothing to look forward to, nothing to expect the next day to be better.

Someone once asked me; "How did you survive?" And I told him, what alternative did we have? You stayed and you survived, that's all.

Document B
The New Nationalism

Practical equality of opportunity for all citizens, when we achieve it, will have two great results. First, every man will have a fair chance to make of himself all that in him lies; to reach the highest point to which his capacities, unassisted by special privilege of his own and unhampered by the special privilege of others, can carry him, and to get for himself and his family substantially what he has earned. Second, equality of opportunity means that the commonwealth will get from every citizen the highest service of which he is capable. No man who carries the burden of the special privileges of another can give to the commonwealth that service to which it is fairly entitled....

Now, this means that our government, national and state, must be freed from the sinister influence or control of special interests. Exactly as the special interests of cotton and slavery threatened our political integrity before the Civil War, so now the great special business interests too often control and corrupt the men and methods of government for their own profit. We must drive the special interests out of politics. That is one of our tasks today....

The true friend of property, the true conservative, is he who insists that property shall be the servant and not the master of the commonwealth; who insists that the creature of man's making shall be the servant and not the master of the man who made it. The citizens of the United States must effectively control the mighty commercial forces which they have themselves called into being....

It has become entirely clear that we must have government supervision of the capitalization, not only of the public service corporations, including, particularly, railways, but of all corporations doing an interstate business. I do not wish to see the nation forced into the ownership of the railways if it can possibly be avoided, and the only alternative is thoroughgoing and effective regulation, which shall be based on a full knowledge of all the facts, including a physical valuation of property....

Combinations in industry are the result of an imperative economic law which cannot be repealed by political legislation. The effort at prohibiting all combination has substantially failed. The way out lies, not in attempting to prevent such combinations, but in completely controlling them in the interest of the public welfare.

Document C
The New Freedom (1913)

The doctrine that monopoly is inevitable and that the only course open to the people of the United States is to submit to and regulate it found a champion during the campaign of 1912 in the new party or branch of the Republican Party, founded under the leadership of Mr. Roosevelt, with the conspicuous aid, —I mention him with no satirical intention, but merely to set the facts down accurately, —of Mr. George W. Perkins, organizer of the Steel Trust and the Harvester Trust, and with the support of patriotic, conscientious and high-minded men and women of the land. The fact that its acceptance of monopoly was a feature of the new party platform from which the attention of the generous and just was diverted by the charm of a social program of great attractiveness to all concerned for the amelioration of the lot of those who suffer wrong and privation, and the further fact that, even so, the platform was repudiated by the majority of the nation, render it no less necessary to reflect on the party in the country's history. It may be useful, in order to relief of the minds of many from an error of no small magnitude, to consider now, the heat of a presidential contest being past, exactly what it was that Mr. Roosevelt proposed.

Mr. Roosevelt attached to his platform some very splendid suggestions as to noble enterprises which we ought to undertake for the uplift of the human race;...If you have read the trust plank in that platform as often as I have read it, you have found it very long, but very tolerant. It did not anywhere condemn monopoly, except in words; its essential meaning was that the trusts have been bad and must be made to be good. You know that Mr. Roosevelt long ago classified trusts for us as good and bad, and he said that he was afraid only of the bad ones. Now he does not desire that there should be any more of the bad ones, but proposes that they should all be made good by discipline, directly applied by a commission of executive appointment. All he explicitly complains of is lack of publicity and lack of fairness; not the exercise of power, for throughout that plank the power of the great corporations is accepted as the inevitable consequence of the modern organization of industry. All that it is proposed to do is to take them under control and deregulation.

The fundamental part of such a program is that the trusts shall be recognized as a permanent part of our economic order, and that the government shall try to make trusts the ministers, the instruments, through which the life of this country shall be justly and happily developed on its industrial side....

Shall we try to get the grip of monopoly away from our lives, or shall we not? Shall we withhold our hand and say monopoly is inevitable, that all we can do is to regulate it? Shall we say that all we can do is to put government in competition with monopoly and try its strength against it? Shall we admit that the creature of our own hands is stronger than we are? We have been dreading all along the time when the combined power of high finance would be greater than the power of the government.

Document Set Nineteen
America at War

When war broke out in 1914 Americans thought the Europeans had gone mad. Wilson, who had been elected because of his domestic policies, found himself forced to develop a foreign policy that would keep the United States out of the conflict. Asking Americans to remain totally neutral, Wilson believed he could keep the nation out of war. In the 1916 Presidential election he ran on a platform that promised, "Peace, Prosperity and Progress." One year later Wilson was asking the Congress for a declaration of war against Germany.

Many Americans perceived of the war as an extension of the Progressive reform movement. By promising them that winning the war would make the world safe for democracy, Wilson lifted the war to the level of a great crusade. George Creel was appointed to head the Committee of Public Information in Washington. This agency was charged with selling the war to America. In speeches, pamphlets, posters, and movies Americans were exhorted to support the war effort.

Document A, "The Boy Scouts Support the War Effort," is a selection from a pamphlet published by the Committee for the American Boy Scouts. They were told that they had been "summoned by their Commander-in-Chief to serve as a dispatch bearer to the American people." Students should note the zeal of the pamphlet as the Boy Scouts are told that "World War is for liberty and democracy." Why does the pamphlet make reference to, "the enemy within." Who is that enemy? Were the Boy Scouts being exploited by the American government?

The Creel Committee, and the passage of the Espionage and Sedition Acts, helped create a domestic environment that associated dissent with treason. Wars demanded loyalty and it was a time when Americans were expected to "rally round the flag." In Document B, "The Treatment of German-Americans," students have an opportunity to read the observations of Secretary of War Baker regarding the treatment of non-natives during that time. Why were Americans taking such drastic actions against foreigners? Was the treatment foreigners received during wartime any different from earlier nativist attacks against them? Was Baker correct in believing that the United States government was not responsible for the actions of its citizens against aliens?

The United States entered the war in 1917 unprepared for military action. The American doughboy quickly learned that Sherman had been right and war was hell. In Document C an American doughboy describes life at the front lines in France. His narration expresses how difficult and dirty war was. There is a tone in his writing of growing hardness to the death and destruction around him. Can war only be glorified by those who don't fight it?

Long before the war was over, Wilson was planning the peace and ways to insure that war would never happen again. Issuing his "Fourteen Points" (Document D), he believed that the world really could be made safe for democracy. How realistic was it for Wilson to assume that he could achieve this goal? Students should note how the points are broken down. How many relate to the causes of the war and which are concerned with creating a new world order? Did most people believe that the nation had entered war as a self sacrifice?

Questions for Document Set Nineteen

1. Does government propaganda have a role in a free society?

2. For most Americans, who did they have the most to fear from?

3. Could the attacks against German-Americans, Socialists, pacifists and other groups within the United States have been prevented?

4. Based on the account of the American doughboy, describe life at the front lines of the war.

5. Was it realistic to assume that the war would make the world safe for democracy?

Document A
Boy Scouts Support the War Effort

To the Members of the Boy Scouts of America!

Attention, Scouts! We are again called upon to do active service for our country! Every one of the 285,661 Scouts and 76,957 Scout Officials has been summoned by President Woodrow Wilson, Commander-in-Chief of the Army and Navy, to serve as a dispatch bearer from the Government at Washington to the American people all over the country. The prompt, enthusiastic, and hearty response of every one of us has been pledged by our [Scout] President, Mr. Livingstone. Our splended record of accomplishments in war activities promises full success in this new job.

This patriotic service will be rendered under the slogan

"EVERY SCOUT TO BOOST AMERICA"

AS A GOVERNMENT DISPATCH BEARER

The World War is for liberty and democracy.

America has long been recognized as the leader among nations standing for liberty and democracy.

American entered the war as a sacred duty to uphold the principles of liberty and democracy.

As a democracy, our country faces great danger—not so much from submarines, battleships and armies, because, thanks to our allies, our enemies have apparently little chance of reaching our shores.

Our danger is from within.

Our enemies have representatives everywhere; they tell lies; they mispresent the truth; they deceive our own people; they are a real menace to our country.

Already we have seen how poor Russian has been made to suffer because her people do not know the truth. Representatives of the enemy have been very effective in their deceitful efforts to make trouble for the Government.

Fortunately here in America our people are better educated—they want the truth. Our President recognized the justice and wisdom of this demand when in the early stages of the war he created the Committee of Public Information. He knew that the Government would need the confidence, enthusiasm and willing service of every man and woman, every boy and girl in the nation. He knew that the only possible way to create a genuine feeling of partnership between the people and its representatives in Washington was to take the people into his confidence by full, frank statements concerning the reasons for our entering the war, the various steps taken during the war and the ultimate aims of the war.

Neither the President as Commander-in-Chief, nor our army and navy by land and sea, can alone win the war.

At this moment the best defense that America has is an enlightened and loyal citizenship. Therefore, we as scouts are going to have the opportunity of rendering real patriotic service under our slogan.

"EVERY SCOUT TO BOOST AMERICA" AS A GOVERNMENT DISPATCH BEARER

Here is where our service begins.

We are to help spread the facts about America and America's part in the World War.

We are to fight lies with truth.

We are to help create public opinion "just as effective in helping to bring victory as ships and guns," to stir patriotism, the great force behind the ships and guns. Isn't that a challenge for every loyal Scout?

'EVERY SCOUT TO BOOST AMERICA' AS A GOVERNMENT DISPATCH BEARER: HOW?

As Mr. George Creel, the Chairman of the Committee on Public Information, says in his letter, scouts are to serve as direct special representatives of the Committee on Public Information to keep the people informed about the War and its causes and progress. The Committee has already prepared a number of special pamphlets and other will be prepared. It places upon the members of the Boy Scouts of America the responsibility of putting the information in these pamphlets in homes of the American people. Every Scout will be furnished a credential card by his Scoutmaster. Under the direction of our leaders, the Boy Scouts of America are to serve as an intelligence division of the citizen's army, always prepared and alert to respond to any call which may come from the President of the United States and the Committee on Public Information at Washington.

...Each Scoutmaster is to be furnished with a complete set of all of the government publications, in order that all of the members of his troop may be completely informed. Each scout and scout official is expected to seize every opportunity to serve the Committee on Public Information by making available authoritative information. It is up to the Boy Scouts to see that as many people as possible have an intelligent understanding of any and all facts incident to our present national crisis and the World War....

PAMPHLETS NOW READY FOR CIRCULATION

Note:—A set will be sent to every Scoutmaster. You will need to know what is in these pamphlets so as to act as a serviceable bureau of information and be able to give each person the particular intelligence he seeks.

Document B
The Treatment of German-Americans

The spirit of the country seems unusually good, but there is a growing frenzy of suspicion and hostility toward disloyalty. I am afraid we are going to have a good many instances of people roughly treated on very slight evidence of disloyalty. Already a number of men and some women have been "tarred and feathered," and a portion of the press is urging with great vehemence more strenuous efforts at detection and punishment. This usually takes the form of advocating "drum-head courts-martial" and "being stood up against a wall and shot," which are perhaps none too bad for real traitors, but are very suggestive of summary discipline to arouse mob spirit, which unhappily does not take time to weigh evidence.

In Cleveland a few days ago a foreign-looking man got into a street car and, taking a seat, noticed pasted in the window next to him a Liberty Loan poster, which he immediately tore down, tore into small bits, and stamped under his feet. The people in the car surged around him with the demand that he be lynched, when a Secret Service man showed his badge and placed him under arrest, taking him in a car to the police station, where he was searched and found to have two Liberty Bonds in his pocket and to be a non-English Pole. When an interpreter was procured, it was discovered that the circular which he had destroyed had had on it a picture of the German Emperor, which had so infuriated the fellow that he destroyed the circular to show his vehement hatred of the common enemy. As he was unable to speak a single word of English, he would undoubtedly have been hanged but for the intervention and entirely accidental presence of the Secret Service agent.

I am afraid the grave danger in this sort of thing, apart from its injustice, is that the German Government will adopt retaliatory measures. While the Government of the United States is not only responsible for these things, but very zealously trying to prevent them, the German Government draws no fine distinctions.

Document C
A "Doughboy" Describes the Fighting Front

Thursday, September 12, 1918. Hiked through dark woods. No light allowed, guided by holding on the pack of the man ahead. Stumbled through underbrush for about half mile into an open field where we waited in soaking rain until about 10:00 p.m. We then started on our hike to the St. Mihiel front, arriving on the crest of a hill at 1:00 a.m. I saw a sight which I shall never forget. It was the zero hour and in one instant the entire front as far as the eye could reach in either direction was a sheet of flame while the heavy artillery made the earth quake. The barrage was so intense that for a time we could not make out whether the Americans or Germans were putting it over. After timing the interval between flash and report we knew that the heaviest artillery was less than a mile away and consequently it was ours. We waded through pools and mud across open lots into a woods on a hill and had to pitch tents in mud. Blankets all wet and we are soaked to the skin. Have carried full pack from 10:00 p.m. to 2:00 a.m., without a rest....Despite the cannonading I slept until 8:00 a.m. and awoke to find every discharge of 14-inch artillery shaking our tent like a leaf. Remarkable how we could sleep. No breakfast....The doughboys had gone over the top at 5:00 a.m. and the French were shelling the back areas toward Metz....Firing is incessant, so is rain. See an air battle just before turning in.

Friday, September 13, 1918. Called at 3:00 a.m. Struck tents and started to hike at 5:00 a.m. with full packs and a pick. Put on gas mask at alert position and hiked about five miles to St. Jean, where we unslung full packs and went on about four miles further with short packs and picks. Passed several batteries and saw many dead horses who gave out at start of push. Our doughboys are still shoving and "Jerry" is dropping so many shells on road into no man's land that we stayed back in field and made no effort to repair shell-torn road. Plenty of German prisoners being brought back....Guns booming all the time....

Thursday, October 17, 1918. Struck tents at 8:00 a.m. and moved about four miles to Chatel. Pitched tents on a side hill so steep that we had to cut steps to ascend. Worked like hell to shovel out a spot to pitch tent on. Just across the valley in front of us about two hundred yards distant, there had occurred an explosion due to a mine planted by the "Bosche" [Germans] and set with a time fuse. It had blown two men (French), two horses, and the wagon into fragments....Arriving on the scene we found Quinn ransacking the wagon. It was full of grub. We each loaded a burlap bag with cans of condensed milk, peas, lobster, salmon, and bread. I started back...when suddenly another mine exploded, the biggest I ever saw. Rocks and dirt flew sky high. Quinn was hit in the knee and had to go to hospital....At 6:00 p.m. each of our four platoons left camp in units to go up front and throw three foot and one artillery bridge across the Aire River. On way to river we were heavily shelled and gassed....We put a bridge across 75-foot span....Third platoon men had to get into water and swim or stand in water to their necks. The toughest job we had so far....

Monday, October 21, 1918. Fragment from shell struck mess-kit on my back....Equipment, both American and German, thrown everywhere, especially Hun helmets and belts of machine gunners....Went scouting...for narrow-gauge rails to replace the ones "Jerry" spoiled before evacuating. Negro engineers working on railroad same as at St. Mihiel, that's all they are good for....

Friday, November 1, 1918. Started out at 4:00 a.m. The drive is on. Fritz is coming back at us. Machine guns cracking, flares and Verry lights, artillery from both sides. A real war and we are walking right into the zone, ducking shells all the way. The artillery is nerve racking and we don't know from which angle "Jerry" will fire next. Halted behind shelter of railroad track just outside of Grand Pre after being forced back off main road by shell fire. Trees splintered like toothpicks. Machine gunners on top of railroad bank...."Jerry" drove Ewell and me into a two-by-four shell hole, snipers' bullets close.

Sunday, November 3, 1918. Many dead Germans along the road. One heap on a manure pile....Devastation everywhere. Our barrage has rooted up the entire territory like a ploughed field. Dead horses galore, many of them have a hind quarter cut off—the Huns need food. Dead men here and there. The sight I enjoy better than a dead German is to see heaps of them. Rain again. Couldn't keep rain out of our faces and it was pouring hard. Got up at midnight and drove stakes to secure shelter-half over us, pulled our wet blankets out of mud and made the bed all over again. Slept like a log with all my equipment in the open. One hundred forty-two planes sighted in evening.

Sunday, November 10, 1918. First day off in over two months....Took a bath and we were issued new underwear but the cooties [lice] got there first....The papers show a picture of the Kaiser entitled "William the Lost," and stating that he had abdicated. Had a good dinner. Rumor at night that armistice was signed. Some fellows discharged their arms in the courtyard, but most of us were too well pleased with dry bunk to get up.

Document D
The Fourteen Points

It will be our wish and purpose that the processes of peace, when they are begun, shall be absolutely open and that they shall involve and permit henceforth no secret understandings of any kind. The day of conquest and aggrandizement is gone by; so is also the day of secret covenants entered into in the interest of particular governments and likely at some unlooked-for moment to upset the peace of the world....

We entered this war because violations of right had occurred which touched us to the quick and made the life of our own people impossible unless they were corrected and the world secure once for all against their recurrence.

What we demand in this war, therefore, is nothing peculiar to ourselves. It is that the world be made fit and safe to live in; and particularly that it be made safe for every peace-loving nation which, like our own, wishes to live its own life, determine its own institutions, be assured of justice and fair dealing by the other peoples of the world as against force and selfish aggressions.

All the peoples of the world are in effect partners in this interest, and for our own part we see very clearly that unless justice be done to others it will not be done to us. The program of the world's peace, therefore, is our program; and that program, the only possible program, as we see it, is this:

1. Open covenants of peace, openly arrived at, after which there shall be no private international understandings of any kind but diplomacy shall proceed always frankly and in the public view.

2. Absolute freedom of navigation upon the seas, outside territorial waters, alike in peace and in war, except as the seas may be closed in whole or in part by international action for the enforcement of international covenants.

3. The removal, so far as possible, of all economic barriers and the establishment of an equality of trade conditions among all the nations consenting to the peace and associating themselves for its maintenance.

4. Adequate guarantees given and taken that national armaments will be reduced to the lowest points consistent with domestic safety.

5. A free, open-minded, and absolutely impartial adjustment of all colonial claims, based upon a strict observance of the principle that in determining all such questions of sovereignty the interests of the populations concerned must have equal weight with the equitable claims of the government whose title is to be determined.

6. The evacuation of all Russian territory and such a settlement of all questions affecting Russia as will secure the best and freest cooperation of the other nations of the world in obtaining for her an unhampered and unembarrassed opportunity for the independent determination of her own political development and national policy and assure her of a sincere welcome into the society of free nations under institutions of her own choosing; and, more than a welcome, assistance also of every kind that she may need and may herself desire. The treatment accorded Russian by her sister nations in the months to come will be the acid test of their good will, of their comprehension of her needs as distinguished from their own interests, and of their intelligent and unselfish sympathy.

7. Belgium, the whole world will agree, must be evacuated and restored, without any attempt to limit the sovereignty which she enjoys in common with all other free nations. No other single act will serve as this will serve to restore confidence among the nations in the laws which they have themselves set and determined for the government of their relations with one another. Without this healing act the whole structure and validity of international law is forever impaired.

8. All French territory should be freed and the invaded portions restored, and the wrong done to France by Prussia in 1871 in the matter of Alsace-Lorraine, which has unsettled the peace of the world for nearly fifty years, should be righted, in order that peace may once more be made secure in the interest of all.

9. A readjustment of the frontiers of Italy should be affected along clearly recognizable lines of nationality.

10. The peoples of Austria-Hungary, whose place among the nations we wish to see safeguarded and assured, should be accorded the freest opportunity of autonomous development.

11. Rumania, Serbia, and Montenegro should be evacuated; occupied territories restored; Serbia accorded free and secure access to the sea; and the relations of the several Balkan states to one another determined by friendly counsel along historically established lines of allegiance and nationality; and international guarantees of the political and economic independence and territorial integrity of the several Balkan states should be entered into.

12. The Turkish portions of the present Ottoman Empire should be assured a secure sovereignty, but the other nationalities which are now under Turkish rule should be assured an undoubted security of life and an absolutely unmolested opportunity of autonomous development, and the Dardanelles should be permanently opened as a free passage to the ships and commerce of all nations under international guarantees.

13. An independent Polish state should be erected which should include the territories inhabited by indisputably Polish populations, which should be assured a free and secure access to the sea, and whose political and economic independence and territorial integrity should be guaranteed by international covenant.

14. A general association of nations must be formed under specific covenants for the purpose of affording mutual guarantees of political independence and territorial integrity to great and small states alike.

In regard to these essential rectifications of wrong and assertions of right we feel ourselves to be intimate partners of all the governments and peoples associated together against the imperialists. We cannot be separated in interest or divided in purpose. We stand together until the end....

An evident principle runs through the whole program I have outlined. It is the principle of justice to all peoples and nationalities, and their right to live on equal terms of liberty and safety with one another, whether they be strong or weak.

Unless this principle be made its foundation no part of the structure of international justice can stand. The people of the United States could act upon no other principle; and to the vindication of this principle they are ready to devote their lives, their honor, and everything that they possess. The moral climax of this the culminating and final war for human liberty has come, and they are ready to put their own strength, their own highest purpose, their own integrity and devotion to the test.

Document Set Twenty
Hard Times

As the 1920s began, Americans wanted to forget the disillusionment of the war and the promises of the Progressive Period. It became the decade in which the nation recognized it was an urban society and searched for normalcy. The transition to a modern society was not easy and some tried hard to hang on to their rural roots. It was a decade which carried over the xenophobia about foreigners, saw a resurgence of the Klu Klux Klan and believed that prohibition could create a moral society. Conspicuous consumption emerged and the American economy was a House of Cards built on consumer credit. When the decade ended with a crash, America entered an economic depression that lasted ten years.

As a direct consequence of World War One, nativism reappeared during the 1920s. No longer would unrestricted immigration from Europe be accepted and, instead, a very selective immigration policy was put into practice. Document A, "The Immigration Act of 1924," details how the new quota system worked. Analysis of the document can be an excellent critical thinking exercise for students. Which countries benefited from the act? Which countries suffered? Why did most native Americans want 1890 as the base year to determine foreign countries' quotas? Was the act a continuation of the postwar hysteria which began during the Red Scare?

The 1929 Stock Market crash became the worst depression in the history of the nation. By the presidential election of 1932, twenty-five per cent of the work force had lost their jobs. The American public was psychologically and economically depressed. The election of Franklin Delano Roosevelt brought renewed hope for them. While his New Deal program did not end the depression, it did restore the nation's confidence and faith in the system. Students will find sections of his First Inaugural Address (Document B) very familiar. In stating, "We Have Nothing To Fear But Fear Itself," what message was he sending to the nation? Students should note how he reminds Americans of their heritage and the spirit which had made the nation great. According to Roosevelt, what is the primary task of government? Why were Americans inspired by the speech? How similar is this speech to President Clinton's call for a new covenant between the American people and the government?

By the mid 1930s New Deal legislation was not effective in ending the depression. While some critics argued Roosevelt had gone too far, others believed he had not gone far enough. In Document C, "Share Our Wealth," one of Roosevelt's most vocal critics, Huey Long, outlines a program that advocates a guaranteed income for every American family. Why was Roosevelt frightened by Long and this plan? Did Long really pose a political threat to Roosevelt? Could Long's program be implemented?

The depression was most difficult for minority groups and, in particular, African Americans. Document D, "We Want to Live," is a poignant letter written by a young African American woman to FDR. As she points out, they were often the last hired and the first fired. As a group, they received few benefits from New Deal legislation. Why was Roosevelt's record so weak on civil rights? Why wasn't he more supportive of the needs of minority groups?

Questions for Document Set Twenty

1. Why did Americans want to restrict immigration in the 1920s? How different was this act from earlier immigration legislation?

2. Why would the public feel a renewed sense of confidence after the First Inaugural Speech? Did it give a plan of action to end the depression?

3. How realistic was Long's "Share The Wealth?" Is Long critical of the Roosevelt administration?

4. Why didn't minorities receive the full benefits of the legislation passed during the New Deal?

Document A
The Immigration Act of 1924

By the President of the United States of America

A Proclamation

Whereas it is provided in the act of Congress approved May 26, 1924, entitled "An act to limit the immigration of aliens into the United States, and for other purposes" that —"The annual quota of any nationality shall be two per centum of the number of foreign-born individuals of such nationality resident in continental Untied States as determined by the United States census of 1890, but the minimum quota of any nationality shall be 100 (Sec. 11 (a))....

"The Secretary of State, the Secretary of Commerce, and the Secretary of Labor, jointly, shall, as soon as feasible after the enactment of this act, prepare a statement showing the number of individuals of the various nationalities resident in continental United States as determined by the United States census of 1890, which statement shall be the population basis for the purposes of subdivision (a) of section 11 (sec. 12 (b)).

"Such officials shall, jointly, report annually to the President the quota of each nationality under subdivision (a) of section 11, together with the statements, estimates, and revisions provided for in this section. The President shall proclaim and make known the quotas so reported." (Sect. 12 (e)).

Now, therefore I, Calvin Coolidge, President of the United States of America acting under and by virtue of the power in me vested by the aforesaid act of Congress, do hereby proclaim and make known that on and after July 1, 1924, and throughout the fiscal year 1924-1925, the quota of each nationality provided in said Act shall be as follows:

COUNTRY OR AREA OF BIRTH
QUOTA 1924-1925

Afghanistan— 100
Albania— 100
Andorra— 100
Arabian peninsula (1, 2)— 100
Armenia— 124
Australia, including Papua, Tasmania, and all islands appertaining to Australia (3, 4)— 121
Austria— 785
Belgium (5)— 512
Bhutan— 100
Bulgaria— 100
Cameroon (proposed British mandate)— 100
Cameroon (French mandate)— 100
China— 100
Czechoslovakia— 3,073
Danzig, Free City of— 228
Denmark (5, 6)— 2,789
Egypt— 100
Esthonia— 124
Ethiopia (Abyssinia)— 100
Finland— 170

COUNTRY OR AREA OF BIRTH
QUOTA 1924-1925

France (1, 5, 6)— 3,954
Germany— 51,227
Great Britain and Northern Ireland (1, 3, 5, 6)— 34,007
Greece— 100
Hungary— 473
Iceland— 100
India (3)— 100
Iraq (Mesopotamia)— 100
Irish Free State (3)— 28,567
Italy, including Rhodes, Dodekanesia, and Castellorizzo (5)— 3,845
Japan— 100
Latvia—142
Liberia— 100
Liechtenstein— 100
Lithuania— 344
Luxemburg— 100
Monaco— 100
Morocco (French and Spanish Zones and Tangier)— 100
Muscat (Oman)— 100
Nauru (proposed British mandate) (4)— 100
Nepal— 100
Netherlands (1, 5, 6)— 1648
New Zealand (including appertaining islands (3, 4)— 100
Norway (5)— 6,453
New Guinea, and other Pacific Islands under proposed Australian mandate (4)— 100
Palestine (with Trans-Jordan, proposed British mandate)— 100
Persia (1)— 100
Poland— 5,982
Portugal (1, 5)— 503
Ruanda and Urundi (Belgium mandate)— 100
Rumania— 603
Russia, European and Asiatic (1)— 2,248
Samoa, Western (4) (proposed mandate of New Zealand)— 100
San Marino— 100
Siam— 100
South Africa, Union of (3)— 100
South West Africa (proposed mandate of Union of South Africa)— 100
Spain (5)— 131
Sweden— 9,561
Switzerland— 2,081
Syria and The Lebanon (French mandate)— 100
Tanganyika (proposed British mandate)— 100
Togoland (proposed British mandate)— 100
Togoland (French mandate)— 100
Turkey— 100
Yap and other Pacific islands (under Japanese mandate) (4)— 100
Yugoslavia— 671

GENERAL NOTE.—The immigration quotas assigned to the various countries and quota-areas should not be regarded as having any political significance whatever, or as involving recognition of new governments, or of new boundaries, or of transfers of territory except as the United States Government has already made such recognition in a formal and official manner....**Calvin Coolidge**.

Document B
First Inaugural Address

I am certain that my fellow Americans expect that on my induction into the Presidency I will address them with a candor and a decision which the present situation of our Nation impels. This is preeminently the time to speak the truth, the whole truth, frankly and boldly. Nor need we shrink from honestly facing conditions in our country today. This great Nation will endure as it has endured, will revive and will prosper. So, first of all, let me assert my firm belief that the only thing we have to fear is fear itself—nameless, unreasoning, unjustified terror which paralyzes needed efforts to convert retreat into advance. In every dark hour of our national life a leadership of frankness and vigor has met with that understanding and support of the people themselves which is essential to victory. I am convinced that you will again give that support to leadership in these critical days.

In such a spirit on my part and on yours we face our common difficulties. They concern, thank God, only material things. Values have shrunken to fantastic levels; taxes have risen; our ability to pay has fallen; government of all kinds is faced by serious curtailment of income; the means of exchange are frozen in the currents of trade; the withered leaves of industrial enterprise lie on every side; farmers find no markets for their produce; the savings of many years in thousands of families are gone.

More important, a host of unemployed citizens face the grim problem of existence, and an equally great number toil with little return. Only a foolish optimist can deny the dark reality of the movement.

Yet our distress comes from no failure or substance. We are stricken by no plague of locusts. Compared with the perils which our forefathers conquered because they believed and were not afraid, we have still much to be thankful for. Nature still offers her bounty and human efforts have multiplied it. Plenty is at our doorstep, but a generous use of it languishes in the very sight of the supply. Primarily this is because rulers of the exchange of mankind's goods have failed through their own stubbornness and their own incompetence, have admitted their failure, and have abdicated. Practices of the unscrupulous money changers stand indicted in the court of public opinion, rejected by the hearts and minds of men.

True they have tried, but their efforts have been cast in the pattern of an outworn tradition. Faced by failure of credit they have proposed only the lending of more money. Stripped of the lure of profit by which to induce our people to follow their leadership, they have resorted to exhortations, pleading tearfully for restored confidence. They have known only the rules of a generation of self-seekers. They have no vision, and when there is no vision the people perish.

The money changers have fled from their high seats in the temple of our civilization. We may now restore that temple to the ancient truths. The measure of the restoration lies in the extent to which we apply social values more noble than mere monetary profit.

Happiness lies not in the mere possession of money; it lies in the joy of achievement, in the thrill of creative effort. The joy and moral stimulation of work no longer must be forgotten in the mad chase of evanescent profits. These dark days will be worth all they cost us if they teach us that our true destiny is not to be ministered unto but to minister to ourselves and to our fellow men.

Recognition of the falsity of material wealth as the standard of success goes hand in hand with the abandonment of the false belief that public office and high political position are to be valued only by the standards of pride of place and personal profit; and there must be an end to a conduct in banking and in business which too often has given to a sacred trust the likeness of callous and selfish wrongdoing. Small wonder that confidence languishes, for it thrives only on honesty, on honor, on the sacredness of obligations, on faithful protection, on unselfish performance; without them it cannot live.

Restoration calls, however not for changes in ethics alone. This Nation asks for action, and action now.

Our greatest primary task is to put people to work. This is no unsolvable problem if we face it wisely and courageously. It can be accomplished in part by direct recruiting by the Government itself, treating the task as we would treat the emergency of a war, but at the same time, through this employment, accomplishing greatly needed projects to stimulate and reorganize the use of our natural resources.

Hand in hand with this we must frankly recognize the overbalance of population in our industrial centers and, by engaging on a national scale in a redistribution, endeavor to provide a better use of the land for those best fitted for the land. The task can be helped by definite efforts to raise the values of agricultural products and with this the power to purchase the output of our cities. It can be helped by preventing realistically the tragedy of the growing loss through foreclosure of our small homes and our farms. It can be helped by insistence that the Federal, State, and local governments act forthwith on the demand that their cost be drastically reduced. It can be helped by the unifying of relief activities which today are often scattered, uneconomical, and unequal. It can be helped by national planning for and supervision of all forms of transportation and of communications and other utilities which have a definitely public character. There are many ways in which it can be helped but it can never be helped merely by talking about it. We must act and act quickly.

Finally, in our progress toward a resumption of work we require two safeguards against a return of the evils of the old order: there must be a strict supervision of all banking an credits and investments, so that there will be an end to speculation with other people's money; and there must be provision for an adequate but sound currency.

These are the lines of attack. I shall presently urge upon a new Congress, in special session, detailed measures for their fulfillment, and I shall seek the immediate assistance of the several States.

Through this program of action we address ourselves to putting our own national house in order and making income balance outgo. Our international trade relations, though vastly important,, are in point of time and necessity secondary to the establishment of a sound national economy. I favor as a practical policy the putting of first things first. I shall spare no effort to restore world trade by international economic readjustment, but the emergency at home cannot wait on that accomplishment.

The basic thought that guides these specific means of national recovery is not narrowly nationalistic. It is the insistence as a first consideration, upon the interdependence of the various elements in and parts of the United States—a recognition of the old and permanently important manifestation of the American spirit of the pioneer. It is the way to recovery. It is the immediate way. It is the strongest assurance that the recovery will endure.

In the field of world policy I would dedicate this Nation to the policy of the good neighbor—the neighbor who respects his obligations and respects the sanctity of his agreements in and with a world of neighbors.

If I read the temper of our people correctly, we now realize as we have never realized before our interdependence on each other; that we cannot merely take but we must give as well; that if we are to go forward, we must move as a trained and loyal army willing to sacrifice for the good of a common discipline, because without such discipline no progress is made, no leadership becomes effective. We are, I know, ready and willing to submit our lives and property to such discipline, because it makes possible a leadership which aims at a larger good. This I propose to offer, pledging that the larger purpose will bind upon us all as a sacred obligation with a unity of duty hitherto evoked only in time of armed strife.

With this pledge taken, I assume unhesitatingly the leadership of this great army of our people dedicated to a disciplined attack upon our common problems.

Action in this image and to this end is feasible under the form of government which we have inherited from our ancestors. Our Constitution is so simple and practical that it is possible always to meet extraordinary needs by changes in emphasis and arrangement without loss of essential form. That is why our constitutional system has proved itself the most superbly enduring political mechanism the modern world has produced. It has met every stress of vast expansion of territory, of foreign wars, of bitter internal strife, of world relations.

It is to be hoped that the normal balance of Executive and legislative authority may be wholly adequate to meet the unprecedented task before us. But it may be that an unprecedented demand and need for undelayed action may call for temporary departure from that normal balance of public procedure.

I am prepared under my constitutional duty to recommend the measures that a stricken Nation in the midst of a stricken world may require. These measures, or such other measures as the Congress may build out of its experience and wisdom, I shall seek, within my constitutional authority to bring to speedy adoption.

But in the event that the Congress shall fail to take one of these two courses and in the event that the national emergency is still critical, I shall not evade the clear course of duty that will then confront me. I shall ask the Congress for the one remaining instrument to meet the crisis—broad Executive power to wage a war against the emergency, as great as the power that would be given to me if we were in fact invaded by a foreign foe.

For the trust reposed in me I will return the courage and the devotion that befit the time. I can do no less.

We face the arduous days that lie before us in the warm courage of national unity; with the clear consciousness of seeking old and precious moral values; with the clear satisfaction that comes from the stern performance of duty by old and young alike. We aim at the assurance of a rounded and permanent national life.

We do not distrust the future of essential democracy. The people of the United States have not failed. In their need they have registered a mandate that they want direct, vigorous action. They have asked for discipline and direction under leadership. They have made me the present instrument of their wishes. In the spirit of the gift I take it.

In this dedication of a Nation we humbly ask the blessing of God. May He protect each and every one of us. May He guide me in the days to come.

Document C
Huey Long, "Share Our Wealth"

Here is the whole sum and substance of the Share Our Wealth movement:

1. Every family to be furnished by the government a homestead allowance, free of debt, of not less than one-third the average family wealth of the country, which means, at the lowest, that every family shall have the reasonable comforts of life up to a value of from $5,000 to $6,000: No person to have a fortune of more than 100 to 300 times the average family fortune, which means that the limit to fortune is between $1,500,000 and 5,000,000, with annual capital levy taxes imposed on all above 1,000,000.

2. The yearly income of every family shall be not less than one-third of the average family income, which means that, according to the estimates of the statisticians of the U. S. Government and Wall Street, no family's annual income would be less than from $2,000 to $2,500: No yearly income shall be allowed to any person larger than from 100 to 300 times the size of the average family income, which means that no person would be allowed to earn in any year more than $600,000 to $1,800,000, all to be subject to present income tax laws.

3. To limit or regulate the hours of work to such an extent as to prevent over-production; the most modern and efficient machinery would be encouraged so that as much would be produced as possible so as to satisfy all demands of the people, but also to allow the maximum time to the workers for recreation, convenience, education, and luxuries of life.

4. An old age pension to the persons over 60.

5. To balance agricultural production with what can be consumed according to the laws of God, which includes the preserving and storing of surplus commodities to be paid for and held by the Government for emergencies when such are needed. Please bear in mind, however, that when the people of America have had money to buy things they needed, we have never had a surplus of any commodity. This plan of God does not call for destroying any of the things raised to eat or wear, nor does it countenance whole destruction of hogs, cattle or milk.

6. To pay the veterans of our wars what we owe them and to care for their disabled.

7. Education and training for all children to be equal in opportunity in all schools, colleges, universities and other institutions for training in the professions and vocations of life; to be regulated on the capacity of children to learn, and not on the ability of parents to pay the costs. Training for life's work to be as much universal and thorough for all walks in life as has been the training in the arts of killing.

8. The raising of revenues and taxes for the support of this program to come from the reduction of swollen fortunes from the top, as well as for the support of public works to give employment whenever there may be any slackening necessary in private enterprise.

Document D
We Want to Live, Not Merely Exist

Dear President Roosevelt:

I really don't know exactly how to begin this letter to you. Perhaps I should first tell you who I am. I am a young married woman. I am a Negro....I believe that you are familiar with the labor situation among the Negroes, but I want you to know how I and many of us feel about it and what we expect of you.

My husband is working for the e W.P.A. doing skilled labor. Before he started on this we were on relief for three months. We were three months trying to get relief. While trying to obtain relief I lost my unborn child. I believe if I had sufficient food this would not have happened. My husband was perfectly willing to work but could not find it. Now I am pregnant again. He is working at Tilden Tech. School where there are more white than colored. Every month more than one hundred persons are given private employment and not one of them are colored. It isn't that the colored men are not as skilled as the white, it is the fact that they are black and therefore must not get ahead.

We are citizens just as much or more than the majority of this country....We are just as intelligent as they. This is supposed to be a free country regardless of color, creed or race but still we are slaves....Won't you help us? I'm sure you can. I admire you and have very much confidence in you. I believe you are a real Christian and non-prejudice. I have never doubted that you would be elected again. I believe you can and must do something about the labor conditions of the Negro.

Why must our men fight and die for their country when it won't even given them a job that they are fitted for? They would much rather fight and die for their families or race. Before it is over many of them might. We did not ask to be brought here as slaves, nor did we ask to be born black. We are real citizens of this land and must and will be recognized as such!...If you are a real Christian you can not stand by and let these conditions exist.

My husband is young, intelligent and very depressed over this situation. We want to live, not merely exist from day to day, but to live as you or any human being desires to do. We want our unborn children to have an equal chance as the white. We don't want them to suffer as we are doing now because of race prejudice. My husband is 22 and I am 18 years of age. We want to own just a comfortable home by the time he reaches his early thirties. Is that asking too much? But how can we do that when the $26 he makes every two weeks don't hardly last the two weeks it should. I can manage money rather well but still we don't have the sufficient amount of food or clothes to keep us warm....I would appreciate it very much if you would give this letter some consideration and give me an answer. I realize that you are a very busy person and have many problems but please give this problem a little thought also.

I will close thanking you in advance.

Sincerely and hopefully yours

Mrs. Henry Weddington

Document Set Twenty-One
Peace and War

American foreign policy in the 1920s and 1930s was reactive in its approach to dealing with the world. The nation was disillusioned with the experience of the first World War and the Treaty of Versailles. Americans had a bunker mentality about world events and believed that the Atlantic Ocean was their Maginot line of defense.

In the 1930s the isolationists in Congress were able to control foreign policy with the enactment of Neutrality Laws that were intended to keep the United States out of war. While the executive branch, under the leadership of F.D.R., was more international in its approach, Roosevelt was unable to direct the course of American foreign policy.

Once war broke out in 1939, Roosevelt was able to gain some control over foreign affairs and, for the next three years, the United States would operate under the "Technicality of Neutrality." By January 1941 only England and Russia remained as bastions against the aggressions of Germany and Italy. Roosevelt's Four Freedoms, (Document A), warned the nation in January of 1941 of the threat to its security from the actions of the Axis powers. Students can compare the Four Freedoms speech to Wilson's Fourteen points. What similarities and differences are there in the two documents? Was Roosevelt influenced by Wilson's idealism of the First World War? What did Roosevelt mean in his statement, "...our domestic problems are now a part of great emergency?" What long-term objective did Roosevelt have in giving this speech?

Even before the United States entered the war, Roosevelt was warned of the potential threat of the German war machine. In Document B, "A Letter to President Roosevelt," Albert Einstein details how science was on the threshold of creating a weapon of destruction beyond human imagination. Students should analyze the letter for its underlying message. What does Einstein want Roosevelt to do? What actions did Roosevelt take as a result of the pressure of Einstein and other scientists? What would be the consequence of these actions for the United States and the rest of the world? It is interesting to note that Einstein would later regret his lobbying efforts.

The Second World War brought dramatic changes to American society. A critical shortage in the labor supply for war production allowed American women to enter the workforce in unprecedented numbers. By the end of the war nineteen million women had gone to work. The war had offered them the opportunity to enter jobs which had been traditionally closed to them. Document C, "A Woman Remembers the War," narrates the experience of one young woman in the war plants of California. This "Rosie the Riveter" found it the best of times and the worst of times. Like others of her gender, it liberated her economically but she continued to find herself discriminated against by her employers and the unions. How was she treated in the war plants? Why did she have a difficult time with the union? Would the war change her economic and social status in American society? Students should take particular note of the last paragraph and her analysis of why the war was important to her.

No group in American society suffered more from World War Two than Japanese-Americans. Over 110,000 Japanese Americans were interned in "relocation centers" in the American west. Document D, "Memories of the Internment Camp," describes life in one of these camps. As Ben Yorita explains, upon being ordered to evacuate his family was notified they, "could take only what we could carry...." The conditions of the camps were horrifying. Class discussion might center on comparing the policies of the United States and Germany during the war. Was the U. S. as racist as Germany in its actions? Why were only Japanese Americans interned? Was there a better solution to the problem?

Questions for Document Set Twenty-One

1. In the "Four Freedoms," why did Roosevelt believe it was important to integrate national and world needs? What were Roosevelt's long-term objectives?

2. What were the consequences of Einstein and other scientists lobbying President Roosevelt?

3. Did American women benefit from the Second World War? Were women expected to maintain their traditional roles and support the war effort?

4. Were there other alternatives to the internment policies of the United States government?

5. Why do we sacrifice our civil liberties during war time?

Document A
The Four Freedoms

Armed defense of democratic existence is now being gallantly waged in four continents. If that defense fails, all the population and all the resources of Europe, Asia, Africa and Australasia will be dominated by the conquerors. The total of those populations and their resources...greatly exceeds the sum total of the population and the resources of the whole of the Western Hemisphere—many times over.

In times like these it is immature—and incidentally untrue—for anybody to brag that an unprepared America, single-handed, and with one hand tied behind its back, can hold off the whole world.

No realistic American can expect from a dictator's peace international generosity, or return of true independence, or world disarmament, or freedom of expression, or freedom of religion—or even good business....

The need of the moment is that our actions and our policy should be devoted primarily—almost exclusively—to meeting this foreign peril. For all our domestic problems are now a part of the great emergency.

Just as our national policy in internal affairs has been based upon a decent respect for the rights and the dignity of all our fellowmen within our gates, so our national policy in foreign affairs has been based on a decent respect for the rights and dignity of all nations, large and small. And the justice of morality must and will win in the end.

Our national policy is this:

First, by an impressive expression of the public will and without regard to partisanship, we are committed to all-inclusive national defense.

Second, by an impressive expression of the public will and without regard to partisanship, we are committed to full support of all those resolute peoples, everywhere, who are resisting aggression and are thereby keeping war away from our hemisphere. By this support, we express our determination that the democratic cause shall prevail, and we strengthen the defense and security of our own nation.

Third, by an impressive expression of the public will and without regard to partisanship, we are committed to the proposition that principles of morality and considerations for our own security will never permit us to acquiesce in a peace dictated by aggressors and sponsored by appeasers. We know that enduring peace cannot be bought at the cost of other people's freedom....

I also ask this Congress for authority and for funds sufficient to manufacture additional munitions and war supplies of many kinds, to be turned over to those nations which are now in actual war with aggressor nations.

Our most useful and immediate role is to act as an arsenal for them as well as for ourselves. They do not need man power. They do need billions of dollars' worth of the weapons of defense....

Let us say to the democracies, "We Americans are vitally concerned in your defense of freedom. We are putting forth our energies, our resources, and our organizing powers to give you the strength to regain and maintain a free world. We shall send you, in ever-increasing numbers, ships, planes, tanks, guns. This is our purpose and our pledge." ....

There is nothing mysterious about the foundations of a healthy and strong democracy. The basic things expected by our people of their political and economic systems are simple.

They are:

Equality of opportunity for youth and for others.
Jobs for those who can work.
Security for those who need it.
The ending of special privilege for the few.
The preservation of civil liberties for all.
The enjoyment of the fruits of scientific progress in a wider and constantly rising standard of living.

These are the simple and basic things that must never be lost sight of in the turmoil and unbelievable complexity of our modern world. The inner and abiding strength of our economic and political systems is dependent upon the degree to which they fulfill these expectations....

In the future days, which we seek to make secure, we look forward to a world founded upon four essential human freedoms.

The first is freedom of speech and expression everywhere in the world.

The second is freedom of every person to worship God in his own way everywhere in the world.

The third is freedom from want, which, translated into world terms, means economic understandings which will secure to every nation a healthy peacetime life for its inhabitants everywhere in the world.

The fourth is freedom from fear—which, translated into world terms, means a world-wide reduction of armaments to such a point and in such a thorough fashion that no nation will be in a position to commit an act of physical aggression against any neighbor—anywhere in the world.

That is no vision of a distant millennium. It is a definite basis for a kind of world attainable in our own time and generation. That kind of world is the very antithesis of the so-called new order of tyranny which the dictators seek to create with the crash of a bomb.

To that new order we oppose the greater conception—the moral order. A good society is able to face schemes of world domination and foreign revolutions alike without fear.

Since the beginning of our American history we have been engaged in change—in a perpetual peaceful revolution—a revolution which goes on steadily, quietly adjusting itself to changing conditions—without the concentration camp or the quicklime in the ditch. The world order which we seek is the cooperation of free countries, working together in a friendly, civilized society.

Document B
A Letter to President Roosevelt

Albert Einstein
Old Grove Rd.
Nassau Point
Peconic, Long Island

August 2nd, 1939
F. D. Roosevelt,
President of the United States,
White House
Washington, D. C.

Sir:

Some recent work by E. Fermi and L. Szilard, which has been communicated to me in manuscript, leads me to expect that the element uranium may be turned into a new and important source of energy in the immediate future. Certain aspects of the situation which has arisen seem to call for watchfulness and, if necessary, quick action on the part of the Administration. I believe therefore that it is my duty to bring to your attention the following facts and recommendations:

In the course of the last four months it has been made probable—through the work of Joliot in France as well as Fermi and Szilard in America—that it may become possible to set up a nuclear chain reaction in a large mass of uranium, by which vast amount of power and large quantities of new radium-like elements would be generated. Now it appears almost certain that this could be achieved in the immediate future.

This new phenomenon would also lead to the construction of bombs, and it is conceivable—though much less certain—that extremely powerful bombs of a new type may thus be constructed. A single bomb of this type, carried by boat and exploded in a port, might very well destroy the whole port together with some of the surrounding territory. However, such bombs might very well prove to be too heavy for transportation by air.

The United States has only very poor ores of uranium in moderate quantities. There is some good ore in Canada and the former Czechoslovakia, while the most important source of uranium is Belgian Congo.

In view of this situation you may think it desirable to have some permanent contact maintained between the Administration and the group of physicists working on chain reactions in America. One possible way of achieving this might be for you to entrust with this task a person who has your confidence and who could perhaps serve in an inofficial capacity. His task might comprise the following:

a) to approach Government Departments, keep them informed of the further development, and put forward recommendations for Government action, giving particular attention to the problem of securing a supply of uranium ore for the United States:

b) to speed up the experimental work, which is at present being carried on within the limits of the budgets of University laboratories, by providing funds, if such funds be required, through his contacts with private persons who are willing to make contributions for this cause, and perhaps also by obtaining the co-operation of industrial laboratories which have the necessary equipment.

I understand that Germany has actually stopped the sale of uranium from the Czechoslovakian mines which she has taken over. That she should have taken such early action might perhaps be understood on the ground that the son of the German Under-Secretary of State, von Weizsacker, is attached to the Kaiser-Wilhelm-Institut in Berlin where some of the American work on uranium is now being repeated.

Yours very truly,
[signed] Albert Einstein

Document C
A Woman Remembers the War

When the war started I was twenty-six, unmarried, and working as a cosmetics clerk in a drugstore in Los Angeles. I was running the whole department, handling the inventory and all that. It seemed asinine, though, to be selling lipstick when the country was at war. I felt that I was capable of doing something more than that toward the war effort.

There was also a big difference between my salary and those in defense work. I was making something like twenty-two, twenty-four dollars a week in the drugstore. You could earn a much greater amount of money for your labor in defense plants. Also it interested me. There was a certain curiosity about meeting that kind of challenge, and here was an opportunity to do that, for there were more and more openings for women.

So I went to two or three plants and took their tests. And they all told me I had absolutely no mechanical ability. I said, "I don't believe that." So I went to another plant, A.D.E.I. I was interviewed and got the job. This particular plant made the hydraulic-valve system for the B-17. And where did they put women? In the burr room. You sat at a workbench, which was essentially like a picnic table, with a bunch of other women, and you worked grinding and sanding machine parts to make them smooth. That's what you did all day long. It was very mechanical and it was very boring. There were about thirty women in the burr room, and it was like being in a beauty shop every day. I couldn't stand the inane talk. So when they asked me if I would like to work someplace else in the shop, I said I very much would.

They started training me. I went to a blueprint class and learned how to use a micrometer and how to draw tools out of the tool crib and everything else. Then one day they said, "Okay, how would you like to go into the machine shop?"

I said, "Terrific."

And they said, "Now, Adele, it's going to be a real challenge, because you'll be the only woman in the machine shop." I thought to myself, well, that's going to be fun, all those guys and Adele in the machine shop. So the foreman took me over there. It was a big room, with a high ceiling and fluorescent lights, and it was very noisy. I walked in there, in my overalls, and suddenly all the machines stopped and every guy in the shop just turned around and looked at me. It took, I think, two weeks before anyone even talked to me. The discrimination was indescribable. They wanted to kill me.

My attitude was, "Okay, you bastards, I'm going to prove to you I can do anything you can do, and maybe better than some of you." And that's exactly the way it turned out. I used to do the rework on the pieces that the guy on the shift before me had screwed up. I finally got assigned to nothing but rework.

Later they taught me to run an automatic screwing machine. It's a big mother, and it took a lot of strength just to throw that thing into gear. They probably thought I wasn't going to be able to do it. But I was determined to succeed. As a matter of fact, I developed the most fantastic biceps from throwing that machine into gear. Even today I still have a little of that muscle left.

Anyway, eventually some of the men became very friendly, particularly the older ones, the ones in their late forties or fifties. They were journeymen tool and die makers and were so skilled that they could work anywhere at very high salaries. They were sort of fatherly, protective. They weren't threatened by me. The younger men, I think, were.

Our plant was an open shop, and the International Association of Machinists was trying to unionize the workers. I joined them and worked to try to get the union in the plant. I proselytized for the union during lunch hour, and

I had a big altercation with the management over that. The employers and my lead man and foreman called me into the office and said, "We have a right to fire you."

I said, "on what basis? I work as well or better than anybody else in the shop except the journeymen."

They said, "No, not because of that. Because you're talking for the union on company property. You're not allowed to do that."

I said, "Well, that's just too bad, because I can't get off the grounds here. You won't allow us to leave the grounds during lunch hour. And you don't pay me for my lunch hour, so that time doesn't belong to you, so you can't tell me what to do." And they backed down.

I had one experience at the plant that really made me work for the union. One day while I was burring I had an accident and ripped some cartilage out of my hand. It wasn't serious, but it looked kind of messy. They had to take me over to the industrial hospital to get my hand sutured. I came back and couldn't work for a day or two because my hand was all bandaged. It wasn't serious, but it was awkward. When I got my paycheck, I saw that they had docked me for time that I was in the industrial hospital. When I saw that I was really mad.

It's ironic that when the union finally got into the plant, they had me transferred out. They were anxious to get rid of me because after we got them in I went to a few meetings and complained about it being a Jim Crow union. So they arranged for me to have a higher rating instead of a worker's rating. This allowed me to make twenty-five cents an hour more, and I got transferred to another plant. By this time I was married. When I became pregnant I worked for about three months more, then I quit.

For me defense work was the beginning of my emancipation as a woman. For the first time in my life I found out that I could do something with my hands besides bake a pie. I found out that I had manual dexterity and the mentality to read blueprints and gauges, and to be inquisitive enough about things to develop skills other than the conventional roles that women had at that time. I had the consciousness-raising experience of being the only woman in this machine shop and having the mantle of challenge laid down by the men, which stimulated my competitiveness and forced me to prove myself. This, plus working in the union, gave me a lot of self-confidence.

Document D
Memories of the Internment Camp

BEN YORITA

"Students weren't as aware of national politics then as they are now, and Japanese-Americans were actually apolitical then. Our parents couldn't vote, so we simply weren't interested in politics because there was nothing we could do about it if we were.

"There were two reasons we were living in the ghettos: Birds of a feather flock together and we had all the traditional aspects of Japanese life—Japanese restaurants, baths, and so forth; and discrimination forced us together. The dominant society prevented us from going elsewhere."

"Right after Pearl Harbor we had no idea what was going to happen, but toward the end of December we started hearing rumors and talk of the evacuation started. We could tell from what we read in the newspapers and the propaganda they were printing—guys like Henry McLemore, who said he hated all Japs and that we should be rounded up, gave us the idea of how strong feelings were against us. So we were expecting something and the evacuation was no great surprise.

...Once the evacuation was decided, we were told we had about a month to get rid of our property or do whatever we wanted to do with it. That was a rough time for my brother, who was running a print shop my parents owned. We were still in debt on it and we didn't know what to do with all the equipment.....We sold the equipment through newspaper classified ads: 'Evacuating: Household goods for sale.' Second-hand dealers and everybody else came in and bought our refrigerator, the piano, and I had a whole bunch of books I sold for $5, which was one of my personal losses. We had to sell our car, and the whole thing was very sad. By the way it was the first time we had ever had a refrigerator and it had to be sold after only a few months.

"We could take only what we could carry, and most of us were carrying two suitcases or duffel bags. The rest of our stuff that we couldn't sell was stored in the Buddhist church my mother belonged to. When we came back, thieves had broken in and stolen almost everything of value from the church."

...."They took all of us down to the Puyallup fairgrounds, Camp Harmony, and everything had been thrown together in haste. They had converted some of the display and exhibit areas into rooms and had put up some barracks on the parking lot."....

"They had also built barbed-wire fences around the camp with a tower on each corner with military personnel and machine guns, rifles, and searchlights. It was terrifying because we didn't know what was going to happen to us. We didn't know where we were going and we were just doing what we were told. No questions asked. If you get an order, you go ahead and do it."

..."There was no fraternization, no contact with the military or any Caucasian except when we were processed into the camp."....

"There was no privacy whatsoever in the latrines and showers, and it was humiliating for the women because they were much more modest then than today. It wasn't so bad for the men because they were accustomed to open latrines and showers....

"From Camp Harmony on, the family structure was broken down. Children ran everywhere they wanted to in the camp, and parents lost their authority. We could eat in any mess hall we wanted, and kids began ignoring their parents and wandering wherever they pleased."

"Eventually they boarded us on army trucks and took us to trains to be transported to the camps inland. We had been in Camp Harmony from May until September."......

"When we got to Twin Falls, we were loaded onto trucks again, and we looked around and all we could see was that vast desert with nothing but sagebrush. When the trucks started rolling, it was dusty, and the camp itself wasn't completed yet. The barracks had been built and the kitchen facilities were there, but the laundry room, showers, and latrines were not finished. They had taken a bulldozer in the good old American style and leveled the terrain and then built the camp. When the wind blew, it was dusty and we had to wear face masks to go to the dining hall. When winter came and it rained, the dust turned into gumbo mud. Until the latrines were finished, we had to use outhouses."

"The administrators were civilians and they tried to organize us into a chain of command to make the camp function. Each block of barracks was told to appoint a representative, who were called block managers. Of course we called them the Blockheads."

"When winter came, it was very cold and I began withdrawing my savings to buy clothes because we had none that was suitable for that climate. Montgomery Ward and Sears Roebuck did a landslide business from the camps because we ordered our shoes and warm clothing from them. The people who didn't have savings suffered quite a bit until the camp distributed navy pea coats. Then everybody in camp was wearing oversize pea coats because we were such small people. Other than army blankets, I don't remember any other clothing issues."

"The barracks were just single-wall construction and the only insulation was tar paper nailed on the outside, and they never were improved. The larger rooms had potbellied stoves, and we all slept on army cots. Only the people over sixty years old were able to get metal cots, which had a bit more spring to them than the army cots, which were just stationary hammocks."

"These camps were technically relocation centers and there was no effort to hold us in them, but they didn't try actively to relocate us until much later. On my own initiative I tried to get out as soon as I could, and started writing letters to friends around the country. I found a friend in Salt Lake City who agreed to sponsor me for room and board, and he got his boss to agree to hire me. I got out in May 1943, which was earlier than most. In fact, I was one of the first to leave Minidoka."

..."I got on the bus with my suitcase, all by myself, my first time in the outside world, and paid my fare and began looking for a seat, then this old guy said: 'Hey, Tokyo, sit next to me.'"

"I thought, Oh, my God, Tokyo! I sat next to him and he was a friendly old guy who meant well."

Document Set Twenty-Two
The Cold War at Home and Abroad

The Cold War emerged from the ashes of the Second World War. At the end of the war only two nations had the military and/or economic power to take positions of leadership. For both these nations, the United States and the Soviet Union, the memories of the 30s and the war would color their actions in the post war period. The United States, under the leadership of Harry Truman, remembered the lessons of the 30s and what could happen if aggression went unchecked. Stalin, and leading party officials in the Soviet Union, were determined to insure that their country would never again suffer the horrors of war. Basing their foreign policy on the principles of geopolitics, the Soviets wanted to ring their nation with buffer states to protect themselves. Each of these nations perceived the other as a threat to either world peace or national security. By 1947, with most of eastern Europe under the control of the communists, Truman had come to believe that an "Iron Curtain," had descended on eastern Europe.

The war had left Europe economically devastated and politically unstable. Among the nations which appeared threatened were Turkey and Greece. President Truman was convinced that if the United States did not come to their aid, these countries would fall under the control of the communists. In 1947 he appeared before Congress to outline his plan to save Turkey and Greece. Document A, "The Truman Doctrine," defines how the United States would act if nations were threatened by subversive elements. Students should note the tone of his speech as he divided the world into good and evil. This tone would prevail throughout the Cold War era. What role did Truman define for the United States? Was the doctrine a scare tactic or was there a real threat to world peace? Would Roosevelt have acted differently?

The economic problems of Western Europe worried Secretary of State George Marshall. Like Truman, Marshall feared that economic instability would lead to political turmoil and provide new political opportunities for the Communists. In a speech given at the Harvard commencement exercises of 1947, Marshall presented his plan for European economic recovery. In Document B, "The Marshall Plan," he explains that if the United States does not provide economic aid, Europe would, "face economic, social and political deterioration of a very grave character..." He assures his audience that, "Our policy is not directed against any country or doctrine..." Why did the Soviet Union object to the plan? Would the United States have been willing to assist any European country? Was the cost of the plan, $15 billion, worth the results?

The Cold War dominated American life at home as well as abroad. The tough talk of Truman, and others, had made American suspicious of anyone who could not be defined as "red, white and blue." In political debates of this period, the Republicans were quick to accuse the Democrats of being soft on communism. Many even believed that F.D.R. had given away eastern Europe to the Soviet Union at the Yalta conference. Truman tried to negate this image by ordering an investigation of the loyalty of all federal employees.

In this climate of suspicion and fear the House on Un-American Activities began a series of hearings on the loyalty of Hollywood writers, directors, actors and actresses. Over a four year period, members of this community were asked to testify about the infiltration of communists into the industry. As President of the Screen Actors Guild, Ronald Reagan was called to testify. Document C outlines some of his testimony to the committee. According to Reagan, was there a subversive element in Hollywood and what were its goals and objectives? Students should note his use of the term, "fifth column." Why would he use this type of term? According to Reagan, how were he and his supporters combating these subversive activities?

By 1954 the internal Red Scare appeared over and the nation's attention was directed toward other domestic issues. Racism still prevailed throughout the nation whether in the form of the Jim Crow laws of the South, or the de facto segregation of the North. In a landmark decision that year, *Brown v Board of Education*, the Supreme Court overturned the separate but equal doctrine which had been in place since 1896. Document D gives students an opportunity to read this decision and discuss its effect on the nation. Why did the Court determine that separate but equal would not work? What consequences did they believe resulted from separating children of different races? The court ordered that the decision be enforced with, "all deliberate speed." Did this occur? How long would it be before segregation ended?

Question for Document Set Twenty-Two

1. How did the Truman Doctrine define American foreign policy for the next thirty years?

2. What role should foreign aid play in a nation's foreign policy?

3. Was there a threat to international security at the time that the Marshall Plan was announced?

4. Why was Hollywood a target of the House on Un-American Activities Committee?

5. Should the Supreme Court play an activist role in American society?

Document A
The Truman Doctrine

At the present moment in world history nearly every nation must choose between alternative ways of life. The choice is too often not a free one.

One way of life is based upon the will of the majority, and is distinguished by free institutions, representative government, free elections, guarantees of individual liberty, freedom of speech and religion, and freedom from political oppression.

The second way of life is based upon the will of a minority forcibly imposed upon the majority. It relies upon terror and oppression, a controlled press and radio, fixed elections, and the suppression of personal freedoms.

I believe that it must be the policy of the United States to support free peoples who are resisting attempted subjugation by armed minorities or by outside pressures.

I believe that we must assist free peoples to work out their own destinies in their own way.

I believe that our help should be primarily through economic and financial aid, which is essential to economic stability and orderly political processes.

The world is not static, and the status quo is not sacred. But we cannot allow changes in the status quo in violation of the Charter of the United Nations by such methods as coercion, or by such subterfuges as political infiltration. In helping free and independent nations to maintain their freedom, the United States will be giving effect to the principles of the Charter of the United Nations....

The seeds of totalitarian regimes are nurtured by misery and want. They spread and grow in the evil soil of poverty and strife. They reach their full growth when the hope of a people for a better life has died.

We must keep that hope alive.

The free peoples of the world look to us for support in maintaining their freedoms.

If we falter in our leadership, we may endanger the peace of the world—and we shall surely endanger the welfare of our own Nation.

Document B
The Marshall Plan

The truth of the Matter is that Europe's requirements for the next three or four years of foreign food and other essential products—principally from America—are so much greater than her present ability to pay that she must have substantial additional help or face economic, social, and political deterioration of a very grave character....

Aside from the demoralizing effect on the world at large and the possibilities of disturbances arising as a result of the desperation of the people concerned, the consequences of the economy of the United Sates should be apparent to all. It is logical that the United States should do whatever it is able to do to assist in the return of normal economic health in the world, without which there can be no political stability and no assured peace. Our policy is directed not against any country or doctrine but against hunger, poverty, desperation, and chaos. Its purpose should be the revival of a working economy in the world so as to permit the emergence of political and social conditions in which free institutions can exist.

Such assistance, I am convinced, must not be on a piecemeal basis as various crises develop. Any assistance that this Government may render in the future should provide a cure rather than a mere palliative. Any government that is willing to assist in the task of recovery will find full cooperation, I am sure, on the part of the United States Government. Any government which maneuvers to block the recovery of other countries cannot expect help from us. Furthermore, governments, political parties, or groups which seek to perpetuate human misery in order to profit there from politically or otherwise will encounter the opposition of the United States.

It is already evident that, before the United States Government can proceed much further in its efforts to alleviate the situation and help start the European world on its way to recovery, there must be some agreement among the countries of Europe as to the requirements of the situation and the part those countries themselves will take in order to give proper effect to whatever action might be undertaken by this Government.

It would be neither fitting nor efficacious for this Government to undertake to draw up unilaterally a program designed to place Europe on its feet economically. This is the business of the Europeans. The initiative, I think, must come from Europe. The role of this country should consist of friendly aid in the drafting of a European program and of later support of such a program so far as it may be practical for us to do so. The program should be a joint one, agreed to by a number, if not all, European nations.

Document C
Ronald Reagan Testifies

Ronald Reagan

October 23, 1947

The Committee met at 10:30 a.m., the Honorable J. Parnell Thomas (Chairman) presiding.

The Chairman: The record will show that Mr. McDowell, Mr. Vail, Mr. Nixon, and Mr. Thomas are present. A Subcommittee is sitting.

Staff members present: Mr. Robert E. Stripling, Chief Investigator; Messrs. Louis J. Russell, H. A. Smith, and Robert B. Gatson, Investigators; and Mr. Benjamin Mandel, Director of Research.

Mr. Stripling: When and where were you born, Mr. Reagan?

Mr. Reagan: Tampico, Illinois, February 6, 1911.

Mr. Stripling: What is your present occupation?

Mr. Reagan: Motion-picture actor.

Mr. Stripling: How long have you been engaged in that profession?

Mr. Reagan: Since June 1937, with a brief interlude of three and a half years—that at the time didn't seem very brief.

Mr. Stripling: What period was that?

Mr. Reagan: That was during the late war.

Mr. Stripling: What branch of the service were you in?

Mr. Reagan: Well, sir, I had been for several years in the Reserve as an officer in the United States Calvary, but I was assigned to the Air Corp.

Mr. Stripling: Are you the president of the guild at the present time?

Mr. Reagan: Yes, sir....

Mr. Stripling: As a member of the board of directors, as president of the Screen Actors Guild, and as an active member, have you at any time observed or noted within the organization a clique of either Communists or Fascists who were attempting to exert influence or pressure on the guild?

Mr. Reagan: Well, sir, my testimony must be very similar to that of Mr. [George] Murphy and Mr. [Robert] Montgomery. There has been a small group within the Screen Actors Guild which has consistently opposed the policy of the guild board and officers of the guild, as evidenced by the vote on various issues. That small clique referred to has been suspected of more or less following the tactics that we associated with the Communist Party.

Mr. Stripling: Would you refer to them as a disruptive influence within the guild?

Mr. Reagan: I would say that at times they have attempted to be a disruptive influence.

Mr. Stripling: You have no knowledge yourself as to whether or not any of them are members of the Communist Party?

Mr. Reagan: No, sir, I have no investigative force, or anything, and I do not know.

Mr. Stripling: Has it ever been reported to you that certain members of the guild were Communists?

Mr. Reagan: Yes, sir, I have heard different discussions and some of them tagged as Communists.

Mr. Stripling: Would you say that this clique has attempted to dominate the guild?

Mr. Reagan: Well, sir, by attempting to put over their own particular views on various issues....

Mr. Stripling: Mr. Reagan, there has been testimony to the effect here that numerous Communist-front organizations have been set up in Hollywood. Have you ever been solicited to join any of those organizations or any organization which you consider to be a Communist-front organization?

Mr. Reagan: Well, sir, I have received literature from an organization called the Committee for a Far-Eastern Democratic Policy. I don't know whether it is Communist or not. I only know that I didn't like their views and as a result I didn't want to have anything to do with them....

Mr. Stripling: Would you say from your observation that this is typical of the tactics or strategy of the Communists, to solicit and use the names of prominent people to either raise money or gain support.

Mr. Reagan: I think it is in keeping with their tactics, yes, sir.

Mr. Stripling: Do you think there is anything democratic about those tactics?

Mr. Reagan: I do not, sir.

Mr. Stripling: Mr. Reagan, what is your feeling about what steps should be taken to rid the motion-picture industry of any Communist influences?

Mr. Reagan: Well, sir, ninety-nine percent of us are pretty well aware of what is going on, and I think, within the bounds of our democratic rights and never once stepping over the rights given us by democracy, we have done a pretty good job in our business of keeping those people's activities curtailed. After all, we must recognize them at present as a political party. On that basis we have exposed their lies when we came across them, we have opposed their propaganda, and I can certainly testify that in the case of the Screen Actors Guild we have been eminently successful in preventing them from, with their usual tactics, trying to run a majority of an organization with a well-organized minority. In opposing those people, the best thing to do is make democracy work....

Mr. Reagan: Sir, I detest, I abhor their philosophy, but I detest more than that their tactics, which are those of the fifth column, and are dishonest, but at the same time I never as a citizen want to see our country become urged, by either fear or resentment of this group that we ever compromise with any of our democratic principles through that fear or resentment. I still think that democracy can do it.

Document D
Brown v Board of Education

MR. Chief Justice Warren delivered the opinion of the Court

These cases come to us from the States of Kansas, South Carolina, Virginia, and Delaware. They are premised on different facts and different local conditions, but a common legal question justifies their consideration together in this consolidated opinion.

In each of the cases, minors of the Negro race, through their legal representatives, seek the aid of the courts in obtaining admission to the public schools of their community on a nonsegregated basis. In each instance, they had been denied admission to schools attended by white children under laws requiring or permitting segregation according to race. This segregation was alleged to deprive the plaintiffs of the equal protection of the laws under the Fourteenth Amendment. In each of the cases other than the Delaware case, a three-judge federal district court denied relief to the plaintiffs on the so-called "separate but equal" doctrine announced by this Court in *Plessy v. Ferguson*, 163 U.S. 537. Under that doctrine, equality of treatment is accorded when the races are provided substantially equal facilities, even though these facilities be separate. In the Delaware case, the Supreme Court of Delaware adhered to that doctrine, but ordered that the plaintiffs be admitted to the white schools because of their superiority to the Negro schools.

The plaintiffs contended that segregated public schools are not "equal" and cannot be made "equal," and that hence they are deprived of the equal protection of the laws....

In the first cases in this Court construing the Fourteenth Amendment, decided shortly after its adoption, the Court interpreted it as proscribing all state-imposed discriminations against the Negro race. The doctrine of "separate but equal" did not make its appearance in this Court until 1896 in the case of *Plessy v. Ferguson*, *supra*, involving not education but transportation. American courts have since labored with the doctrine for over half a century. In this Court, there have been six cases involving the "separate but equal" doctrine in the field of public education....In none of these cases was it necessary to examine the doctrine to grant relief to the Negro plaintiff. And in *Sweatt v. Painter*, *supra*, the Court expressly reserved decision on the question of whether *Plessy v. Ferguson* should be held inapplicable to public education.

In the instant cases, that question is directly presented. Here, unlike *Sweatt v. Painter*, there are findings below that the Negro and white schools involved have been equalized, or are being equalized, with respect to buildings, curricula, qualifications and salaries of teachers, and other "tangible" factors. Our decision, therefore, cannot turn on merely a comparison of these tangible factors in the Negro and white schools involved in each of the cases. We must look instead to the effect of segregation itself on public education.

In approaching this problem, we cannot turn the clock back to 1868 when the Amendment was adopted, or even to 1896 when *Plessy v. Ferguson* was written. We must consider public education in the light of its full development and its present place in American life throughout the Nation. Only in this way can it be determined if segregation in public schools deprives these plaintiffs of the equal protection of the laws.

Today, education is perhaps the most important function of state and local governments. Compulsory school attendance laws and the great expenditures for education both demonstrate our recognition of the importance of education to our democratic society. It is required in the performance of our most basic public responsibilities, even service in the armed forces. It is the very foundation of good citizenship. Today it is a principal instrument in awakening the child to cultural values, in preparing him for later professional training, and in helping him to adjust normally to his environment. In these days, it is doubtful that any child may reasonably be expected to succeed in life if he is denied the opportunity of an education. Such an opportunity, where the state has undertaken to provide it, is a right which must be made available to all on equal terms.

WE come then to the question presented: Does segregation of children in public schools solely on the basis of race, even though the physical facilities and other "tangible" factors may be equal, deprive the children of the minority group of equal education opportunities? We believe that it does.

In *Sweatt v. Painter, supra*, in finding that a segregated law school for Negroes could not provide them equal education opportunities, the Court relied in large part on "those qualities which are incapable of objective measurement but which make for greatness in a law school." In *McLaurin v. Oklahoma State Regents, supra*, the Court, in requiring that a Negro admitted to a white graduate school be treated like all other students, again resorted to intangible considerations: "...his ability to study, to engage in discussions and exchange views with other students, and in general, to learn his profession." Such considerations apply with added force to children in grade and high schools. To separate them from others of similar age and qualifications solely because of their race generates a feeling of inferiority as to their status in the community that may affect their hearts and minds in a way unlikely ever to be undone. The effect of this separation on their educational opportunities was well stated by a finding in the Kansas case by a court which nevertheless felt compelled to rule against the Negro plaintiffs:

Segregation of white and colored children in public schools has a detrimental effect upon the colored children. The impact is greater when it has the sanction of the law; for the policy of separating the races is usually interpreted as denoting the inferiority of the negro group. A sense of inferiority affects the motivation of a child to learn. Segregation with the sanction of law, therefore, has a tendency to retard the education and mental development of negro children and to deprive them of some of the benefits they would receive in a racial[ly] integrated school system.

Whatever may have been the extent of psychological knowledge at the time of *Plessy v. Ferguson*, this finding is amply supported by modern authority. Any language in *Plessy v. Ferguson* contrary to this finding is rejected.

We conclude that in the field of public education the doctrine of "separate but equal" has no place. Separate educational facilities are inherently unequal. Therefore, we hold that the plaintiffs and others similarly situated for whom the actions have been brought are, by reason of the segregation complained of, deprived of the equal protection of the laws guaranteed by the Fourteenth Amendment. This disposition makes unnecessary any discussion whether such segregation also violates the Due Process Clause of the Fourteenth Amendment.

Document Set Twenty-Three
Vietnam and the Crises of Authority

Foreign policy dominated the Presidencies from 1960 to 1976. While changes were occurring in domestic life, issues abroad colored the administrations of Kennedy, Johnson, Nixon, and Ford. In the end they caused the downfall of one President (Johnson) and the resignation of another (Nixon). For each of the Presidents no issue was more important than Vietnam. United States actions in Vietnam foreshadowed all the rest of American life during this period.

This was a generation of Presidents who remembered the lessons of World War Two and the early years of the Cold War. American policy in Southeast Asia was centered around the domino theory, a theory whose foundation lay in American fears of unchecked aggression and its consequences. Ironically Vietnam had a greater effect on American domestic life than it did on its other foreign policies.

The decade of the 1960s opened on a note of hope and change. John F. Kennedy's election brought a promise of a new society, of a New Frontier where the country could resolve its problems at home and provide leadership abroad. The dreams of a new "Camelot" began with his inaugural speech (Document A) on January 20th, 1961. With phrases such as, "Ask not what your country can do for you..." Kennedy challenged the American public to rise to new levels of greatness. Students should find the speech interesting and it can give them insight into understanding why Kennedy's greatest legacy was the rhetoric of this speech. They should analyze the foreign policy implications of it. What warnings does he make to foreign powers and promise to allies? Who were the "common enemies" he cites? Why did the speech have a powerful impact on the American public and influence a generation of youth?

Less than a year in office Kennedy experienced his first failure, the Bay of Pigs. Badly planned and a disaster in its implementation, the invasion strengthened the alliance between Cuba and the Soviet Union. This association led to the Cuban Missile Crisis in October, 1962. Given the experience of the Bay of Pigs, it could be argued whether or not Khrushehev under estimated the determination of the United States. Document B is the speech by Ambassador Adali Stevenson at the United Nations. It expressed America's conviction to prohibit the extension of Soviet power in the Western Hemisphere. Students should take note of Stevenson's perception of the world and balance of power. What implicit warning to the Soviets can be found in the speech? Using terms like, "Until hell freezes over..." Why is Stevenson angry at the Soviets?

When did the Vietnam war begin? Students are often perplexed by the war and its origins. It is difficult for them to understand that Vietnam was not a "real war." If there was an official beginning, it started with the passage of the Tonkin Gulf Resolution. (Document C) President Johnson used the resolution to justify continued military build up in the region. It could be argued that the fall of his presidency began with the resolution. Why did he have overwhelming support in the Congress for the resolution? Was the incident enough to justify increased American involvement? Students should note in his speech phrases like, "...support freedom...protect peace in Southeast Asia." What impact would these phrases have on the American public? In his argument, how did Johnson take the war out of the realm of an internal conflict?

When did President Johnson lose public support for the war? Anti war protest began with college students who challenged the morality of the war. It was a war they "Opposed and Despised." Like other students of the time, Bill Clinton had difficulty reconciling his beliefs to the call to military service. Document D is a letter written to the director of the ROTC program at the University of Arkansas. It captures the feelings of the anti war student movement. Like others of this generation, Clinton differentiates between wars that are necessary for national survival (World War II) and Vietnam. Did Clinton provide a cogent argument against the draft? Is it possible to separate wars into good and bad?

Questions for Document Set Twenty-Three

1. In is inaugural speech does John Kennedy carry on the tradition of the Progressive Movement and the New Deal?

2. According to Adali Stevenson, what role does the United States play in world affairs?

3. How does the Tonkin Gulf Resolution lead to the extension of the powers of the Executive branch?

4. What is the relationship between the Resolution and the passage of the War Powers Act.

5. What arguments does Bill Clinton have against the draft?

6. According to the Clinton letter, what alternatives to the war were students taking?

Document A
Inaugural Address

My fellow citizens:

We observe today not a victory of party but a celebration of freedom—symbolizing an end as well as a beginning—signifying renewal as well as change. For I have sworn before you and Almighty God the same solemn oath our forebears prescribed nearly a century and three quarters ago.

The world is very different now. For man holds in his mortal hands the power to abolish all form of human poverty and to abolish all form of human life. And, yet, the same revolutionary beliefs for which our forebears fought are still at issue around the globe—the belief that the rights of man come not from the generosity of the state but from the hand of God.

We dare not forget today that we are the heirs of that first revolution. Let the word go forth from this time and place, to friend and foe alike, that the torch has been passed to a new generation of Americans—born in this century, tempered by war, disciplined by a cold and bitter peace, proud of our ancient heritage—and unwilling to witness or permit the slow undoing of those human rights to which this nation has always been committed, and to which we are committed today.

Let every nation know, whether it wish us well or ill, that we shall pay any price, bear any burden, meet any hardship, support any friend or oppose any foe in order to assure the survival and success of liberty.

This much we pledge—and more.

To those old allies whose cultural and spiritual origins we share, we pledge the loyalty of faithful friends. United, there is little we cannot do in a host of new co-operative ventures. Divided, there is little we can do—for we dare not meet a powerful challenge at odds and split asunder.

To those new states whom we now welcome to the ranks of the free, we pledge our world that one form of colonial control shall not have passed merely to be replaced by a far more iron tyranny. We shall not always expect to find them supporting our every view. But we shall always hope to find them strongly supporting their own freedom—and to remember that, in the past, those who foolishly sought to find power by riding on the tiger's back inevitably ended up inside.

To those peoples in the huts and villages of half the globe struggling to break the bonds of mass misery, we pledge our best efforts to help them help themselves, for whatever period is required—not because the Communists are doing it, not because we seek their votes, but because it is right. If the free society cannot help the many who are poor, it can never save the few who are rich.

To our sister republics south of our border, we offer a special pledge—to convert our good words into good deeds—in a new alliance for progress—to assist free men and free Governments in casting off the chains of poverty. But this peaceful revolution of hope cannot become the prey of hostile powers. Let all our neighbors know that we shall join with them to oppose aggression or subversion anywhere in the Americas. And let every other power know that this Hemisphere intends to remain the master of its own house.

To that world assembly of sovereign states, the United Nations, our last best hope in an age where the instruments of war have far outpaced the instruments of peace, we renew our pledge of support—to prevent its becoming merely a forum for invective—to strengthen its shield of the new and the weak—and to enlarge the area to which its writ may run.

Finally, to those nations who would make themselves our adversary, we offer not a pledge but a request: that both sides begin anew the quest for peace, before the dark powers of destruction unleashed by science engulf all humanity in planned or accidental self-destruction.

We dare not tempt them with weakness. For only when our arms are sufficient beyond doubt can we be certain beyond doubt that they will never be employed.

But neither can two great and powerful groups of nations take comfort from their present course—both sides overburdened by the cost of modern weapons, both rightly alarmed by the steady spread of the deadly atom, yet both racing to alter that uncertain balance of terror that stays the hand of mankind's final war.

So let us begin anew—remembering on both sides that civility is not a sign of weakness and sincerity is always subject to proof. Let us never negotiate out of fear. But let us never fear to negotiate.

Let both sides explore what problems unite us instead of belaboring the problems that divide us.

Let both sides for the first time, formulate serious and precise proposals for the inspection and control of arms—and bring the absolute power to destroy other nations under the absolute control of all nations.

Let both sides join to invoke the wonders of science instead of its terrors. Together let us explore the stars, conquer the deserts, eradicate disease, tap the ocean depths and encourage the arts and commerce.

Let both sides unite to heed in all corners of the earth the command of Isaiah—to "undo the heavy burdens...(and) let the oppressed go free."

And if a beachhead of co-operation can be made in the jungles of suspicion, let both sides join in the next task: creating, not a new balance of power, but a new world of law, where the strong are just and the weak secure and the peace preserved forever.

All this will not be finished in the first 100 days. Nor will it be finished in the first 1,000 days, nor in the life of this Administration, nor even perhaps in our lifetime on this planet. But let us begin.

In your hands, my fellow citizens, more than in mine, will rest the final success or failure of our course. Since this country was founded, each generation has been summoned to give testimony to its national loyalty. The graves of young Americans who answered that call encircle the globe.

Now the trumpet summons us again—not as a call to battle, though embattled we are—but a call to bear the burden of a long twilight struggle, year in and year out, "rejoicing in hope, patient in tribulation"—a struggle against the common enemies of man: tyranny, poverty, disease and war itself.

Can we forge against these enemies a grand and global alliance, north and south, east and west, that can assure a more fruitful life for all mankind? Will you join in that historic effort?

In the long history of the world, only a few generations have been granted the role of defending freedom in its hour of maximum danger. I do not shrink from this responsibility—I welcome it. I do not believe that any of us would exchange places with any other people or any other generation. The energy, the faith and the devotion which we bring to this endeavor will light our country and all who serve it—and the glow from that fire can truly light the world.

And so, my fellow Americans: Ask not what your country will do for you—ask what you can do for your country.

My fellow citizens of the world: Ask not what America will do for you, but what together we can do for the freedom of man.

Finally, whether you are citizens of America or of the world, ask of us the same high standards of strength and sacrifice that we shall ask of you. With a good conscience our only sure reward, with history the final judge of our deeds, let us go forth to lead the land we love, asking His blessing and His help, but knowing that here on earth God's work must truly be our own.

Document B
The Cuban Missile Crisis

I want to say to you, Mr. Zorin, that I do not have your talent for obfuscation, for distortion, for confusing language and for double-talk. And I must confess to you that I am glad that I do not!

But if I understood what you said, it was that my position had changed, that today I was defensive because we did not have the evidence to prove our assertions that your government had installed long-range missiles in Cuba.

Well, let me say something to you, Mr. Ambassador—we do have evidence. We have it, and it is clear and it is incontrovertible. And let me say something else—those weapons must be taken out of Cuba! Next, if I understood you, you said—with a trespass on credibility that excels your best—that our position had changed since I spoke here the other day because of the pressures of world opinion and the majority of the United Nations. Well, let me say to you, sir—you are wrong again. We have had no pressure from anyone whatsoever. We came here today to indicate our willingness to discuss U Thant's proposals, and that is the only change that has taken place.

But let me also say to you, sir, that there has been a change. You—the Soviet Union has sent these weapons to Cuba. You—the Soviet Union has upset the balance of power in the world. You—the Soviet Union has created this new danger, not the United States.

And you ask with a fine show of indignation why the President did not tell Mr. Gromyko on last Thursday about our evidence, at the very time that Mr. Gromyko was blandly denying to the President that the U.S.S.R. was placing such weapons on sites in the new world.

Well, I will tell you why—because we are assembling the evidence, and perhaps it would be instructive to the world to see how far the Soviet official would go in perfidy. Perhaps we wanted to know if this country faced another example of nuclear deceit like that one a year ago when, in stealth, the Soviet Union broke the nuclear test moratorium.

And while we are asking questions, let me ask you why your government your Foreign Minister deliberately, cynically deceived us about the nuclear build-up in Cuba?

And, finally, the other day, Mr. Zorin, I remind you that you did not deny the existence of these weapons. Instead, we heard that they had suddenly become defensive weapons. But today, again, if I heard you correctly, you now say, with another fine flood of rhetorical scorn, they do not exist, or that we haven't proved they exist.

All right, sir, let me ask you one simple question: Do you, Ambassador Zorin, deny that the U.S.S.R. has placed and is placing medium and intermediate-range missiles and sites in Cuba? Yes or no? Don't wait for the translation. Yes or No?

[Ambassador Zorin refused to answer, maintaining that he was "not in an American courtroom."]

You are in the courtroom of world opinion. You have denied they exist, and I want to know if I understood you correctly.

I am prepared to wait for my answer until hell freezes over, if that's your decision. And I am also prepared to present the evidence in this room—now!....[Stevenson then displayed and explained the photographic evidence.]

I have not had a direct answer to my question. The representative of the Soviet Union says that the official answer of the U.S.S.R. was a statement carried by Tass that it does not need to locate missiles in Cuba. I agree—the U.S.S.R. does not need to. But the question is not whether the U.S.S.R. needs missiles in Cuba; the question is: Has the U.S.S.R. missiles in Cuba? And that question remains unanswered. I knew it would remain unanswered.

As to the authenticity of the photographs which Mr. Zorin has spoken about with such scorn, I wonder if the Soviet Union would ask its Cuban colleague to permit a United Nations team to go to these sites. If so, Mr. Zorin, I can assure you that we can direct them to the proper places very quickly.

And now I hope that we can get down to business, that we can stop this sparring. We know the facts and so do you, sir, and we are ready to talk about them. Our job here is not to score debating points. Our job, Mr. Zorin, is to save the peace. And if you are ready to try, we are.

Document C
The Tonkin Gulf Incident
1964

1. President Johnson's Message to Congress
August 5, 1964
(Department of State Bulletin, August 24, 1964)

Last night I announced to the American people that North Vietnamese regime had conducted further deliberate attacks against US. naval vessels operating in international waters, and that I had therefore directed air action against gunboats and supporting facilities used in these hostile operations. This air action has now been carried out with substantial damage to the boats and facilities. Two US. aircraft were lost in the action.

After consultation with the leaders of both parties in the Congress, I further announced a decision to ask the Congress for a resolution expressing the unity and determination of the United States in supporting freedom and in protecting peace in southeast Asia.

These latest actions of the North Vietnamese regime have given a new and grave turn to the already serious situation in southeast Asia. Our commitments in that area are well known to the Congress. They were first made in 1954 by President Eisenhower. They were further defined in the Southeast Asia Collective Defense Treaty approved by the Senate in February 1955.

This treaty with its accompanying protocol obligates the United States and other members to act in accordance with their constitutional processes to meet Communist aggression against any of the parties or protocol states.

Our policy in southeast Asia has been consistent and unchanged since 1954. I summarized it on June 2 in our simple propositions:

1. America keeps her word. Here as elsewhere, we must and shall honor our commitments.

2. The issue is the future of southeast Asia as a whole. A threat to any nation in that region is a threat to all, and a threat to us.

3. Our purpose is peace. We have no military, political, or territorial ambitions in the area.

4. This is not just a jungle war, but a struggle for freedom on every front of human activity. Our military and economic assistance to South Vietnam and Laos in particular has the purpose of helping these countries to repel aggression and strengthen their independence.

The threat to the free nations of southeast Asia has long been clear. The North Vietnamese regime has constantly sought to take over South Vietnam and Laos. This Communist regime has violated the Geneva accords for Vietnam. It has systematically conducted a campaign of subversion, which included the direction, training, and supply of personnel and arms for the conduct of guerrilla warfare in South Vietnamese territory. In Laos, the North Vietnamese regime has maintained military forces, used Laotian territory for infiltration into South Vietnam, and most recently carried out combat operations—all in direct violation of the Geneva agreements of 1962.

In recent months, the actions of the North Vietnamese regime have become steadily more threatening....

As President of the United States I have concluded that I should now ask the Congress, on its part, to join in affirming the national determination that all such attacks will be met, and that the United States will continue in its basic policy of assisting the free nations of the area to defend their freedom.

As I have repeatedly made clear, the United States intends no rashness, and seeks no wider war. We must make it clear to all that the United States is united in its determination to bring about the end of Communist subversion and aggression in the area. We seek the full and effective restoration of the international agreements signed in Geneva in 1954, with respect to South Vietnam, and again in Geneva in 1962, with respect to Laos....

2. Joint Resolution of Congress
H. J. Res. 1145
August 7, 1964
(Department of State Bulletin, August 24, 1964)

To promote the maintenance of international peace and security in southeast Asia.

Whereas naval units of the Communist regime in Vietnam, in violation of the principles of the Charter of the United Nations and of international law, have deliberately and repeatedly attacked United States naval vessels lawfully present in international waters, and have thereby created a serious threat to international peace; and

Whereas these attacks are part of a deliberate and systematic campaign of aggression that the Communist regime in North Vietnam has been waging against its neighbors and the nations joined with them in the collective defense of their freedom; and

Whereas the United States is assisting the peoples of southeast Asia to protect their freedom and has no territorial, military or political ambitions in that area, but desires only that these peoples should be left in peace to work out their own destinies in their own way; Now, therefore, be it

Resolved by the Senate and House of Representatives of the United States of America in Congress assembled, that the Congress approves and supports the determination of the President, as Commander in Chief, to take all necessary measures to repel any armed attack against the forces of the United States and to prevent further aggression.

SEC. 2. The United States regards as vital to its national interest and to world peace the maintenance of international peace and security in southeast Asia. Consonant with the Constitution of the Untied States and the Charter of the United Nations and in accordance with its obligations under the Southeast Asia Collective Defense Treaty, the Untied States is, therefore, prepared, as the President determines, to take all necessary steps, including the use of armed force, to assist any member or protocol state of the Southeast Asia Collective Defense Treaty requesting assistance in defense of its freedom.

SEC. 3. This resolution shall expire when the President shall determine that the peace and security of the area is reasonably assured by international conditions created by action of the United Nations or otherwise, except that it may be terminated earlier by concurrent resolution of the Congress.

Document D
A War I Opposed and Despised

Bill Clinton

I am sorry to be so long in writing. I know I promised to let you hear from me at least once a month, and from now on you will, but I have had to have some time to think about this first letter. Almost daily since my return to England I have thought about writing about what I want to and ought to say.

First, I want to thank you, not just for saving me from the draft, but for being so kind and decent to me last summer, when I was as low as I have ever been. One thing which made the bond we struck in good faith somewhat palatable to me was my high regard for you personally. In retrospect, it seems that the admiration might not have been mutual had you known a little more about me, about my political beliefs and activities. At least you might have thought me more fit for the draft than for R.O.T.C.

Let me try to explain. As you know, I worked for two years in a very minor position on the Senate Foreign Relations Committee. I did it for the experience and the salary but also for the opportunity, however small, of working every day against a war I opposed and despised with a depth of feeling I had reserved solely for racism in America before Vietnam. I did not take the matter lightly but studied it carefully, and there was a time when not many people had more information about Vietnam at hand than I did.

I have written and spoken and marched against the war. One of the national organizers of the Vietnam Moratorium is a close friend of mine. After I left Arkansas last summer, I went to Washington to work in the national headquarters of the Moratorium, then to England to organize the Americans here for demonstrations Oct. 15 and Nov. 16.

Interlocked with the war is the draft issue, which I did not begin to consider separately until early 1968. For a law seminar at Georgetown I wrote a paper on the legal arguments for and against allowing, within the Selective Service System, the classification of selective conscientious objection, for those opposed to participation in a particular war, not simply to "participation in war in any form."

From my work I came to believe that the draft system itself is illegitimate. No government really rooted in limited, parliamentary democracy should have the power to make its citizens fight and kill and die in a war they may oppose, a war which even possibly may be wrong, a war which, in any case, does not involve immediately the peace and freedom of the nation.

The draft was justified in World War II because the life of the people collectively was at stake. Individuals had to fight, if the nation was to survive, for the lives of their countrymen and their way of life. Vietnam is no such case. Nor was Korea an example, where, in my opinion, certain military action was justified but the draft was not, for the reasons stated above.

Because of my opposition to the draft and the war, I am in great sympathy with those who are not willing to fight, kill, and maybe die for their country (i.e. the particular policy of a particular government) right or wrong. Two of my friends at Oxford are conscientious objectors. I wrote a letter of recommendation for one of them to his Mississippi draft board, a letter which I am more proud of than anything else I wrote at Oxford last year. One of my roommates is a draft resister who is under possible indictment and may never be able to go home again. He is one of the bravest, best men I know. His country needs men like him more than they know. That he is considered a criminal is an obscenity.

The decision not to be a resister and the related subsequent decisions were the most difficult of my life. I decided to accept the draft in spite of my beliefs for one reason: to maintain my political viability within the system. For years I have worked to prepare myself for a political life characterized by both practical political ability and concern for rapid social progress. It is a life I still feel compelled to try to lead. I do not think our system of government is by definition corrupt, however dangerous and inadequate it has been in recent years. (The society may be corrupt, but that is not the same thing, and it is true we are all finished anyway.)

When the draft came, despite political convictions, I was having a hard time facing the prospect of fighting a war I had been fighting against, and that is why I contacted you. R.O.T.C. was the one way left in which I could possibly, but not positively, avoid both Vietnam and resistance. Going on with my education, even coming back to England, played no part in my decision to join R.O.T.C. I am back here, and would have been at Arkansas Law School because there is nothing else I can do. In fact, I would like to have been able to take a year out perhaps to teach in a small college or work on some community action project and in the process to decide whether to attend law school or graduate school and how to begin putting what I have learned to use.

But the particulars of my personal life are not nearly as important to me as the principles involved. After I signed the R.O.T.C. letter of intent I began to wonder whether the compromise I had made with myself was not more objectionable than the draft would have been, because I had no interest in the R.O.T.C. program in itself and all I seemed to have done was to protect myself from physical harm. Also, I began to think I had deceived you, not by lies—there were none—but by failing to tell you all the things I'm writing now. I doubt that I had the mental coherence to articulate them then.

At that time, after we had made our agreement and you had sent my I-D deferment to my draft board, the anguish and loss of my self-regard and self-confidence really set in. I hardly slept for weeks and kept going by eating compulsively and reading until exhaustion brought sleep. Finally, on Sept. 12 I stayed up all night writing a letter to the chairman of my draft board, saying basically what is in the preceding paragraph, thanking him for trying to help in a case where he really couldn't, and stating that I couldn't do the R.O.T.C. after all and would he please draft me as soon as possible.

I never mailed the letter, but I did carry it on me every day until I got on the plane to return to England. I didn't mail the letter because I didn't see, in the end, how my going in the army and maybe going to Vietnam would achieve anything except a feeling that I had punished myself and gotten what I deserved. So I came back to England to try to make something of this second year of my Rhodes scholarship.

And that is where I am now, writing to you because you have been good to me and have a right to know what I think and feel. I am writing too in the hope that my telling this one story will help you to understand more clearly how so many fine people have come to find themselves still loving their country but loathing the military, to which you and other good men have devoted years, lifetimes, of the best service you could give. To many of us, it is no longer clear what is clear, the conclusion is likely to be illegal.

Forgive the length of this letter. There was much to say. There is still a lot to be said, but it can wait. Please say hello to Col. Jones for me.

Merry Christmas.

Sincerely,

Bill Clinton

Document Set Twenty-Four
Liberty for All

Dissenting voices were heard throughout the 1960s as demands were placed upon American society to widen the political, economic and social enfranchisement. African Americans, Hispanics, Women and Native Americans believed the time had come for them to share in the "American Pie." Under the leadership of Lyndon Johnson, the government initiated legislation to make the nation a "Great Society," for all Americans.

Lyndon Johnson understood the power of government. Nurtured on the spirit of the New Deal, he believed in twentieth century liberalism and the concept of the General Welfare State. Upon taking office in 1963, he embarked on a program to provide a minimum standard of life for all Americans. Known as the Great Society, this legislative package became the most massive reform movement in the history of the country. Its effects would touch more groups than any other reform movement and it changed the face of American society.

Documents A and B are two of the most important laws passed during this period. The Economic Opportunity Act was a 947.5 million appropriation to wage war on poverty. It included establishing a Job Corps, Vista and new educational opportunities. In Document A, Johnson outlines the importance of this law. According to him, who would benefit from the legislation? Why did the country have a responsibility to enact it?

The Civil Rights Act of 1964 (Document B) was a capstone of the Great Society program. It used the power of the federal government to prohibit discrimination in housing, employment and voting. While it was intended primarily for the African American community, it affected all disadvantaged groups in American society. Students should consider the relationship of the act to the activism of the civil rights movement during this period. Would the act have passed without events like the March on Washington? Can the government end discrimination through legislation? Did the law achieve its objectives?

The last three documents provide students with the opportunity to hear the voices of the underside of American society. It was these voices who demanded change and caused a social and economic revolution in the nation. Martin Luther King symbolized the essence of the early Civil Rights movement. From 1956 until 1968, he led the African American community on a quest for equality and justice. Believing in the philosophy of non-violent direct action, King made his dream the American dream. Many consider the March on Washington, in 1963, to be the pinnacle of his career. Standing before 100,000 Americans, King talked of his dream for America. The eloquence of this speech (Document C) reminded Americans of the roots of the republic. Undaunted by the frustrations of inequality, he spoke of the dream that, "...one day this nation will rise up and live out the true meaning...that all men are created equal." What was King's dream? Why would some African Americans later criticize his approach to the problems they faced? Who was King speaking to in the speech? How much impact did he have on changing the conditions within the nation?

Though much of the Civil Rights legislation had been written for the Black Civil Rights movement, other groups were able to utilize it to improve their conditions. For the first time since the passage of the 19th Amendment, women found their voice in the 1960s. Touching upon many of the same concerns as other disenfranchised groups, their revolution would mean a shift in the value system of the society as male-female roles were re-defined. Like other groups, there was not one voice that spoke for women in the 60s and 70s. However, as the largest organization, the National Organization of Women focused on correcting the legal, economic and political inequities facing women. Organized in 1966, it used the Equal Employment Act, and the Civil rights Act of 1964, to initiate changes for women. Document D is the statement of purpose that was drawn up when NOW was organized in 1966. What was the status of women in 1966? What problems did they face? According to NOW, are women second class citizens?

Among the silent voices who were suddenly heard in the 1960s was the Hispanic community. Concentrated primarily in the Southwest, they had suffered centuries of economic, social, and political discrimination.

However, this began to change as they realized the power they could have by organizing their community. La Raza Unida became a strong political force in the Southwest. Other groups were able to pressure for bi-lingual education in the public schools. Perhaps no one better symbolized this new militancy than Cesar Chavez. He took on what appeared to be an impossible task, the unionization of migrant workers. Throughout this period, he led strikes and boycotts to improve their working conditions. Document E, "Harvest of Discontent," describes the conditions of the workers and how Chavez fought to rectify the situation. Were the conditions of the farm workers worse than other labor groups? What alternatives did Chavez and the union have to achieve their goals? Why was Chavez able to win public support for his cause?

Questions for Document Set Twenty-Four

1. Was the Great Society the culmination of twentieth century American liberalism?

2. What actions could the federal government take if the Civil Rights Act of 1964 was disobeyed?

3. Did the laws achieve their objectives?

4. Was Martin Luther King a realist? Were his dreams achieved?

5. Why did militant organizations oppose King's philosophy?

6. Was NOW a militant organization?

7. What long-term goals did Cesar Chavez have for his organization?

Document A
The War on Poverty

I have called for a national war on poverty. Our objective: total victory.

There are millions of Americans—one fifth of our people—who have not shared in the abundance which has been granted to most of us, and on whom the gates of opportunity have been closed.

What does this poverty mean to those who endure it?

It means a daily struggle to secure the necessities for even a meager existence. It means that the abundance, the comforts, the opportunities they see all around them are beyond their grasp.

Worst of all, it means hopelessness for the young.

The young man or woman who grows up without a decent education, in a broken home, in a hostile and squalid environment, in ill health or in the face of racial injustice—that young man or woman is often trapped in a life of poverty.

He does not have the skills demanded by a complex society. He does not know how to acquire those skills. He faces a mounting sense of despair which drains initiative and ambition and energy....

The war on poverty is not a struggle simply to support people, to make them dependent on the generosity of others.

It is a struggle to give people a chance.

It is an effort to allow them to develop and use their capacities, as we have been allowed to develop and use ours, so that they can share, as others share, in the promise of this nation.

We do this, first of all, because it is right that we should.

For the establishment of public education and land grant colleges through agricultural extension and encouragement to industry, we have pursued the goal of a nation with full and increasing opportunities for all its citizens.

The war on poverty is a further step in that pursuit.

We do it also because helping some will increase the prosperity of all.

Our fight against poverty will be an investment in the most valuable of our resources—the skills and strength of our people.

And in the future, as in the past, this investment will return its cost many fold to our entire economy.

If we can raise the annual earnings of 10 million among the poor by only $1,000 we will have added 14 billion dollars a year to our national output. In addition we can make important reductions in public assistance payments which now cost us 4 billion dollars a year, and in the large costs of fighting crime and delinquency, disease and hunger.

This is only part of the story.

Our history has proved that each time we broaden the base of abundance, giving more people the chance to produce and consume, we create new industry, higher production, increased earnings and better income for all.

Giving new opportunity to those who have little will enrich the lives of all the rest.

Because it is right, because it is wise, and because, for the first time in our history, it is possible to conquer poverty submit, for the consideration of the Congress and the country, the Economic Opportunity Act of 1964.

The Act does not merely expand old programs or improve what is already being done.

It charts a new course.

It strikes at the causes, not just the consequences of poverty.

It can be a milestone in our one-hundred-eighty year search for a better life for our people.

Document B
Civil Rights Act of 1964
July 2, 1964

Title I

Voting Rights

Sec. 101 (2). No person acting under color of law shall—

(A) in determining whether any individual is qualified under State law or laws to vote in any Federal election, apply any standard, practice, or procedure different form the standards, practices, or procedures applied under such law or laws to other individuals within the same county, parish, or similar political subdivision who have been found by State officials to be qualified to vote;....

(C) employ any literacy test as a qualification for voting in any Federal election unless (i) such test is administered to each individual wholly in writing; and (ii) a certified copy of the test and of the answers given by the individual is furnished to him within twenty-five days of the submission of his request made within the period of time during which records and papers are required to be retained and preserved pursuant to title III of the civil Rights Act of 1960....

TITLE II
Injunctive Relief Against Discrimination in Places of Public Accommodation

Sec. 201. (a) All persons shall be entitled to the full and equal enjoyment of the goods, services, facilities, privileges, advantages, and accommodations of any place of public accommodation, as defined in this section, without discrimination or segregation on the ground of race, color, religion, or national origin.

(b) Each of the following establishments which serves the public is a place of public accommodation within the meaning of this title if its operations affect commerce, or if discrimination or segregation by it is supported by State action:

(1) any inn, motel, or other establishment which provides lodging to transient guests, other than an establishment located within a building which co... is not more than five rooms for rent or hire and which is actually occupied by the proprietor of such establishment as his residence;

(2) any restaurant, cafeteria, lunch room, lunch counter, soda fountain, or other activity principally engaged in selling food for consumption on the premises....

(3) any motion picture house, theater, concert hall, sports arena, stadium or other place of exhibition or entertainment....

(d) Discrimination or segregation by an establishment is supported by State action within the meaning of this title if such discrimination or segregation (1) is carried on under color of any law, statute, ordinance, or regulation; or (2) is carried on under color of any custom or usage required or enforced by officials of the State or political subdivision thereof....

SEC. 202. All persons shall be entitled to be free, at any establishment or place, from discrimination or segregation of any kind on the ground of race, color, religion, or national origin, if such discrimination or segregation is or purports to be required by any law, statute, ordinance, regulation, rule, or order of a State or any agency or political subdivision thereof....

SEC. 206 (a) Whenever the Attorney General has reasonable cause to believe that any person or group of persons is engaged in a pattern of practice of resistance to the full enjoyment of any of the rights secured by this title, the Attorney General may bring a civil action in the appropriate district court of the United States by filing with it a complaint...requesting such preventive relief, including an application for a permanent or temporary injunction, restraining order or other order against the person or persons responsible for such pattern or practice, as he deems necessary to insure the full enjoyment of the rights herein described.

TITLE IV
Nondiscrimination in Federally Assisted Programs

SEC. 601. No person in the United States shall, on the ground of race, color, or national origin, be excluded from participation in, be denied the benefits of, or be subjected to discrimination under any program or activity receiving Federal financial assistance.

Document C
Martin Luther King, Jr.
"I Have a Dream"

Five score years ago, a great American, in whose symbolic shadow we stand, signed the Emancipation Proclamation. This momentous decree came as a great beacon light of hope to millions of Negro salves who had been seared in the flames of withering injustice. It came as a joyous daybreak to end the long night of captivity.

But one hundred years later, we must face the tragic fact that the Negro is still not free. One hundred years later, the Negro lives on a lonely island of poverty in the midst of a vast ocean of material prosperity. One hundred years later the Negro is still languished in the corners of American society and finds himself an exile in his own land. So we have come here today to dramatize an appalling condition.

In a sense we have come to our nation's Capital to cash a check. When the architects of our republic wrote the magnificent words of the Constitution and the Declaration of Independence, they were signing a promissory note to which every American was to fall heir. This note was a promise that all men would be guaranteed the unalienable rights of life, liberty, and the pursuit of happiness....

But there is something that I must say to my people who stand on the warm threshold which leads to this palace of justice. In the process of gaining our rightful place we must not be guilty of wrongful deeds. Let us not seek to satisfy our thirst for freedom by drinking from the cup of bitterness and hatred. We must forever conduct our struggle on the high plane of dignity and discipline. We must not allow our creative protest to degenerate into physical violence. Again and again we must rise to the majestic heights of meeting physical force with soul force. The marvelous new militancy which has engulfed the Negro community must not lead us to a distrust of all white people, for many of our white brothers, as evidenced by their presence here today, have come to realize that their destiny is tied up with our destiny and their freedom is inextricably bound to our freedom. We cannot walk alone.

And as we walk, we must make the pledge that we shall march ahead. We cannot turn back. There are those who are asking the devotees of civil rights, "When will you be satisfied?" We can never be satisfied as long as the Negro is the victim of the unspeakable horrors of police brutality. We can never be satisfied as long as our bodies, heavy with the fatigue of travel, cannot gain lodging in the motels of the highways and the hotels of the cities. We cannot be satisfied as long as the Negro's basic mobility is from a smaller ghetto to a larger one. We can never be satisfied as long as a Negro in Mississippi cannot vote and a Negro in New York believes he has nothing for which to vote. No, no we are not satisfied, and we will not be satisfied until justice rolls down like waters and righteousness like a mighty stream....

I say to you today, my friends, that in spite of the difficulties and frustrations of the moment I still have a dream. It is a dream deeply rooted in the American dream.

I have a dream that one day this nation will rise up and live out the true meaning of its creed: "We hold these truths to be self-evident; that all men are created equal."

I have a dream that one day on the red hills of Georgia the sons of former slaves and the sons of former slave owners will be able to sit down together at the table of brotherhood.

I have a dream that one day even the state of Mississippi, a desert state sweltering with the heat of injustice and oppression, will be transformed into an oasis of freedom and justice.

I have a dream that my four little children will one day live in a nation where they will not be judged by the color of their skin but by the content of their character.

I have a dream today.

I have a dream that one day the state of Alabama, whose governor's lips are presently dripping with the words of interposition and nullification, will be transformed into a situation where little black boys and black girls will be able to join hands with little white boys and white girls and walk together as brothers and sisters.

I have a dream today.

I have a dream that one day every valley shall be exalted, every hill and mountain shall be made low, the rough places will be made plains, and the crooked places will be made straight, and the glory of the Lord shall be revealed, and all flesh shall see it together.

Document D
National Organization for Women

Statement of Purpose
(Adopted at the organizing conference in Washington, D.C., October 29, 1966)

We, men and women who hereby constitute ourselves as the National Organization for Women, believe that the time has come for a new movement toward true equality for all women in America, and toward a fully equal partnership of the sexes, as part of the worldwide revolution of human rights now taking place within and beyond our national borders.

The purpose of **NOW** is to take action to bring women into full participation in the mainstream of American society now, exercising all the privileges an responsibilities thereof in truly equal partnership with men.

WE BELIEVE the time has come to move beyond the abstract argument, discussion and symposia over the status and special nature of women which have raged in America in recent years; the time has come to confront, with concrete action, the conditions that now prevent women from enjoying the equality of opportunity and freedom of choice which is their right, as individual Americans, and as human beings.

NOW is dedicated to the proposition that women, first and foremost, are human beings, who, like all other people in our society, must have the chance to develop their fullest human potential. We believe that women can achieve such equality only by accepting to the full the challenges and responsibilities they share with all other people in our society, as part of the decision-making mainstream of American political, economic, and social life.

WE ORGANIZE to initiate or support action, nationally, or in any part of this nation, by individuals or organizations, to break through the silken curtain of prejudice and discrimination against women in government, industry, the professions, the churches, the political parties, the judiciary, the labor unions, in education, science, medicine, law, religion, and every other field of importance in American society....

Despite all the talk about the status of American women in recent years, the actual position of women in the United States has declined, and is declining, to an alarming degree throughout the 1950's and 1960's....Working women are becoming increasingly—not less—concentrated on the bottom of the job ladder. As a consequence full-time women workers today earn on the average only 60% of what men earn, and that wage gap has been increasing over the past twenty-five years in every major industry group....

Further, with higher education increasingly essential in today's society, too few women are entering and finishing college or going on to graduate or professional school...

In all the professions considered of importance to society, and in the executive ranks of industry and government, women are losing ground. Where they are present it is only a token handful....

Official pronouncement of the advance in the status of women hide not only the reality of this dangerous decline, but the fact that nothing is being done to stop it. The excellent reports of the President's Commission on the Status of Women and of the State Commissions have not been fully implemented. Such Commissions have power only to advise. They have no power to enforce their recommendations; nor have they the freedom to organize American women and men to press for action on them. The reports of these commissions have, however, created a basis upon which it is now possible to build.

Discrimination in employment on the basis of sex is now prohibited by federal law, in Title VII of the Civil Rights Act of 1964....Until now, too few women's organizations and official spokesmen have been willing to speak out against these dangers facing women. Too many women have been restrained by the fear of being called "feminist."

There is no civil rights movement to speak for women, as there has been for Negroes and other victims of discrimination. The National Organization for Women must therefore begin to speak.

WE BELIEVE that the power of American law, and the protection guaranteed by the U.S. Constitution to the civil rights of all individuals, must be effectively applied and enforced to isolate and remove patterns of sex discrimination, to ensure equality of opportunity in employment and education, and equality of civil and political rights and responsibilities on behalf of women, as well as for Negroes and other deprived groups.

WE REALIZE that women's problems are linked to many broader questions of social justice; their solution will require concerted action by many groups....

WE DO NOT ACCEPT the token appointment of a few women to high-level positions in government and industry as a substitute for a serious continuing effort to recruit and advance women according to their individual abilities. To this end, we urge American government and industry to mobilize the same resources of ingenuity and command with which they have solved problems of far greater difficulty than those now impeding the progress of women.

WE BELIEVE that this nation has a capacity at least as great as other nations, to innovate new social institutions which will enable women to enjoy true equality of opportunity and responsibility in society, without conflict with their responsibilities as mothers and homemakers....

...WE REJECT the assumption that these problems are the unique responsibility of each individual woman, rather than a basic social dilemma which society must solve....

WE BELIEVE that it is an essential for every girl to be educated to her full potential of human ability as it is for every boy—with the knowledge that such education is the key to effective participation in today's economy and that, for a girl as for a boy, education can only be serious where there is expectation that it will be used in society....

WE REJECT the current assumptions that a man must carry the sole burden of supporting himself, his wife, and family, and that a woman is automatically entitled to lifelong support by a man upon her marriage, or that marriage, home, and family are primarily woman's world and responsibility—hers to dominate—his to support. We believe that a true partnership between the sexes demands a different concept of marriage, and equitable sharing of the responsibilities of home and children and of the economic burdens of their support. We believe that proper recognition should be given to the economic and social value of homemaking and child care....

WE BELIEVE that women must now exercise their political rights and responsibilities as American citizens. They must refuse to be segregated on the basis of sex into separate-and-not-equal ladies' auxiliaries in the political parties, and they must demand representation according to their numbers in the regularly constituted party committees—at local, state, and national levels—and in the informal power structure, participating fully in the selection of candidates and political decision making, and running for office themselves....

NOW WILL HOLD ITSELF INDEPENDENT OF ANY POLITICAL PARTY in order to mobilize the political power of all women and men intent on our goals....

WE BELIEVE that women will do most to create a new image of women by acting now, and by speaking out in behalf of their own equality, freedom, and human dignity—not in pleas for special privilege, nor in enmity toward men, who are also victims of the current, half-equality between the sexes—but in an active, self-respecting partnership with men. By so doing, women will develop confidence in their own ability to determine actively, in partnership with men, the conditions of their life, their choices, their future, and their society.

Document E
Harvest of Discontent

UNION DRIVE RIPENS IN VINEYARDS

The broiling summer sun bakes this central California valley with one-hundred-ten-degree temperatures.

It's preharvest time. And out in the hot, muggy fields a lush grape crop and a labor movement are ripening together.

At stake is a half-million dollars in grapes and the fortunes of eighty thousand migrants who pick them.

What happens may force a redirection of California's $3.8-billion-a-year agricultural economy, which peaks right here in this fiery furnace in late August and September.

Cesar Chavez's farm labor union has been picking up momentum for two years—since its dramatic grape strike here in the fall of 1965. At the same time, [the] migrant workers' civil rights movement also crystallized.

CONTRACT PUSH PLANNED

Now with tens of thousands of acres of fruit ready for harvesting, the union plans its greatest push ever for collective-bargaining contracts.

Some three hundred growers in the San Joaquin Valley will be under pressure. Many may be forced to sign with the union or lose their crop for lack of labor.

Other factors make this perhaps the most meaningful harvest ever for the growers. In recent years, their profits have steadily dwindled as overhead soared. Higher labor costs, forced by unionization, could drive some growers out of business.

A successful union thrust in the next few weeks could mean[for the migrants] higher wages,...a better standard of living, improved housing, and a boost from society's cellar.

But if the union drive fails, the entire farm labor movement and its attendant civil rights cause may be set back for a decade....

LA CAUSA HITS

Then came La Causa.

...The Mexican farm worker, virtually silent and anonymous for more than half a century, sprang from beneath the arbors and demanded a share of "the good life." He called his uprising La Causa.

He was prodded by the simple but pungent dialogue of one of his own kind, soft-spoken Cesar Chavez, a man whom an admirer called "a quiet explosion." ...

INROADS MADE

Through his new union, the migrant asked for reform. From the grower, he demanded guaranteed wages, better working conditions, and collective-bargaining agreements with a union contract and closed shop. From the government, he demanded coverage under the National Labor Relations Act, unemployment and disability insurance, and Social Security....

GOAL DESCRIBED

For the migrant, Cesar embodies the *Huelga*—the union's two-year-long strike for recognition by three hundred growers in California's lush San Joaquin Valley.

And he embodies La Causa—the dramatic civil rights-type movement aimed at pulling the poverty-stricken, uneducated, and up to now almost ignored, Spanish-speaking migrant into labor's mainstream.

Cesar is short and sturdy. He has wavy, black hair and a dark, youthful complexion.

His eyes are searching and penetrating. And they seem to add to the credibility of the simple but sometimes explosively eloquent phrases which verbalize La Causa.

"We are more than a union," he says. "But we are also less than a union."

In the first instance, he is talking about an extra dimension which most other unions don't possess. Some of the Chavez associates here call this "social conscience." He himself refers to it as "personalized service."

ACTIVITIES LISTED

...In some ways, Cesar Chavez, as a union leader, is reminiscent of the past. He is the union—much in the tradition of Samuel Gompers and, later, John L. Lewis.

BATTLE ALREADY WON

...The migratory worker is not covered under the National Labor Relations Act. He is usually ineligible for unemployment insurance. He is without specific health and welfare protection. And he has no guaranteed minimum wage.

RECOGNITION SOUGHT

Against this backdrop, La Causa fights the migrant's battle on three fronts. It presses the grower for union recognition and collective-bargaining contracts. It lobbies the state and federal governments for legislation to protect the agricultural worker. And it makes a broad appeal to the public to end social discrimination against the migrant.

"Our aims are still very elementary," explains Mr. Chavez. "The big goal is union recognition by the growers. And even when we get this, we have to teach the growers the very meaning of negotiations. Hopeful, they will then get together themselves and set up management-labor relations departments. Now they have no such thing."

Legislation giving benefits to migrants as a group [is] almost nonexistent.

"What we need in a state like California," says Mr. Chavez, "is a Little Wagner Act which would spell out our right to organize and engage in collective bargaining."

"On the national level—for the past thirty years—federal policy has said that workers in general have a right to join a union. We want this extended specifically to farm workers."

The soft-spoken migrant leader is optimistic that such coverage will come. "We have history on our side," he says.

CHANGE ANSWERED

...Cesar Chavez is a patient man. He realizes that it may take ten years or longer for his union to make real headway. In its first two years of operation, UFWOC has signed with only three of the three hundred growers in central California.

And although he doesn't particularly like to think of La Causa as a civil rights movement, Mr. Chavez knows that constant public exposure of the abject poverty and deprivation of the farm worker is essential to the momentum of his movement.

"Our situation," he says, "is really no different from that which exists in the Negro ghettos in other parts of the country."...

Document Twenty-Five
The End of the U.S. Century

The resignation of Richard Nixon haunted the administration of Gerald Ford. Ford's decision to pardon Nixon led to his defeat in 1976 to Jimmy Carter. Carter, the Governor of Georgia, came to power on the anti-government sentiments of the public. Unfortunately, his outsider role hurt his ability to lead the nation through difficult economic and diplomatic times. Like his predecessor, he would be voted out of office in 1980 by strong negative public reaction to his presidency.

The Carter administration was haunted by traumas of the Vietnam war, Watergate and a deteriorating economic situation. By 1979 Carter recognized that the American public had lost faith in itself. His concern led to a speech known as the "The Malaise Speech." (Document A) In it Carter warns the nation about a "crisis of confidence," and the threat it poses to the nation. Why did many analysts believe that this speech helped him lose the election in 1980? Was Carter correct in his perceptions about the state of the nation?

The election of Ronald Reagan in 1980 was seen as the "Triumph of Conservatism." Though he had promised the voters fiscal responsibility, by the end of his administration Ronald Reagan had produced the largest deficit in the history of the country. It was an era in which conspicuous consumption was in vogue and American society became polarized into the rich and the poor. As a result of these dramatic changes in the economy the number of Americans who had become homeless exploded and included increasing numbers of families who could no longer maintain an income to sustain themselves. Document B, "A Welfare Hotel," is from a work by Jonathan Kozol entitled *Rachel and Her Children: Homeless Families in America*. It is a poignant piece about the lifestyle of people who have few alternatives left to them. As Kozol points these are people who, "...live with the peace of resignation." Students should consider why these families are living under these conditions. Were there alternatives for them? Did they want to live this way? What would be the long-term effects for their children?

During the Reagan-Bush years the Old World Order fell and the Cold War was finally over. As communism ended throughout eastern Europe and the Soviet Union it caused a power vacuum on the world scene. Many Third World nations believed they now had carte blanche to act any way they chose. In August of 1990 Iraqi dictator Saddam Hussein sent troops into neighboring Kuwait. He believed the American public was no longer interested in maintaining world order and therefore would not interfere with his plans. As Document C points he was incorrect in his analysis. After Hussein did not obey a January 16th deadline to withdraw, President Bush, with the support of the Congress, announced that a military action in the Persian Gulf had begun. According to Bush, what were the objectives for the war? How is Hussein depicted by the President? Students should note that Bush emphasized that twenty-eight nations participated in the war. Why was there strong public support for the war effort?

Questions for Document Set Twenty-Five

1. What fundamental threat does Jimmy Carter see for American society?

2. What results did Carter want from his speech?

3. Describe life in a welfare hotel?

4. Why do families end up homeless?

5. What alternatives are there for these families?

6. What were the goals of the war against Hussein?

7. Why was the American public receptive to the war?

Document A
"Malaise" Speech

Jimmy Carter

Good evening.

This is a special night for me. Exactly three years ago, on July 15, 1976, I accepted the nomination of my party to run for President of the United States. I promised you a President who is not isolated from the people, who feels your pain, and who shared your dreams and who draws his strength and his wisdom from you....

Ten days ago I had planned to speak to you again about a very important subject—energy. For the fifth time I would have described the urgency of the problem and laid out a series of legislative recommendations to the Congress. But as I was preparing to speak, I began to ask myself the same question that I now know has been troubling many of you. Why have we not been able to get together as a nation to resolve our serious energy problem?

It's clear that the true problems of our Nation are much deeper—deeper than gasoline lines or energy shortages, deeper even than inflation or recession. And I realize more than ever that as President I need your help. So, I decided to reach out and listen to the voices of America.

I invited to Camp David people from almost every segment of our society—business and labor, teachers and preachers, Governors, mayors, and private citizens. And then I left Camp David to listen to other Americans, men and women like you. It has been an extraordinary ten days, and I want to share with you what I've heard....

These ten days confirmed my belief in the decency and the strength and the wisdom of the American people, but it also bore out some of my long-standing concerns about our Nation's underlying problems.

I know, of course, being president, that government actions and legislation can be very important. That's why I've worked hard to put my campaign promises into law—and I have to admit, with just mixed success. But after listening to the American people I have been reminded again that all the legislation in the world can't fix what's wrong with America. So, I want to speak to you first tonight about a subject even more serious than energy or inflation. I want to talk to you right now about a fundamental threat to American democracy.

I do not mean our political and civil liberties. They will endure. And I do not refer to the outward strength of America, a nation that is at peace tonight everywhere in the world, with unmatched economic power and military might.

The threat is nearly invisible in ordinary ways. It is a crisis of confidence. It is a crisis that strikes at the very heart and soul and spirit of our national will. We can see this crisis in the growing doubt about the meaning of our own lives and in the loss of a unity of purpose for our Nation.

The erosion of our confidence in the future is threatening to destroy the social and the political fabric of America....

The symptoms of this crisis of the American spirit are all around us. For the first time in the history of our country a majority of our people believe that the next five years will be worse than the past five years. Two-thirds of our people do not even vote. The productivity of American workers is actually dropping, and the willingness of Americans to save for the future has fallen below that of all other people in the Western world....

Often you see paralysis and stagnation and drift. You don't like it, and neither do I. What can we do?

First of all, we must face the truth, and then we can change our course. We simply must have faith in each other, faith in our course. We simply must have faith in each other, faith in our ability to govern ourselves, and faith in the future of this Nation. Restoring that faith and that confidence to America is now the most important task we face. It is a true challenge of this generation of Americans....

We are at a turning point in our history. There are two paths to choose. One is a path I've warned about tonight, the path that leads to fragmentation and self-interest. Down that road lies a mistaken idea of freedom, the right to grasp for ourselves some advantage over others. That path would be one of constant conflict between narrow interests ending in chaos and immobility. It is a certain route to failure.

All the traditions of our past, all the lessons of our heritage, all the promises of our future point to another path, the path of common purpose and the restoration of American values. That path leads to true freedom for our Nation and ourselves. We can take the first steps down that path as we begin to solve our energy problems....

Document B
A Welfare Hotel

There are families in this building whose existence, difficult though it may be, still represents an island of serenity and peace. Annie Harrington's family has a kind of pained serenity. Gwen and her children live with the peace of resignation. I think of these families like refugees who, in the midst of war, cling to each other and establish a small zone of safety. Most people here do not have resources to create a zone of safety. Terrorized already on arrival, they are quickly caught up in a vortex of accelerating threats and are tossed about like bits of wood and broken furniture and shattered houses in an Arkansas tornado. Chaos and disorder alternate with lethargy and nearly absolute bewilderment in face of regulations they cannot observe or do not understand....

Far from any zone of safety live a man named Mr. Allesandro. He's six feet tall and weighs 120 pounds—down 20 pounds from late September. When he came to the hotel a year ago he weighed 165. I first met him in the ballroom before Christmas when I handed him an apple. One bright apple. One week later he does not forget and, when he sees me in the lobby, asks me if I have some time to talk.

His two daughters are asleep. Christopher, his nine-year-old, is lying on the top bunk, fully dressed and wrapped beneath a pile of blankets, but he is awake and vigilant and almost belligerently alert. It's a cold night and the room appears to be unheated. Mr. Allesandro shows me a cracked pane of glass that he has covered over with a sheet of garbage plastic and Scotch tape. The two coils of the hot plate offer a symbolic reassurance ("heat exists") But they do not provide much warmth. He's wearing a coat and woolen hat. His mother, who is seventy-three, lives with them; for some reason, she's not here.

There aren't many men as heads of households in this building; this fact, I think, adds to his feeling of humiliation. His story, quickly told, remains less vivid for me later on than certain details like his trembling hands, the freezing room, the strange sight of his watchful boy, unsleeping on the bed. The boy reminds me of a rabbit staring from a thicket or caught in the headlights of a car.

These, as Mr. Allesandro tells me, are the facts: He was one of several maintenance workers in a high-rise building in Manhattan owned by one of the well-known developers. It was early autumn and his wife, for reasons I don't learn until much later, just picked up one day and disappeared. He tried to keep his job and home by rising early, feeding the children, bringing them to school, then rushing to his job. But his shift required him to be on duty very early. He was reprimanded and, when he explained his problem, was permitted to stay on but cut back to a half-time job. Half-time work was not enough to pay the rent. He was evicted. In the subsequent emergency he had to take leave from his job....

He searches the ads, walks the pavement, rides the subway; but he cannot find a job that pays enough to rent a home and feed three children. His rent allowance is $281. He's seen apartments for $350 and $400. If he takes an apartment over his rent limit he will have to make the difference up by cutting back on food and clothes. His mother's pension is too small to offer them a safety margin. "I wouldn't risk it. I'm afraid to take a chance. Even if I got a job, what if I lost it? I'd be back there with the children in the barracks."....

November 1986: I'm in New York and visit with the Allesandros. Grandma's back. She says her health is good. But Christopher looks frighteningly thin. Food was scarce before. The situation's worsened since I was here last. Families in the homeless shelters of New York have been cut back on their food-stamp allocations. The White House has decided to consider money paid for rental to the hotel owners as a part of family income. By this standard, families in the Martinique are very rich. "Tightening of eligibility requirements" has an abstract sound in Washington. On the twelfth floor of the Martinique what does it mean?

I study the computerized receipts that Mr. Allesandro has received. In June, his food-stamp allocation was $145. In August, the first stage in government reductions lowered this to $65. In October: $50. As of December it will be $33.

Mrs. Allesandro does not speak in ambiguities about the lives of her grandchildren. I ask her what the cuts will mean. "They mean," she says, "that we aren't going to eat." New York announces it will help make up the difference but, at the time I visit, no supplemental restaurant allowances have been received.

Document C
Address to the Nation Announcing
Allied Military Action in the Persian Gulf
January 16, 1991

Just 2 hours ago, allied air forces began an attack on military targets in Iraq and Kuwait. These attacks continue as I speak. Ground forces are not engaged.

This conflict started August 2d when the dictator of Iraq invaded a small and helpless neighbor. Kuwait—a member of the Arab League and a member of the United Nations—was crushed; its people, brutalized. Five months ago, Saddam Hussein started this cruel war against Kuwait. Tonight, the battle has been joined.

This military action, taken in accord with United Nations resolutions and with the consent of the Untied States Congress, follows months of constant and virtually endless diplomatic activity on the part of the United Nations, the United States, and many, many other countries. Arab leaders sought what became known as an Arab solution, only to conclude that Saddam Hussein was unwilling to leave Kuwait. Others traveled to Baghdad in a variety of efforts to restore peace and justice. Our Secretary of State, James Baker, held an historic meeting in Geneva, only to be totally rebuffed. This past weekend, in a last-ditch effort, the Secretary-General of the United Nations went to the Middle East with peace in his heart—his second such mission. And he came back from Baghdad with no progress at all in getting Saddam Hussein to withdraw from Kuwait.

Now the 28 countries with forces in the Gulf area have exhausted all reasonable efforts to reach a peaceful resolution—have no choice but to drive Saddam from Kuwait by force. We will not fail.

As I report to you, air attacks are underway against military targets in Iraq. We are determined to knock out Saddam Hussein's nuclear bomb potential. We will also destroy his chemical weapons facilities. Much of Saddam's artillery and tanks will be destroyed. Our operations are designed to best protect the lives of all the coalition forces by targeting Saddam's vast military arsenal. Initial reports from General Schwarzkopf are that our operations are proceeding according to plan.

Our objectives are clear: Saddam Hussein's forces will leave Kuwait. The legitimate government of Kuwait will be restored to its rightful place, and Kuwait will once again be free. Iraq will eventually comply with all relevant United Nations resolutions, and then, when peace is restored, it is our hope that Iraq will live as a peaceful and cooperative member of the family of nations, thus enhancing the security and stability of the Gulf.

Some may ask: Why act now? Why not wait? The answer is clear: The world could wait no longer. Sanctions, though having some effect, showed no signs of accomplishing their objective. Sanctions were tried for well over 5 months, and we and our allies concluded that sanctions alone would not force Saddam from Kuwait.

While the world waited, Saddam Hussein systematically raped, pillaged, and plundered a tiny nation, no threat to his own. He subjected the people of Kuwait to unspeakable atrocities—and among those maimed and murdered, innocent children.

While the world waited, Saddam sought to add to the chemical weapons arsenal he now possesses, and infinitely more dangerous weapon of mass destruction—a nuclear weapon. And while the world waited, while the world talked peace and withdrawal, Saddam Hussein dug in and moved massive forces into Kuwait.

While the world waited, while Saddam stalled, more damage was being done to the fragile economies of the Third World, emerging democracies of Eastern Europe, to the entire world, including to our own economy.

The United States, together with the United Nations, exhausted every means at our disposal to bring this crisis to a peaceful end. However, Saddam clearly felt that by stalling and threatening and defying the United Nations, he could weaken the forces arrayed against him.

While the world waited, Saddam Hussein met every overture of peace with open contempt. While the world prayed for peace, Saddam prepared for war.

I had hoped that when the United States Congress, in historic debate, took its resolute action, Saddam would realize the could not prevail and would move out of Kuwait in accord with the United Nation resolutions. He did not do that. Instead, he remained intransigent, certain that time was on his side.

Saddam was warned over and over again to comply with the will of the United Nations: Leave Kuwait, or be driven out. Saddam has arrogantly rejected all warnings. Instead, he tried to make this a dispute between Iraq and the United States of America.

Well, he failed. tonight, 28 nations—countries from 5 continents, Europe and Asia, Africa, and the Arab League—have forces in the Gulf area standing shoulder to shoulder against Saddam Hussein. These countries had hoped the use of force could be avoided. Regrettably, we now believe that only force will make him leave.

Prior to ordering our forces into battle, I instructed our military commanders to take every necessary step to prevail as quickly as possible, and with the greatest degree of protection possible for American and allied service men and women. I've told the American people before that this will not be another Vietnam, and I repeat this here tonight. Our troops will have the best possible support in the entire world, and they will not be asked to fight with one hand tied behind their back. I'm hopeful that this fighting will not go on for long and that casualties will be held to an absolute minimum.

This is an historic moment. We have in this past year made great progress in ending the long era of conflict and cold war. We have before us the opportunity to forge for ourselves and for future generations a new world order—a world where the rule of law, not the law of the jungle, governs the conduct of nations. When we are successful—and we will be—we have a real chance at this new world order, an order in which a credible United Nations can use its peacekeeping role to fulfill the promise and vision of the U.N.'s founders.

We have no argument with the people of Iraq. Indeed, for the innocents caught in this conflict, I pray for their safety. Our goal is not the conquest of Iraq. It is the liberation of Kuwait. It is my hope that somehow the Iraqi people can, even now, convince their dictator that he must lay down his arms, leave Kuwait and let Iraq itself rejoin the family of peace-loving nations.

Thomas Paine wrote many years ago: "These are the times that try men's souls." Those well-known words are so very true today. But even as planes of the multinational forces attack Iraq, I prefer to think of peace, not war. I am convinced not only that we will prevail but that out of the horror of combat will come the recognition that no nation can stand against a world united. No nation will be permitted to brutally assault its neighbor.

No president can easily commit our sons and daughters to war. They are the Nation's finest. Ours is an all-volunteer force, magnificently trained, highly motivated. The troops know why they're there. And listen to what they say, for they've said it better than any President or Prime Minister ever could.

Listen to Hollywood Huddleston, Marine lance corporal. He says, "Let's free these people, so we can go home and be free again." And he's right. The terrible crimes and tortures committed by Saddam's henchmen against the innocent people of Kuwait are an affront to mankind and a challenge to the freedom of all.

Listen to one of our great officers out there, Marine Lieutenant General Walter Boomer. He said: "There are things worth fighting for. a world in which brutality and lawlessness are allowed to go unchecked isn't the kind of world we're going to want to live in."

Listen to Master Sergeant J. P. Kendall of the 82d Airborne: "We're here for more than just the price of a gallon of gas. What we're doing is going to chart the future of the world for the next 100 years. It's better to deal with this guy now than 5 years from now."

And finally, we should all sit up and listen to Jackie Jones, an Army lieutenant, when she says, "If we let him get away with this, who knows what's going to be next?"

I have called upon Hollywood and Walter and J. P. and Jackie and all their courageous comrades-in-arms to do what must be done. Tonight, America and the world are deeply grateful to them and to their families. And let me say to everyone listening or watching tonight: When the troops we've sent in finish their work, I am determined to bring them home as soon as possible.

Tonight, as our forces fight, they and their families are in our prayers. May God bless each and every one of them, and the coalition forces at our side in the Gulf, and may He continue to bless our nation, the United States of America.

NOTE: President Bush spoke at 9:01 p.m. from the Oval Office at the White House. In his address, he referred to President Saddam Hussein of Iraq and Gen. H. Norman Schwarzkopf, commander of the U. S. Forces in the Persian Gulf. The address was broadcast live on nationwide radio and television.

Credits

Document Set One

Pages 3-4: Spanish Letter of Columbus to Luis de Sant' Angel, *Escribano de Racion of the Kingdom of Atagon*, Dated 15 February 1493, Reprinted in Facsimile, Translated and Edited from the Unique Copy of the Original Edition. (London, 1891), pp. 22-27.

Pages 5-6: *The Journal of Alvar Nunez Cabeza de Vaca and His Companions from Florida to the Pacific*, 1528-1536. Translated from His Own Narrative by Fanny Bandelier. Edited with an Introduction by A.F. Bandelier (New York: A.S. Barnes & Company, 1905), pp. 91, 94, 108, 143-145, 149-151, 167-168.

Page 7: Rawdon, Brown, ed., *Calendar of State Papers...Venice...* (1864), I, 262.

Pages 8-9: Thomas Mun, England's Treasure by Foreign Trade. In *Early English Tracts on Commerce*, Edited by J.R. McCulloch. (Cambridge: University Press, 1954), pp. 121-26, 134-41).

Pages 10-11: "Articles, Lawes, and Orders, Divine, Politique, and Martiall for the Colony of Virginea," in William Strachey, *For the Colony in Virginea Britannia: Lawes, Divine, Morall and Martiall, Etc.* (London: Walter Barre, 1612), pp. 1-7, 19.

Document Set Two

Pages 15-16: Gottlieb Mittelberger, *Journey to Pennsylvania in the Year 1750 and Return to Germany in the Year 1754*. Translated from the German by Carl Theo. Eben.

Pages 17-18: Alexander Falconbridge, *An Account of the Slave Trade on the Coast of Africa* (London, 1788), pp. 12-32.

Page 19: Minutes of the Provincial Council of Pennsylvania... (1852), I, 30-31. As cited in Thomas A. Bailey, *The American Spirit: U.S. History as Seen by Contemporaries* (Boston: D.C. Heath and Company, 1963), pp. 40-41.

Pages 20-21: As cited in "Declaration of Nathaniel Bacon in the Name of the People of Virginia, July 30, 1676," in Keith Kavenagh, ed., *Foundations of Colonial America: A Documentary History, Southern Colonies* (New York: Chelsea House Publishers, 1973), pp. 1783-1784.

Pages 22-23: William H. Goetzmann, ed., *The Colonial Horizon: America in the Sixteenth and Seventeenth Centuries*, 1969, by Addison Wesley Publishing Company. Reprinted by permission by Addison-Wesley Publishing Co., Inc., Reading, MA.

Page 24: As cited in J.C. Fitzpatrick, ed., *The Writings of George Washington* (1931), I, 150-52. See also Stanley Parsellis, "Braddock's Defeat," *American History Review*, XLI (1936), 253-69.

Document Set Three

Pages 27-28: *The Parliamentary History of England...*(1813), XVI, 138-59, passim.

Page 29: From *Letters from a Farmer in Pennsylvania to the Inhabitants of the British Colonies* (Boston: John Mein, 1768), pp. 5-35.

Page 30: William I. Saunders, ed., *The Colonial Records of North Carolina, Volume IX, 1771-to 1775* (Raleigh, North Carolina Printers, 1890), pp. 1161-1164).

Pages 31-32: Patrick Henry, "Speech in the Virginia Commonwealth, March 23, 1775," from Charles D. Warner, ed., *Library of the World's Best Literature, Ancient and Modern, Volume XII* (New York: R.S. Peale and J.A. Hill, 1897), pp. 7242-7244.

Page 33: L.H. Butterfield et al., eds., *The Adams Family Correspondence* (Cambridge Belknap Press of Harvard University Press, 1963), Vol. 1, 29-31).

Document Set Four

Pages 36-37: W. C. Ford, et al. (eds.), *Journals of the Continental Congress*, 34 vols. (Washington, D.C., 1904-37), XXIV, 295-297.

Pages 38-39: *Massachusetts Archives*, 190, 317-320. As cited in Richard B. Morris, *Basic Documents on the Confederation and the Constitution*, Robert Krieger Publishing Co., 1985, pp. 145-148.

Pages 40-41: Richard B. Morris, *Basic Documents on the Confederation and Constitution--Anvil Series*. Reprint Edition 1985, Krieger Publishing Company, Malabar, Florida.

Pages 42-43: As cited in James Madison, The Federalist, Number 10, November 22, 1787, in Robert Rutland et al., eds., *The Papers of James Madison, Volume 10*, 27 May 1787-3 March 1788 (Chicago: University of Chicago Press, 1977), pp. 267-270.

Document Set Five

Page 46: J.D. Richardson, ed., *Messages and Papers of the Presidents*, National Archives and Records Administration, (1896), I, 221-23.

Pages 49-50: As cited in *The Journals of Lewis and Clark* by Barnard DeVoto, pp. 202-206, 207-211, 213-214. Copyright 1953.

Page 51: J.D. Richardson, ed., *Messages and Papers of the Presidents*, National Archives and Records Administration, (1896), I, 500-04.

Document Set Six

Page 55: 4 Wheaton 316 (pp. 432-33, 436, 437). As cited in Thomas A. Bailey, ed., *The American Spirit: U.S. History as Seen by Contemporaries* (Boston: D.C. Heath and Company, 1963), pp. 220-221.

Pages 56-57: J.D. Richardson, ed., *Messages and Papers of the Presidents*, National Archives and Records Administration, (1896), II, 209, 218-19.

Page 58: J.D. Richardson, ed., *Messages and Papers of the Presidents*, National Archives and Records Administration, (1896), II, 456-59 (Dec. 8, 1829).

Page 59: David Crockett, *Exploits and Adventures in Texas*...(1836), pp. 56-59.

Page 60: Charles Dickens, *American Notes*, Ch. 18

Document Set Seven

Page 63: As cited in Richard B. Morris and James Woodress, eds., *Voices from America's Past* (New York: E.P. Dutton & Co., 1961, 1962, 1963), 2: 46-47.

Page 64: From Twelfth Annual Report, 1848, *Annual Reports on Education* (Boston: Horace B. Fuller, 1868), pp. 650-754.

Page 65: Charles Lyell, *A Second Visit to the United States of North America* (1849), II, 126-27. The Liberator (Boston), Jan. 1, 1831.

Document Set Eight

Pages 69-70: The Arthur Clark Company, from *A Documentary History of American Industrial Society*, ed. John R. Commons et al (Cleveland, 1910), VI, 78, 76-77, 79-81.

Pages 71-72: *The Harbinger*, Nov. 14, 1836, in H.R. Warfel et al., eds. *The American Mind* (1937), 390-91.

Page 73: Quoted in *Niles Weekly Register*, XLVI, 437, (Aug. 23, 1834).

Page 74: As cited in "The Confession of Nat Turner," in John B. Duff and Peter M. Mitchell, eds., *The Nat Turner Rebellion: The Historical Event and the Modern Controversy* (New York: Harper & Row, 1971), pp. 16-18.

Pages 75-76: George Fitzhugh, *Cannibals All! or Slaves Without Masters* (Richmond, Virginia: A. Morris, 1857), pp. 291-299.

Document Set Nine

Pages 79-80: *The United States Magazine and Democratic Review*, VI (November, 1839), 2-3, 6.

Pages 81-82: As cited in Diane Ravitch, ed., *The American Reader: Words That Moved a Nation* (New York: HarperCollins, 1991), pp. 77-79.

Pages 83-84: As cited in Diane Ravitch, ed., *The American Reader: Words That Moved a Nation* (New York: HarperCollins, 1991), pp. 92-94.

Document Set Ten

Pages 87-88: Harriet B. Stowe, *Uncle Tom's Cabin*, Ch. 33.

Page 89: 19, Howard 393 (pp. 451-52, 454). As cited in Thomas A. Bailed, ed., *The American Spirit: U.S. History as Seen by Contemporaries* (Boston: D.C. Heath and Company, 1963), pp. 400-401.

Pages 90: *Political Debates between Hon. Abraham Lincoln and Hon. Stephen A. Douglas*...(Columbus, Ohio, 1860), Published as a campaign document by the Ohio Republican State Central Committee.

Document Set Eleven

Pages 93-94: Perry H. Epler, *Life of Clara Barton* (Macmillan, 1915), pp. 31-32, 35-43, 45, 59, 96-98.

Page 95: *Abraham Lincoln, Complete Works*..., ed. John G. Nicolay and John Hay (New York, 1905), IX, 209-210.

Pages 96-97: As cited in Herbert Aptheker, ed., *A Documentary History of the Negro People in the U.S.* (New York: Citadel Press, 1951), 482-84.

Document Set Twelve

Pages 100-101: *Mississippi, Laws of the State...*, 1865 (Jackson, Miss., 1866), pp. 82-86.

Pages 102-103: From the *Grimes Family Papers* (#3357), 1882. Held in the Southern Historical Collection, University of North Carolina, Chapel Hill.

Page 104: As cited in "The Fourteenth Amendment," in Albert P. Blaustein and Robert L. Zangrando, *Civil Rights and the American Negro: A Documentary History* (New York: Trident Press, 1968), pp. 226-227.

Page 105: Excerpted from George Rawick, ed., *The American Slave: A Composite Autobiography* (Westport: Connecticut: 1977, 1979), Greenwood Press, supp. 1, vol. 5, p. 426, supp. 2, vol. 4, part 3, p. 957, supp. 2, vol. 5, part 4, pp. 1648-1649. Copyright 1979 by George Rawick. Reprinted by permission.

Document Set Thirteen

Page 108: Samuel Clemens [Mark Twain] and Charles Dudley Warner, *The Gilded Age: A Tale of Today* (Hartford: American Publishing Company, 1874), pp. 250-257, 260-261.

Pages 109-110: Andrew Carnegie, "Wealth," *North American Review*, 1889.

Pages 111-112: Helen Hunt Jackson, Letters to the Editor, *New York Tribune*, 1879.

Pages 113-114: Reprinted from *Black Elk Speaks*, by John G. Neihardt, by permission of the University of Nebraska Press. Copyright 1932, 1959, 1972, by John G. Neihardt. Copyright © 1961 by the John G. Neihardt Trust.

Document Set Fourteen

Page 117: John Spargo, *The Bitter Cry of Children* (New York: Macmillan, 1906), pp. 163-165.

Pages 118-119: From *A Bintel Brief* by Isaac Metzker. Copyright © 1971 by Isaac Metzker. Forward and notes copyright © 1971 by Doubleday, a division of Bantam, Doubleday, Dell Publishing Group, Inc. Used by permission of Doubleday, a division of Bantam, Doubleday, Dell Publishing Group, Inc.

Page 120: From Jacob Riis, *How the Other Half Lives* (New York: Charles Scribner's Sons, 1901), reprint of 1890 ed., Chapter 9.

Page 122: As cited in T. Ellis, ed., *Documents of American Catholic History* (1956), Michael Glazier, Inc., pp. 500-01.

Document Set Fifteen

Page 125: Reprinted with the permission of Charles Scribner's Sons, an imprint of Macmillan Publishing Company from *Selected Readings in American History Volume II Main Themes 1865 to the Present*, by John A. DeNovo, General Editor, Copyright 1969 Charles Scribner's Sons.

Pages 126-127: George W. Waring, Jr., *Street Cleaning* (New York: Doubleday and McClure, 1897), pp. 13-31.

Page 128: Richard K. Fox, *Bathing at Coney Island, Coney Island Frolics: How New York's Gay Girls and Jolly Boys Enjoy Themselves by the Sea*, Police Gazette, New York, 1883, pp. 33-35, 37-38.

Pages 129-130: As cited in Ann Banks, ed., Doc Porter's Kickapoo Indian Medicine Show, *First-Person America*, Alfred A. Knopf, 1980, pp. 194-198. Reprinted by permission of Ann Banks.

Document Set Sixteen

Pages 133-134: Reprinted with the permission of Charles Scribner's Sons, an imprint of Macmillan Publishing Company from *Selected Readings in American History Volume II Main Themes 1865 to the Present*, by John A. DeNovo, General Editor, Copyright 1969 Charles Scribner's Sons.

Pages 135-136: The March of the Flag, Printed in the Indianapolis Journal, September 17, 1898. From Albert J. Beveridge, *The Meaning of the Times* (Indianapolis: Bobbs-Merill, 1908), pp. 47-49, 56-57.

Page 137: As cited in William Graham Sumner, *War and Other Essays*, Ayer Co. Publications, Inc., 1911.

Page 138: This document is a report of an interview with McKinley at the White House, November 21, 1899, written by one of the interviewers and confirmed by others present. Published in The Christian Advocate, January 22, 1903, it is here cited from C.S. Olcott, *The Life of William McKinley* (1916), vol. 2, pp. 110-111.

Document Set Seventeen

Page 141: As cited in William Riordon, *Plunkitt of Tammany Hall*, Dutton, 1963.

Pages 142-143: Excerpts from *Giants in the Earth* by O.E. Rolvaag. Copyright 1927 by Harper & Row, Publishers, Inc. Copyright renewed 1955 by Jennie Marie Berdahl Rolvaag. Reprinted by permission of HarperCollins Publishers.

Pages 144-145: The Omaha Platform, from Edward McPherson, *A Handbook of Politics for 1892*, Da Capo Press.

Page 146: *Plessy vs. Ferguson*, from Supreme Court, 163, 537 (1896). As cited in J.R. Conlin, ed., *An America Harvest, Vol. 2* (Ft. Worth: Harcourt, Brace Jovrnovich, 1986), pp. 68-70.

Page 147: Booker T. Washington, *Atlanta Exposition Address*, 1895.

Document Set Eighteen

Pages 150-151: As cited in *We Were There, The Story of Working Women in America*, by Barbara Wertheimer. Copyright 1977 by Barbara Wertheimer, pp. 294-295.

Page 152: Theodore Roosevelt, *The New Nationalism*, 1910.

Page 153: Woodrow Wilson, *The New Freedom: A Call for the Emancipation of the Generous Energies of a People*, 1913.

Document Set Nineteen

Page 156: From a pamphlet entitled *Committee on Public Information*, Boy Scouts of America, 1917.

Page 158: As cited in Frederick Palmer, *Newton D. Baker*, Dodd, Mead and Company (1931), vol. 2, pp. 162-163.

Pages 159-160: From the diary of *Eugene Kennedy*. Courtesy of Eugene Kennedy Collection, Hoover Institution on War, Revolution, and Peace, Stanford University.

Pages 161-162: Woodrow Wilson, *Message to Congress*, January 8, 1918.

Document Set Twenty

Pages 165-167: U.S. Bureau of Immigration, *Annual Report of the Commissioner-General of Immigration*, 1924, p. 24 ff.

Pages 168-170: Franklin D. Roosevelt, *Inaugural Address*, March 4, 1933.

Page 171: From *Voices of Protest* by Alan Brinkley. Copyright © 1982 by Alan Brinkley. Reprinted by permission of Alfred A. Knopf, Inc.

Page 172: As cited in Gerda Lerner, ed., *Black Women in White America* (New York: Pantheon Books), 1972, pp. 300-302.

Document Set Twenty-One

Pages 175-176: The Four Freedoms, from *Annual Message to Congress*, January 6, 1941, Congressional Record, 77th Congress, 1st Session, LXXVII, Part I, 45-47.

Pages 177-178: As cited in *Einstein on Peace*, Otto Nathan and Heinz Norden, eds. (New York: Simon and Schuster, 1960), p. 290.

Pages 179-180: Reprinted by permission of The Putnam Publishing Group for *The Homefront: America During World War II* by Mark Jonathan Harris, Franklin D. Mitchell, and Steven J. Schechter. Copyright © 1984 by Mark Jonathan Harris, Franklin D. Mitchell, and Steven J. Schechter.

Pages 181-182: As cited in Archie Satterfield, *The Home Front: An Oral History of the War Years in America* (Chicago: Playboy Press), 1981, pp. 330-338.

Document Set Twenty-Two

Page 186: Reprinted with the permission of Charles Scribner's Sons, an imprint of Macmillan Publishing Company from *Selected Readings in American History Volume II Main Themes 1865 to the Present*, by John A. DeNovo, General Editor, Copyright 1969 Charles Scribner's Sons.

Page 187: *Department of State Bulletin 16* (June 15, 1947; speech of June 5, 1947): 1159-1160.

Pages 188-189: Testimonies from the proceedings of the House of Representatives, Committee on Un-American Activities, 1947, 1952. As cited in Elliot J. Gorn, ed., *Constructing the American Past, Vol. 2*, (New York: HarperCollins, 1991), pp. 372-376.

Pages 190-191: Reprinted with the permission of Charles Scribner's Sons, an imprint of Macmillan Publishing Company from *Selected Readings in American History Volume II Main Themes 1865 to the Present*, by John A. DeNovo, General Editor, Copyright 1969 Charles Scribner's Sons.

Document Set Twenty-Three

Pages 194-196: John F. Kennedy, *Inaugural Address*, January 20, 1961.

Page 197: As cited in Adlai E. Stevenson, *Looking Outward: Years of Crisis at the United Nations*, ed., Robert L. and Selma Schiffer (New York: Harper & Row, 1963), pp. 107-108, 111-112.

Pages 199-200: President Johnson's *Message to Congress*, August 24, 1964, Department of State Bulletin and the Joint Resolution of Congress, H.J. Res. 1145.

Page 201: Bill Clinton, *A War I Opposed and Despised*, The Associated Press, New York, February 3, 1992. Reprinted by permission.

Document Set Twenty-Four

Pages 206-207: Office of the Federal Register, National Archives and Records Service, *Public Papers of the Presidents of the United States*, Lyndon B. Johnson, 1965.

Pages 208-209: 78 *U.S. Statutes at Large*, 2241 ff. Public law 88-352.

Pages 210-211: Martin Luther King, Jr., *Why We Can't Wait* (New York: The New American Library), 1963.

Pages 212-214: *Statement of Purpose* drawn up by the National Organization for Women (NOW) at their organizing conference in Washington, D.C., October 29, 1966.

Pages 215-217: Curtis Sitomer, *Harvest of Discontent*. Reprinted by permission from The Christian Science Monitor. Copyright 1967 by The Christian Science Publishing Society. All rights reserved.

Document Set Twenty-Five

Pages 220-221: Jimmy Carter, "Malaise" speech, 1979, *National Archives and Records Service, Public Papers of the Presidents of the United States*.

Pages 222-223: From *Rachel and Her Children: Homeless Families in America* by Jonathan Kozol. Copyright © 1988 by Jonathan Kozol. Reprinted by permission of Crown Publishers, Inc.

Pages 224-226: Office of the Federal Register, *National Archives and Records Service, Public Papers of the Presidents of the United States*, George Bush, 1991.